THE
BAKING
BOOK

Linda Collister & Anthony Blake

THE BAKING BOOK

SMITHMARK

TO ALAN, BOBBY, AND NICKY

In the recipes, measurements for ingredients
are given in standard U.S. cups and spoons as well as in metric
weights and volume measures. The two sets of measurements
are not exact conversions.

This edition published in 1996 by SMITHMARK Publishers,
a division of U.S. Media Holdings, Inc., 16 East 32nd Street,
New York, NY 10016

SMITHMARK books are available for bulk purchase for sales promotion
and premium use. For details write or call the manager of special sales,
SMITHMARK Publishers, 16 East 32nd Street, New York, NY 10016

Produced by
Conran Octopus Limited
37 Shelton Street
London WC2H 9HN

Text copyright © 1996 Linda Collister
Photography copyright © 1996 Anthony Blake
Design and layout copyright © 1996 Conran Octopus Ltd

Commissioning Editor Louise Simpson
Project Editor Norma MacMillan
Designer Paul Welti
Production Julia Golding
Typeset by Peter Howard

ISBN 0-765-19663-8

Printed in China

10 9 8 7 6 5 4 3 2 1

Library of Congress CIP

CONTENTS

INTRODUCTION

Baking sweet things combines many pleasures: there is creative pride in the making, social satisfaction in the sharing, and sensual delight in the eating. But baking is also a craft, and like other crafts it has its subtleties and secrets. So one of the great joys of writing this book has been learning new techniques and recipes. I have sought out professional bakers to find out how they make their pastry so light and their fillings so succulent, and I have asked home cooks to teach me how to make the tastiest brownies, the most luxurious chocolate cakes, the least resistible cookies.

My recipes make food to share, not to impress. I am not keen on elaborate cakes, on layers of complex confection and swirls of rich buttercream. I prefer honest sponge cake that tastes of good butter, fresh eggs, and real vanilla; pastry that truly melts in the mouth; bread with real flavor, a good texture, and a chewy crust. Like many simple things, these are hard to find nowadays.

Children enjoy working in the kitchen. These two young members of the Meyer family always help their mother, Dee Dee, with the cooking (see also pages 50–51).

INGREDIENTS

Most people who care about their craft are fussy about their materials: me too! For cake-making, all ingredients – including the fat and eggs – must be at room temperature before starting. And you need high-quality ingredients for a high-quality result.

I usually use unsalted butter, which I buy on special offer and freeze. It has a taste all its own, and I would not make a cake or pastry with anything else. My supermarket sells its own-label organic flour, and I rely on Mike Thurlow at Letheringsett Mill for superlative bread flour. Both my local baker and health food store sell fresh yeast; it's cheap and freezes well. For baking I prefer unrefined pure cane sugar, including granulated and golden confectioners' sugar – my supermarket has its own-label range. I normally use large eggs from cage-free or free-range hens; occasionally a recipe will specify extra large eggs.

Nuts should be as fresh as possible; the oils in them start to turn rancid as soon as they are exposed to air, so it is best to store them in the freezer. Finally, there is no substitute for real chocolate. I never use anything but the very best-quality chocolate with a high proportion of cocoa butter. Well-known brands of European chocolate are usually very good quality and value. See page 118 for more information about chocolate.

EQUIPMENT

For making pastry and cakes, precise measurements are vital – after all, it's chemistry! So I think accurate kitchen scales plus sets of measuring cups and spoons are essential. All cups and spoons should be measured level unless the recipe calls for a rounded or heaped spoon. A clear measuring cup is very useful for liquids.

You cannot bake well without a good, controllable oven. This summer I made my best pies ever on a bottled gas stove in an island log cabin, which must prove that ultra-modern, top-of-the-range appliances are not necessarily better than their cheaper, simpler ancestors. An oven thermometer is essential: thermostats are often unreliable, and you need to learn how your own oven behaves – and to trust your knowledge. The cooking instructions given in these recipes are guidelines; your oven handbook and your experience will teach you which shelf works best. Baking times should usually be reduced for convection ovens; again, please check your handbook. But I always preheat the oven, despite what many manufacturers say.

An electric mixer makes cake batters and kneads bread doughs efficiently and quickly. Care must be taken not to overbeat mixtures, so consult the handbook for speeds and times.

Hard though this is to admit, I would not make pastry without a food processor – my machine does it better than my hands.

If you do a lot of baking, heavy-duty professional-quality pans and baking sheets are a good investment. They will not buckle or scorch in the oven or rust after washing, and they should last a lifetime. See page 190 for some suggested mail-order suppliers.

Non-stick parchment paper is particularly useful for lining baking sheets when making meringues or delicate cookies.

A large wire cooling rack is very convenient, though you can also use the rack from a broiler pan or an oven shelf.

Airtight containers or tins are handy for storing cakes, cookies, and pastries after they have cooled completely.

Happy baking – and even happier eating!

All over the world, beautifully decorated breads are an important part of seasonal feast day and holiday celebrations. Here, a Bulgarian harvest loaf completes the traditional repast of cheese, wine, fruit, and nuts.

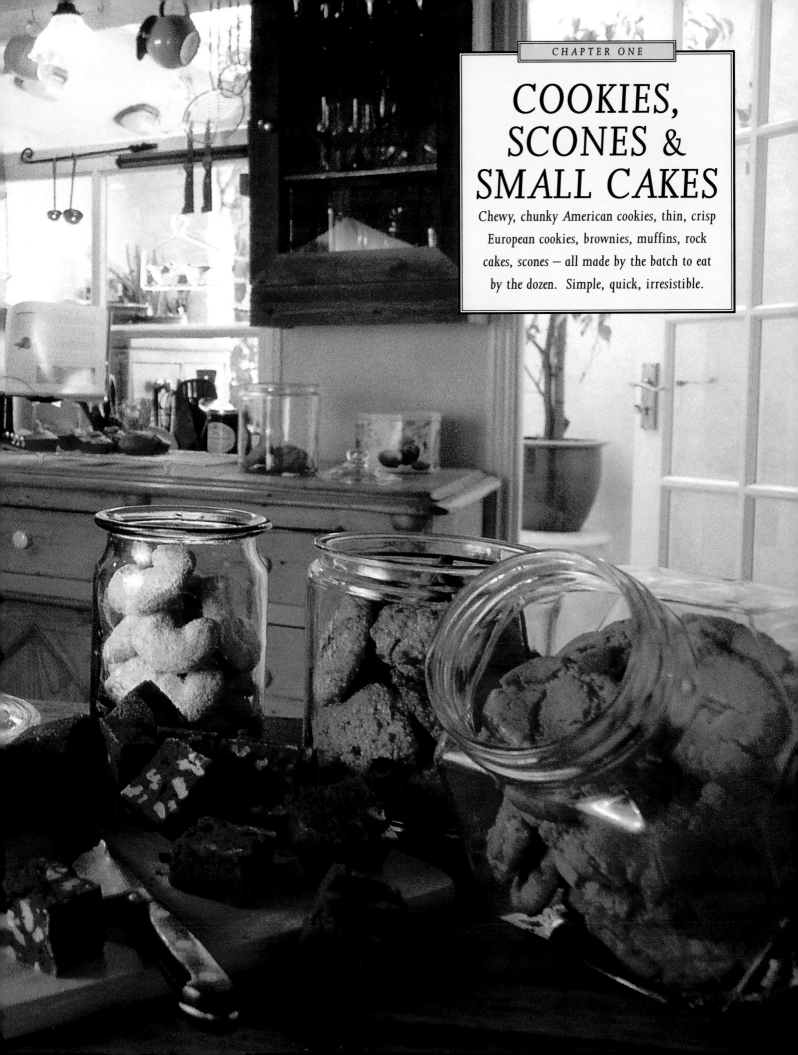

CHAPTER ONE

COOKIES, SCONES & SMALL CAKES

Chewy, chunky American cookies, thin, crisp
European cookies, brownies, muffins, rock
cakes, scones — all made by the batch to eat
by the dozen. Simple, quick, irresistible.

SHORTBREAD THINS

Makes about 2 dozen
³/₄ cup (170g) unsalted butter, at room temperature
7 tablespoons (85g) sugar
1²/₃ cups (230g) all-purpose flour
¹/₄ cup (30g) rice flour, ground rice, or cornstarch
a little sugar for sprinkling

a 2⁵/₈-inch fluted round cookie cutter
several baking sheets, lightly greased

A crisp, buttery Shortbread Thin.

The traditional recipe for shortbread is three parts flour to two of butter and one of sugar. Most good shortbread bakers, who are usually Scots, like to replace some of the flour with rice flour, ground rice, or cornstarch, to give a lighter, shorter, and sandier texture. The flavor is largely determined by the type and quality of the butter. Good unsalted butter and lactic butter give superb taste as well as texture; whey butter – made by cheese-makers as a by-product – makes a very light, crisp shortbread; while well-salted blended butter tends to make the shortbread heavy and greasy. Several older Scottish bakers told me they mix their local country butter with shortening or margarine to get a lighter, shorter, more delicate cookie. I prefer shortbread thin and crisp; however, the same dough can be rolled out thicker or simply pressed into a lightly greased shortbread mold or shallow cake pan, to make it anything from ¹/₄ to 1 inch thick. In this case it is best to score the dough into sections before baking, to make it easier to remove afterward.

Beat the butter until soft and creamy, using a wooden spoon or electric mixer. Add the sugar and beat until the mixture is pale and fluffy. Sift the all-purpose flour with the rice flour and mix in. When the mixture comes together, turn it onto a lightly floured work surface and knead briefly to make a smooth but not sticky dough. (If it seems sticky, chill until firm.)

Roll out the dough to just under ¹/₄ inch thick and cut out rounds using the fluted cutter. Gently knead together the trimmings, then re-roll and cut more rounds. Arrange the rounds slightly apart on the prepared baking sheets. Prick the rounds with a fork, and chill for 15 minutes.

Preheat the oven to 350°F.

Bake the cookies in the preheated oven for 12–15 minutes or until just firm and barely colored. Sprinkle with sugar and let cool on the sheets for a minute or two. When firm enough, transfer to a wire rack to cool completely. Store in an airtight tin, and eat within a week.

VARIATION: CHOCOLATE SHORTBREAD Replace 3¹/₂ tablespoons (30g) of the all-purpose flour with unsweetened cocoa powder, and sift with the flours. As chocolate shortbread scorches more easily, make it thicker and bake it in a pan.

1 *WORK THE ALL-PURPOSE AND RICE FLOURS INTO THE CREAMED BUTTER MIXTURE.*

2 *TRANSFER THE ROUNDS TO A GREASED BAKING SHEET WITH A METAL SPATULA.*

PREVIOUS PAGE (left to right) Cranberry Muffins, Brownies, Almond Crescents, Chocolate Chunk Oat Cookies, Tolcarne Ginger Cookies.

MILLIONAIRE'S SHORTBREAD

INGREDIENTS

Makes 2 dozen
FILLING:
a 14-oz (400-g) can condensed milk

BASE:
³/₄ cup (170g) unsalted butter, at room temperature
7 tablespoons (85g) sugar
1²/₃ cups (230g) all-purpose flour
¹/₄ cup (30g) rice flour, ground rice, or cornstarch

TOPPING:
6oz (170g) good semisweet chocolate, chopped
2 tablespoons (30g) butter
about 2oz (60g) white chocolate, for decoration

*a 9-inch square cake pan, about 2 inches deep,
  greased*

Super rich — an extravagance of dark chocolate, caramel, and butter shortbread.

To make the caramel filling, put the unopened can of condensed milk in a heavy saucepan and cover with water. Bring to a boil, then simmer, without covering the pan, for 3½ hours, replenishing the water as necessary — the can should always be covered. Let cool before opening the can. The condensed milk will have turned to a fudgy, dark-golden caramel.

Meanwhile, make the shortbread base. Preheat the oven to 350°F. Beat the butter until creamy, using a wooden spoon or electric mixer. Add the sugar and beat until the mixture is light and fluffy. Sift the all-purpose flour with the rice flour, add to the butter mixture, and knead gently for a few seconds until smooth. Press the dough into the prepared pan to make an even layer. Prick all over with a fork, then bake in the preheated oven for 20–30 minutes or until crisp and golden. Cool completely.

When the shortbread base is cold, spread the cooled caramel filling evenly over the top. Chill until firm — about 1 hour.

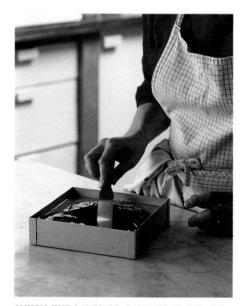

WHEN THE LAYER OF CARAMEL IS SET AND FIRM, SPREAD THE CHOCOLATE TOPPING OVER USING A SMALL SPATULA.

To finish, gently melt the semisweet chocolate in a heatproof bowl set over a pan of hot but not boiling water. Remove from the heat and stir in the butter until melted and smooth. Spread the mixture evenly over the caramel and let set. Melt the white chocolate in the same way, then use a fork or small spoon to drizzle it over the dark chocolate layer in a zigzag pattern (this can also be done using a paper piping cone). Leave until set and firm before cutting into fingers or squares.

VARIATION To make a quick and even richer caramel, melt ³/₄ cup (170g) unsalted butter with ³/₄ cup + 2 tablespoons (170g) sugar in a heavy saucepan (non-stick is best). Add the contents of the can of condensed milk — unboiled — and bring the mixture to a boil. Boil, stirring constantly, until the mixture turns a golden caramel color. Pour the hot mixture over the cooled shortbread base, and leave until cold and set before finishing.

GRASMERE SHORTBREAD

Cuts into about 2 dozen pieces
2¹/₂ cups (340g) all-purpose flour
1¹/₂ teaspoons ground ginger
³/₄ teaspoon baking soda
³/₄ cup (170g) slightly salted butter, chilled
³/₄ cup packed (170g) dark or light brown sugar, sifted

BUTTERCREAM:
¹/₂ cup (110g) slightly salted butter, at room temperature
2 cups (230g) confectioners' sugar, sifted
1 teaspoon ground ginger
2 teaspoons minced candied ginger
2 teaspoons syrup from the jar of ginger

a shallow cake pan, 8–8³/₄ x 12–12¹/₂ inches, or a 12- x 7-inch jelly-roll pan that is ³/₄ inch deep, greased

ABOVE You should not miss the famous Sarah Nelson gingerbread shop on a visit to Grasmere.

RIGHT The view across Lake Windermere to Grasmere, in England's beautiful Lake District.

This recipe comes from our friend and fellow English food writer, Sallie Morris, who describes herself as a Lake District girl, like her mother before her. Sallie says that it was long the tradition in the Grasmere area to give gingerbread, or ginger shortbread, to the children who cut rushes to cover the earthen floor of the local churches. This evolved into an annual rush-bearing ceremony, in August, and those who took part were given a piece of gingerbread stamped with the local Saint's name plus a penny to buy beer. The most famous gingerbread was made by Mrs. Sarah Nelson, and it is still sold in her tiny cottage near the church. The recipe is kept under lock and key in the local bank; indeed, the people who now run the shop had to pay a deposit before they were allowed to see the recipe. There are many theories about the lovely sandy texture of the gingerbread — some claim it contains fine oatmeal, or whole-wheat flour.

This is Sallie's mother's recipe, and was quoted in a book about Sarah Nelson. We think it is more than equal to the original: rich, sandy, and nicely "hot." The shortbread can be served plain, cut into fingers or squares, or sandwiched in pairs with a ginger buttercream filling.

SALLIE PRESSES MOST OF THE SHORTBREAD MIXTURE INTO THE PREPARED PAN (ABOVE RIGHT) AND THEN SCATTERS THE REST EVENLY OVER THE SURFACE (TOP). SHE SANDWICHES PAIRS OF BAKED SHORTBREAD FINGERS WITH GINGER CREAM (ABOVE).

Preheat the oven to 350°F.

Sift the flour, ginger, and baking soda into a mixing bowl. Cut the butter into small pieces, add to the flour, and rub in using the tips of your fingers. When the mixture looks like fine sand, stir in the sugar.

Put three-quarters of the mixture into the prepared pan and press down to make an even layer. Scatter the rest of the mixture evenly over the surface to make a crumbly topping. Use a knife to mark into fingers or squares.

Bake in the preheated oven for 35–40 minutes or until pale golden (if using a jelly-roll pan, increase the cooking time slightly). Cool slightly, then cut into fingers or squares along the marked lines. Leave in the pan until completely cold.

To make the buttercream, beat the butter until creamy using a wooden spoon. Gradually add the confectioners' sugar and ground ginger, beating well, then mix in the minced candied ginger and syrup to make a spreadable cream. Use to sandwich together pairs of shortbread fingers or squares. Once assembled, eat within 3 days.

TOLCARNE GINGER COOKIES

Makes 2¹/₂ dozen
2¹/₂ cups (340g) self-rising flour
1 cup (200g) sugar
1 tablespoon ground ginger
1 teaspoon baking soda
¹/₂ cup (110g) unsalted butter
¹/₄ cup (85g) golden syrup
1 egg, beaten
2 pieces of candied ginger, drained of syrup, minced
　(optional)

several baking sheets, greased

My favorite cookies — crisp and very gingery. The recipe came from my grandmother, who learned to bake at school a hundred years ago. Sometimes I add a teaspoon or two of chopped candied ginger — the kind preserved in syrup — when I add the egg.

Preheat the oven to 325°F.

Put all the dry ingredients into a mixing bowl and stir until thoroughly combined. Gently melt the butter with the golden syrup. Pour onto the dry ingredients, then add the egg and minced ginger and mix well with a wooden spoon to make a dough.

Using your hands, roll walnut-sized pieces of the dough into balls — you should have about 30. Place well apart on the prepared baking sheets, then slightly flatten each ball with your fingers. Bake in the preheated oven for 15–20 minutes or until crisp and golden. Let cool on the sheets for a minute before lifting onto a wire rack to cool completely. Store in an airtight tin, and eat within a week.

PRESS EACH BALL OF DOUGH TO FLATTEN IT SLIGHTLY; THIS HELPS THE COOKIE SPREAD AND BAKE EVENLY IN THE OVEN.

LEFT A charming cottage in Devon, England, worthy of a picture postcard.

A selection of freshly baked treats (clockwise from the top): Tolcarne Ginger Cookies, Shortbread Thins, Chocolate Chunk Oat Cookies, Millionaire's Shortbread.

SWEDISH PEPPER COOKIES

INGREDIENTS

Makes about 5 dozen

1¹/₂ cups (300g) sugar

1 cup (230g) unsalted butter, at room temperature

1 tablespoon honey

1 egg, beaten

2 cups (280g) all-purpose flour

¹/₂ teaspoon salt

1 teaspoon ground ginger

1 teaspoon ground cloves

extra sugar for flattening

several baking sheets, greased

These cookies were baked for us by Rosemary Underdahl, when we visited her in Maine. The recipe comes from her mother-in-law. Although Rosemary's husband was born and raised in Minnesota, his Swedish and Norwegian origins emerge in these, his favorite cookies. Rosemary trained to be a teacher — indeed, she had my little ones under control and eager to please within minutes. She's a natural cook and baker, and is always busy catering for special events and fund-raising galas where her eye-catching and delicate Scandinavian dishes are in demand.

The recipe doesn't actually contain pepper, but the cookies certainly taste spicy. The recipe makes a big batch of cookies — if more convenient, you can bake one of the three portions and keep the other two in the fridge or freezer to bake another time.

Beat the sugar with the butter until pale and fluffy, using a wooden spoon, electric mixer, or food processor. Beat in the honey and the egg. Sift the flour with the salt, ground ginger, and ground cloves, then work into the mixture to make a firm dough.

Divide the dough into three. Shape each portion into a disk and wrap tightly in wax paper. Chill until firm — about 2 hours. The dough can also be frozen for up to a month or kept in the fridge up to 5 days, ready to be shaped for baking.

When ready to bake, preheat the oven to 375°F. Roll marble-size pieces of dough into balls and place them well apart on the prepared baking sheets. Dip the base of a glass in cold water and then into a dish of sugar; press it gently on top of each ball to flatten it into a wafer-thin disk. Re-sugar the glass frequently, when it starts to stick.

Bake for 7–10 minutes or until barely colored and firm. Set each baking sheet on a wire rack to cool for a minute or so, until the cookies are firm enough to lift off onto a cold baking sheet to cool completely. Store in an airtight tin, and eat within 4 days.

1 WORKING QUICKLY, ROSEMARY ROLLS THE WELL-CHILLED DOUGH INTO SMOOTH BALLS THE SIZE OF LARGE MARBLES.

2 SHE FLATTENS THE BALLS USING THE BASE OF A GLASS DIPPED IN SUGAR (THE SUGAR PREVENTS THE DOUGH STICKING).

SWEDISH COCONUT COOKIES

INGREDIENTS

Makes about 6 dozen

$^1/_2$ cup (110g) unsalted butter, at room temperature

$^1/_2$ cup (110g) shortening

$^1/_2$ cup (100g) sugar

$1^1/_2$ cups (230g) all-purpose flour

$^1/_2$ teaspoon baking soda

$^1/_2$ teaspoon baking powder

$^1/_2$ teaspoon pure vanilla extract

$^1/_2$ cup (50g) unsweetened shredded coconut

several baking sheets, greased

Right ROSEMARY CUTS THE ROLL OF THOROUGHLY CHILLED DOUGH INTO WAFER-THIN SLICES.

BELOW My nephew Lucas is a big fan of Rosemary's cookies.

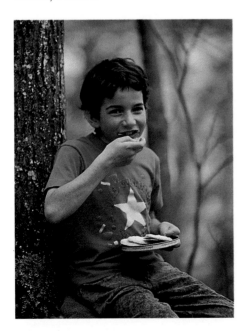

VARIATION: ALMOND COOKIES
Add $^1/_4$ cup (40g) finely chopped almonds with the coconut.

This recipe also comes from Rosemary Underdahl's mother-in-law, and is very popular with her daughters, Caitlin and Hannah. Rosemary likes the contrast between American and Scandinavian cookies: the former are large, chewy, and packed with ingredients; the latter are thin, small, and crisp.

Beat the fats together until evenly blended, using a wooden spoon or electric mixer. Add the sugar and beat again until the mixture is light and fluffy. Sift the flour with the baking soda and baking powder, then add to the mixture with the vanilla and coconut. Work the mixture with your hand until it comes together to make a firm dough.

Divide the dough in half and form each portion into a sausage-like roll with your hands – the roll should be about $2^3/_8$ inches in diameter. Wrap the rolls of dough in wax paper and chill overnight. The dough can be kept in the fridge for up to 5 days or frozen up to a month, so you can bake one portion and keep the other.

When ready to bake, preheat the oven to 350°F. Using a very sharp knife dipped in hot water, cut very thin slices from the roll of dough – no thicker than about $^1/_{16}$ inch if possible. Rosemary says you shouldn't worry if the slices tear or fall apart; just push them together as you arrange them on the prepared baking sheet, or cut thicker slices.

Bake in the preheated oven for 6–8 minutes or until very pale gold and just lightly brown on the edges – you need to watch the cookies carefully as they can brown very quickly. Set each sheet on a wire rack and let the cookies firm up for a minute or two, then lift the cookies carefully onto a cold baking sheet to cool. Store in an airtight tin, and eat within 5 days.

GERMAN CHRISTMAS SPICE COOKIES

INGREDIENTS

Makes about 2 dozen

1¼ cups (170g) all-purpose flour

1½ teaspoons ground ginger

½ teaspoon ground cinnamon

½ teaspoon apple-pie spice

4 tablespoons (60g) unsalted butter, chilled and diced

7 tablespoons (85g) sugar

2 tablespoons golden syrup

2 tablespoons milk

1 egg yolk

TO DECORATE:

1½ cups (170g) confectioners' sugar, sifted

1 egg white

cookie cutters – star, Christmas tree, bell, Santa, holly leaf, etc.

several baking sheets, greased

a paper piping cone or a small plastic bag

thin ribbon

You can shape these crisp, spicy cookies into stars, Christmas trees, bells, or Santas. Then decorate them and thread them onto thin red ribbon to hang on the Christmas trees or in windows.

Preheat the oven to 375°F.

Sift the flour, ginger, cinnamon, and apple-pie spice into a mixing bowl. Add the diced butter and rub into the dry ingredients using the tips of your fingers, to give fine crumbs. Stir in the sugar. Mix the golden syrup with the milk and egg yolk, add to the bowl, and mix with the dry ingredients to make a soft dough.

Turn the dough onto a floured work surface and knead gently for a few seconds until smooth. Roll out ⅛–¼ inch thick, then cut out shapes with the cookie cutters. Using a skewer or toothpick, make a hole at the top of each shape large enough to thread a ribbon through. Arrange the cookies on the prepared baking sheets and chill for 10 minutes.

Bake for 10–12 minutes or until golden. Leave on the sheets to cool slightly, then, when the cookies are firm enough, transfer them to a wire rack to cool completely.

To decorate, gradually beat the sifted confectioners' sugar into the egg white to make a smooth icing of piping consistency. Put into the paper piping cone or plastic bag and snip off the point. Pipe a decorative edge on the cookies, or pipe wavy patterns, names, messages, or whatever you fancy. Let set, then thread on ribbons for hanging.

ABOVE The Christmas market in Nürnberg, Germany.

RIGHT During Advent, the Albrecht Dürer stübe restaurant in Nürnberg is lavishly decorated.

OPPOSITE The festive window at the Albrecht Dürer stübe, with decorated spice cookies and traditional ornaments hung on thin ribbons from copper piping.

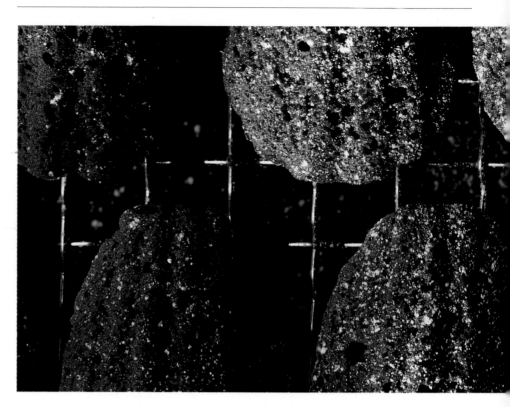

RIGHT Chocolate Madeleines, made with good semisweet chocolate and cocoa powder.

CHOCOLATE MADELEINES

INGREDIENTS

Makes 2 1/2 dozen
1/2 cup + 2 tablespoons (140g) unsalted butter
3oz (85g) good semisweet chocolate, chopped
1 cup (140g) all-purpose flour
2 tablespoons unsweetened cocoa powder
a pinch of salt
4 eggs
2/3 cup (140g) sugar
confectioners' sugar for sprinkling

madeleine molds, well buttered (see recipe)

As Marcel Proust dipped a madeleine into his tilleul, all his memories of childhood flooded back, and he began his search for lost time. If he had been tasting chocolate madeleines instead, the world's longest novel might never have been written — or it might have been even longer, for these are even more of a delight than the traditional lemon-flavored madeleines.

The chocolate version is made by adding melted chocolate and replacing some of the flour with cocoa powder. Madeleines are traditionally baked in shallow shell-shaped molds (look out for the non-stick type), which are sold in specialist kitchenware stores.

Preheat the oven to 375°F.

With a pastry brush, give the molds a thin coating of melted butter. Chill or freeze until firm, then add a second coat of butter.

To make the madeleines, put the butter and chocolate in a heatproof bowl set over a pan of hot but not boiling water and melt gently. Remove the bowl from the pan and stir until the mixture is smooth. Let cool slightly while preparing the other ingredients. Sift the flour twice with the cocoa powder and salt. Beat the eggs with the sugar using an electric mixer, until the mixture becomes pale and very thick — when the beaters are lifted out, the mixture should make a ribbon-like trail on the surface. Using a large metal spoon, fold the flour mixture into the egg mixture in three batches, then carefully fold in the chocolate mixture until thoroughly combined — the batter will lose a little bulk.

Spoon a heaped teaspoon or so of the batter into each madeleine mold — it should be about two-thirds full. Bake for 10–12 minutes or until just firm to the touch. Cool in the molds for a minute, then gently loosen each madeleine with a round-bladed knife and turn out onto a wire rack to cool completely. Serve dusted with confectioners' sugar. Store in an airtight tin, and eat within a week.

VARIATION: TRADITIONAL LEMON MADELEINES Melt $^1/_2$ cup + 2 tablespoons (140g) unsalted butter and cool slightly. Sift 1 cup + 2 tablespoons (155g) all-purpose flour with a pinch of salt, and beat 4 eggs with $^2/_3$ cup (140g) sugar as above. Fold the flour into the egg mixture, with the grated rind of 1 lemon, then fold in the butter. Bake and cool as above.

BRIGITTE'S ALMOND SQUARES

INGREDIENTS

Makes 3$^1/_2$ dozen small squares
PASTRY:
1$^1/_4$ cups (170g) all-purpose flour
$^1/_2$ cup (110g) unsalted butter, chilled and diced
2$^1/_2$ tablespoons (30g) sugar
1 egg yolk
a few drops of pure vanilla extract

TOPPING:
1$^3/_4$ cups (170g) sliced almonds
6 tablespoons (85g) unsalted butter
3 tablespoons (40g) sugar
2 tablespoons (40g) set honey
2 tablespoons cream

a shallow cake pan, 8–8$^3/_4$ x 12–12$^1/_2$ inches, or
   a 7- x 12-inch jelly-roll pan that is $^3/_4$ inch
   deep, greased

Brigitte Friis, who comes from Berlin, is a marvelous cook. This is one of her triumphs — a German confection of thin pastry covered with a sticky combination of honey and almonds.

To make the pastry base, sift the flour into a mixing bowl or food processor bowl. Add the diced butter and rub in using your fingertips, or process, until the mixture looks like bread crumbs. Stir in the sugar. Add the egg yolk and vanilla and work with your hands, or process, to make a smooth, shortbread-like dough.

Press the dough into the prepared pan in an even layer, then prick all over with a fork. Chill for 10–15 minutes or until firm.

Preheat the oven to 375°F.

Bake the pastry base for about 10 minutes or until firm and golden.

For the topping, put the almonds, butter, sugar, and honey into a wide heavy pan — Brigitte uses a non-stick frying pan — and cook over low heat, stirring constantly, until the mixture is a pale straw-gold. Stir in the cream and cook for a few more seconds, then pour over the pastry base and spread in an even layer. Bake for about 10 minutes or until the topping is a deep golden brown.

Let cool in the pan, then cut into small squares. Store in an airtight tin, and eat within 5 days.

CHOCOLATE MACAROONS

INGREDIENTS

Makes 8 filled macaroons
MACAROONS:
3^1/$_2$ oz (100g) good semisweet chocolate, chopped
2 egg whites
1^2/$_3$ cups (140g) very finely ground unblanched
  almonds
^{2}/$_3$ cup (140g) superfine sugar

FILLING:
4oz (110g) good semisweet chocolate, chopped
^{1}/$_2$ cup (100ml) heavy cream or crème fraîche

a baking sheet, lined with parchment paper

One of my favorite pastry shops is Ladurée in the Rue Royale in Paris. It is the pâtisserie of your dreams: gilt and marble fittings, velvet banquettes, cakes displayed like Cartier necklaces, chic dowagers perched on tiny chairs and attended by pretty young men or immaculate, lace-trimmed grandchildren. Ladurée's cakes are legendary, and best of all are their chocolate macaroons — sheer heaven with chocolat chaud on a cold day.

This is my version of their recipe. It is best made with top-quality semisweet chocolate — one that contains a high proportion of cocoa solids and cocoa butter. Unblanched almonds are the ones that still have the thin papery brown skin. If you can't find them already ground, you can grind them with the sugar in a food processor or blender.

Preheat the oven to 275°F.

Put the chocolate in a heatproof bowl set over a pan of hot but not boiling water and melt very gently; remove from the heat and stir until smooth. Using an electric mixer or whisk, beat the egg whites until they form soft peaks. Gradually beat in the almonds combined with the sugar. Gently fold in the melted chocolate using a metal spoon.

Put a heaped tablespoon of the mixture on the prepared baking sheet and spread to form a round about 3 inches in diameter. Repeat with the rest of the mixture to make 16 rounds. Bake for 1 hour or until firm. Cool slightly on the baking sheet, then transfer to a wire rack to cool completely.

To make the mousse filling, put the chopped chocolate in a small heavy pan with the cream and heat gently, stirring occasionally, until melted. Remove from the heat and let cool, then beat well with a wooden spoon until thick and fluffy. Chill until firm.

Sandwich pairs of macaroons together with the mousse filling, spreading it generously. Leave for about an hour before serving.

I like these macaroons best when they are a couple of days old, and they have become wonderfully sticky.

CHOCOLATE CHUNK OAT COOKIES

Makes about 2 dozen
6oz (170g) good semisweet chocolate
¹/₂ cup (110g) unsalted butter, at room temperature
6 tablespoons (85g) light brown sugar
1 egg, beaten
7 tablespoons (60g) self-rising flour
¹/₂ teaspoon baking powder
1¹/₃ cups (110g) rolled oats
¹/₂ teaspoon pure vanilla extract

several baking sheets, greased

Top-quality semisweet chocolate, chopped into large pieces, makes the best chocolate chip cookies — the taste is unrivaled because good chocolate contains far less sugar than commercial chocolate chips. As you bite into a thick chunk of rich chocolate you will realize that bought chocolate chip cookies can never compete with homemade.

Preheat the oven to 350°F.

Using a large sharp knife, coarsely chop the chocolate; set aside. Beat the butter until creamy using a wooden spoon or electric mixer. Add the sugar and beat until light and fluffy. Gradually beat in the egg and continue beating for 1 minute. Sift the flour with the baking powder and stir into the mixture with the oats and vanilla. When thoroughly combined, add the chocolate and mix well.

Place heaped teaspoons of the mixture, well spaced apart, on the prepared baking sheets. Lightly flatten the mounds, then bake in the preheated oven for 12–15 minutes or until golden and just firm. Let cool on the sheets for a minute, then transfer to a wire rack to cool completely. Store in an airtight tin, and eat within a week.

VARIATION: CHOCOLATE NUT COOKIES Omit the oats, increase the flour by 3¹/₂ tablespoons (30g), and add ³/₄ cup (90g) chopped hazelnuts.

USE A HEAVY, SHARP KNIFE TO CHOP THE CHOCOLATE INTO LARGE CHUNKS.

HAZELNUT COOKIES

Makes about 2$\frac{1}{2}$ dozen

$\frac{1}{2}$ cup (70g) hazelnuts

$\frac{1}{2}$ cup (110g) unsalted butter, at room temperature

$\frac{1}{2}$ teaspoon pure vanilla extract

6 tablespoons (85g) light brown sugar

5 tablespoons (60g) granulated sugar

1 egg, beaten

2 cups (280g) all-purpose flour

1$\frac{1}{2}$ teaspoons baking powder

a pinch of salt

several baking sheets

Toasting nuts changes their taste from mild and creamy to an almost caramel, bittersweet richness. These cookies can be made with toasted pecans or untoasted walnuts, but I think hazelnuts give them the best flavor.

Preheat the oven to 350°F.

Spread the hazelnuts on an ungreased baking sheet and toast in the preheated oven for 10–15 minutes or until they turn a rich golden brown and the skin is starting to crack and peel. Gather up the hazelnuts in a clean dish towel so they are held as if in a purse and rub them together to loosen the skins. Chop the skinned nuts coarsely, using a large sharp knife or in a food processor.

Beat the butter with the vanilla until creamy, using a wooden spoon or electric mixer. Add the light brown sugar and the granulated sugar and beat again until the mixture is light and fluffy. Gradually beat in the egg. Sift the flour with the baking powder and salt, and stir into the mixture with the chopped hazelnuts to make a firm dough.

Turn the dough onto a lightly floured work surface and form into a log shape about 8$\frac{1}{2}$ x 2$\frac{1}{4}$ inches. Wrap in wax paper or parchment paper and chill until firm – about 2 hours. The dough can be kept in the refrigerator for up to a week.

When ready to bake, preheat the oven to 375°F. Using a large sharp knife, cut the log into slices just under $\frac{1}{4}$ inch thick. Arrange them slightly apart on greased baking sheets and bake for about 15 minutes or until golden and just firm to the touch. Transfer to wire racks to cool.

Store the cookies in an airtight tin, and eat within 5 days.

LEFT (from left to right): Somerset Easter Cookies, Belgian Spice Cookies, Hazelnut Cookies.

1 GATHER THE TOASTED HAZELNUTS IN A DISH TOWEL AND RUB THEM TOGETHER.

2 THE FRICTION CREATED BY RUBBING THE NUTS WILL LOOSEN THEIR PAPERY SKINS.

ALMOND CRESCENTS

Makes about 2 dozen

½ cup (110g) unsalted butter, at room temperature

2-3 drops of pure almond extract (optional)

½ cup (60g) confectioners' sugar, sifted

a pinch of salt

½ cup + 2 tablespoons (85g) all-purpose flour, sifted

1⅓ cups (110g) ground almonds

extra confectioners' sugar for dredging

several baking sheets, greased

ABOVE Almond trees in blossom.

OPPOSITE Sugar-dredged Almond Crescents are well-partnered by a glass of sweet wine.

Every Christmas, a Czech friend used to make a wonderful big box of these snow-white cookies for my mother but wouldn't divulge the recipe. I've since enjoyed them at holiday time in the houses of Polish, German, and Dutch friends, and my American mother-in-law says the recipe is an old Jewish one. From clues dropped here and there I've gradually worked out the proportions — the method is very simple. I like to serve the cookies with fruit desserts such as oranges in caramel, poached pears, or strawberries and cream, as well as with coffee.

Preheat the oven to 325°F.

Using a wooden spoon or electric mixer, beat the butter with the almond extract until very light and creamy. Add the sugar and mix slowly until combined, then beat until fluffy. Add the remaining ingredients and mix thoroughly using a wooden spoon. Knead lightly to bring the dough together — it should be firm.

Take a heaping teaspoon-sized portion of dough and roll it with your hands to make a sausage about 3 inches long, then curve to make a crescent. Place on a prepared baking sheet. Repeat with the rest of the dough, spacing the crescents well apart. Bake in the preheated oven for 15–18 minutes or until firm. The cookies should remain pale with only the tips slightly colored.

Dredge with confectioners' sugar, then let cool on the sheets for a couple of minutes. Transfer to a wire rack to cool completely. Store in an airtight tin, and eat within a week. The flavor develops if the cookies are kept at least a day after baking.

CURVE THE SAUSAGES OF DOUGH INTO NEAT CRESCENT SHAPES USING YOUR FINGERTIPS.

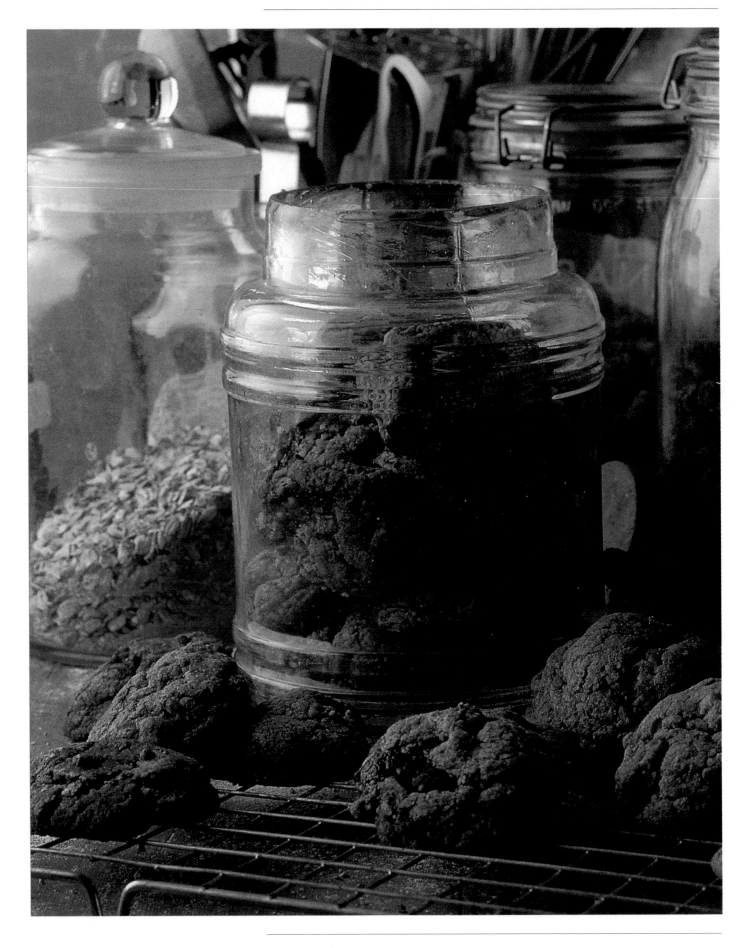

DOUBLE-CHOCOLATE PECAN COOKIES

Makes about 2¹/₂ dozen

1¹/₄ cups (100g) rolled oats

1 cup (140g) all-purpose flour

a pinch of salt

¹/₂ teaspoon baking powder

¹/₂ teaspoon baking soda

7oz (200g) good semisweet chocolate

¹/₂ cup (110g) unsalted butter, at room
temperature

7 tablespoons (85g) granulated sugar

6 tablespoons (85g) light brown sugar

1 egg, beaten

1 cup (110g) coarsely chopped pecans

several baking sheets

Really good chocolate, grated and chopped into large chunks, makes the richest, darkest, most luxurious cookies. I like to add pecans — my favorite nut when cooking with chocolate — but chopped walnuts or a mixture of nuts are also good. To make white-chocolate nut cookies, still use the grated semisweet chocolate, but replace the chopped semisweet chocolate with an equal quantity of good white chocolate.

Preheat the oven to 375°F.

Spread the oats on an ungreased baking sheet and toast in the preheated oven, stirring occasionally, for about 15 minutes or until golden. Let cool, then put into the food processor with the flour, salt, baking powder, and baking soda. Process until the mixture has the texture of sand.

Finely grate 2oz (50g) of the chocolate, and chop the remainder into large chunks using a heavy, sharp knife.

Beat the butter until creamy, using an electric mixer or wooden spoon. Add the sugars and beat again until light and fluffy. Gradually beat in the egg, then continue beating for 1 minute. Stir in the oat mixture, grated and chopped chocolate, and pecans to make a stiff dough — in cold weather, you may need to use your hands to work it together.

Roll walnut-sized pieces of dough into balls with your hands. Place the balls well spaced apart on greased baking sheets and bake for about 12 minutes or until almost firm. Let cool on the sheets for a minute, then transfer the cookies to a wire rack to cool completely. Store in an airtight tin, and eat within 5 days.

Nuts go rancid quite quickly, so when making Double-Chocolate Pecan Cookies use the freshest pecans you can find — just shelled if possible.

SOMERSET EASTER COOKIES

Makes about 1¹/₂ dozen
¹/₂ cup (110g) unsalted butter, at room
    temperature
7 tablespoons (85g) sugar
1 egg yolk
1¹/₂ cups (200g) all-purpose flour
a pinch of salt
¹/₈ teaspoon baking powder
¹/₈ teaspoon grated nutmeg
¹/₂ teaspoon apple-pie spice
¹/₂ teaspoon ground cinnamon
6 tablespoons (60g) raisins or currants
1 teaspoon minced mixed candied peel

TO FINISH:
1 egg white, lightly beaten
sugar for sprinkling

a 2⁵/₈-inch fluted round cookie cutter
several baking sheets, greased

*ABOVE A spicy Somerset Easter Cookie, with its
sugary glaze.*

*TOP RIGHT The River Parrot on Sedgemoor in
Somerset, England.*

I spent many a happy Easter on a farm in Somerset, so I always associate these short, slightly spicy cookies with England's West Country. My friend Michael Sealey has a passion for afternoon tea, and serves these cookies in stacks of three, tied with yellow ribbon. He likes to use currants, but I prefer raisins. The choice is yours.

Preheat the oven to 400°F.
   Beat the butter until creamy, using a wooden spoon or electric mixer. Add the sugar and beat until the mixture is light and fluffy. Add the egg yolk and beat for a further minute. Sift the flour with the salt, baking powder, nutmeg, apple-pie spice, and cinnamon. Add to the butter mixture and stir until thoroughly combined. Add the fruit and peel and mix well with your hands. If the dough seems very stiff or dry and doesn't come together, add a tablespoon of milk.
   Turn the dough onto a floured work surface and knead lightly for a few seconds or until smoothly combined. Roll out slightly less than ¹/₄ inch thick. Cut out rounds with the fluted cookie cutter, then re-roll the trimmings and cut out more rounds. Arrange the cookie rounds, spaced a little apart, on the prepared baking sheets.
   Bake in the preheated oven for 10 minutes or until pale golden and firm. Remove from the oven. Lightly brush each cookie with egg white, then sprinkle with a little sugar. Return the cookies to the oven and bake for a further 3–5 minutes or until the tops turn golden and crunchy. Transfer to a wire rack to cool.
   Store the cookies in an airtight tin, and eat within 5 days.

BELGIAN SPICE COOKIES

Makes about 3¹/₂ dozen

1¹/₂ cups (200g) all-purpose flour

¹/₂ teaspoon ground ginger

¹/₂ teaspoon ground cinnamon

¹/₂ teaspoon apple-pie spice

¹/₂ teaspoon baking powder

¹/₂ cup (110g) unsalted butter, chilled and diced

6 tablespoons (85g) light brown sugar

about ¹/₃ cup (45g) split (halved) almonds

several baking sheets, lined with parchment paper

These thin, crisp, fragile cookies are of the "ice-box" variety — the dough is shaped into a brick, wrapped, chilled, and then sliced when ready to bake. I like them best with a cup of coffee after dinner, but they are a treat at any time of day.

Sift the flour with the ginger, cinnamon, apple-pie spice, and baking powder. Tip into a food processor, add the diced butter, and process until the mixture looks like fine crumbs. Add the sugar and process until the mixture comes together to make a firm dough — in cold weather you may have to knead the dough a little by hand. The dough can also be made by rubbing the fat into the flour mixture with your fingers, then stirring in the sugar, and finally kneading the dough together.

Turn the dough onto a work surface and form it into a brick shape measuring about 7 x 3 x 1¹/₄ inches. Wrap in wax paper and chill until firm at least 2 hours. The dough can be kept in the refrigerator for up to 5 days and then baked when convenient.

When ready to bake, preheat the oven to 400°F. Using a large sharp knife, cut the dough into very thin slices — you should have about 40. Arrange slightly apart on the prepared baking sheets and press an almond half into the middle of each slice. Bake for 5–7 minutes or until golden. Cool on the sheets for a minute, then transfer to a wire rack to cool completely. Store in an airtight tin, and eat within 4 days.

Crisp Belgian Spice Cookies can be freshly baked whenever you want them.

THE DOUGH MUST BE VERY FIRM SO THAT IT CAN BE CUT INTO WAFER-THIN SLICES.

PLAIN SCONES

INGREDIENTS

Makes 8

1²/₃ cups (230g) self-rising flour

a pinch of salt

3 tablespoons (40g) sugar

3 tablespoons (40g) unsalted butter, chilled and diced

1 egg, made up to ²/₃ cup (140ml) with milk

extra flour for rolling out

a 2³/₈-inch fluted round cookie cutter

a baking sheet, greased

I'm quite proud of my scones, if only because they got me my first job. Over the last 20 years I've tried every recipe I've come across – ones using soured milk or buttermilk; risen with various combinations of baking soda and cream of tartar, or baking powder; made with cream, or with golden syrup, with or without eggs. To get a moist, well-flavored scone that is light and well-risen you need a leavening agent or agents – but use too much and you just get a huge scone with a nasty chemical aftertaste. I found it quite difficult to get the proportions to my liking, so I went back to the simplest recipe, using self-rising flour, and got the best results. A light touch is also required here – too much kneading or overworking will develop the gluten in the flour and make the dough elastic, so it becomes tough and hard when baked. Making the dough in the food processor overcomes this to a certain extent – it is also very quick.

I think scones spread thickly with clotted or whipped rich cream and good strawberry preserves make the finest afternoon tea yet invented.

Preheat the oven to 425°F.

Sift the flour and salt into a bowl, then tip into the bowl of a food processor. Add the sugar and run the machine for a few seconds just to combine the ingredients. Add the diced butter and process until there are no lumps and the mixture looks like sand. Beat the egg with the milk just until mixed. Slowly pour into the processor through the feed tube while the machine is running; stop pouring and turn off the machine as soon as the mixture forms a rather soft but not sticky ball of dough. If the dough seems dry and stiff, add a little extra milk.

Turn the dough onto a well-floured work surface. If the dough feels sticky and is hard to handle, sprinkle it with a little flour and work this in by gentle kneading; however, try not to work the dough more than necessary. Lightly knead the dough until it forms a rough-looking ball, then using your fingers pat it out ³⁄₄ inch thick. Dip the cutter in flour and cut out as many rounds as possible. Gather up the trimmings into a ball, then pat out again and cut more rounds.

Arrange the rounds of dough well apart on the prepared baking sheet and bake immediately. They will take 12–15 minutes and should be a good golden brown, risen, and firm. Transfer from the baking sheet to a wire rack. Eat warm the same day, or split and toast. When completely cold, the scones can be frozen for up to a month.

TO MAKE SCONES WITHOUT A PROCESSOR, sift the flour and salt into a bowl, mix in the sugar, and add the diced butter. Rub the butter into the dry ingredients using the tips of your fingers. When the mixture resembles fine crumbs, add the egg and milk mixture. Stir in using a round-bladed knife to make a soft dough. Finish as above.

1 PROCESS THE BUTTER WITH THE DRY INGREDIENTS TO A SAND-LIKE TEXTURE.

2 ADD ENOUGH EGG AND MILK TO MAKE A SOFT DOUGH THAT IS NOT STICKY.

3 TURN OUT THE DOUGH ONTO A WELL-FLOURED WORK SURFACE.

4 KNEAD THE DOUGH LIGHTLY TO BLEND THE INGREDIENTS, THEN FORM A BALL.

5 PAT OUT THE DOUGH WITH YOUR FINGERS TO A DISK ³⁄₄ INCH THICK.

6 CUT OUT ROUNDS WITH A FLOURED CUTTER AND PLACE ON A BAKING SHEET.

STRAWBERRY SHORTCAKE

INGREDIENTS

Serves 4—5

1 lb (450g) ripe strawberries, hulled

1—2 tablespoons sugar, to taste

about 6 tablespoons (85g) unsalted butter, at room temperature, for spreading

SHORTCAKE:

1³/₄ cups (250g) self-rising flour

¹/₂ teaspoon baking powder

¹/₈ teaspoon salt

6¹/₂ tablespoons (80g) sugar

5¹/₂ tablespoons (80g) unsalted butter, chilled and diced

about 1 cup (230ml) heavy cream, chilled

a few drops of pure vanilla extract

a 3-inch plain round cookie cutter

a baking sheet, greased

When planning my American father-in-law's 70th birthday dinner, I asked him to name his favorite dessert. "Strawberry Shortcake — but hold the shortcake," was the reply. Will loves strawberries, but finds that too often the shortcake tastes like cardboard. "It should be warm, rich with butter and cream, but also light and flaky," he says. Eventually I came up with this recipe — and it got the smacked lips of approval. The shortcake is similar to British scones (see previous page), but is made with cream instead of egg and milk, giving a texture and taste somewhere between a scone, shortbread, and spongecake. Serve with thick cream.

Preheat the oven to 425°F.

Thickly slice the strawberries and toss with a little sugar. Put aside.

Sift the flour, baking powder, salt, and sugar into a mixing bowl. Add the diced butter and quickly rub into the dry ingredients with the tips of your fingers until the mixture resembles large crumbs. Add the cream and vanilla and mix with a round-bladed knife until the mixture comes together to form a stiff dough.

Turn onto a lightly floured work surface, and pat into a brick. Using a rolling pin, roll out the dough to a rectangle ¹/₂ inch thick. Fold the dough into three: fold the bottom third of the rectangle up to cover the center third, then fold the top third down over this, to make three layers. Roll or pat out the dough again until it is 1 inch thick. Cut out rounds using the cookie cutter, then gently knead and re-roll the trimmings to give four or five rounds in all.

Place the dough rounds on the prepared baking sheet and bake in the preheated oven for 10 minutes. Reduce the oven temperature to 350°F, and bake for a further 10—15 minutes or until firm and golden. Leave on the sheet to cool slightly, then carefully transfer the shortcakes to a wire rack to cool completely.

When ready to serve, preheat the oven to 350°F. Split the shortcakes in half horizontally and butter the cut surfaces. Divide two-thirds of the strawberries among the shortcake bases. Cover with the lids and arrange the rest of the berries on top. Put the assembled shortcakes on a baking sheet and heat in the oven for 3—4 minutes or until they are warm and the butter is starting to melt. Eat immediately, with cream.

OPPOSITE *Strawberry Shortcake, an all-American favorite.*

ARRANGE MOST OF THE STRAWBERRY SLICES ON THE BUTTERED SHORTCAKE BASES.

CRANBERRY MUFFINS

INGREDIENTS

Makes 1 dozen

1 cup (140g) unbleached all-purpose flour
1 cup (140g) stoneground whole-wheat bread flour
1 tablespoon baking powder
$^1/_8$ teaspoon salt
$^1/_3$ cup (85g) sugar
the grated rind of $^1/_2$ unwaxed orange
1 extra large egg, beaten
1$^1/_4$ cups (280ml) whole milk
2 teaspoons orange juice
$^1/_4$ cup (60ml) soybean oil
1$^1/_4$ cups (140g) fresh or frozen cranberries – use
    straight from freezer

a 12-cup muffin tin, well greased or lined
    with paper muffin cases (see note)

In New England, white-painted churches like this
are a familiar sight. The one shown above is in
Mackerel Bay, Maine.

To me, muffins mean New England, and the best ones are made with the tart, juicy fruit of that region – cranberries and wild blueberries, either fresh or frozen. This is my mother-in-law's recipe. The combination of white and stoneground whole-wheat flours gives a good texture and prevents these muffins tasting like cupcakes; the orange contrasts well with the mouth-puckering tartness of the cranberries. Eat warm, preferably on the day of baking.

Preheat the oven to 400°F.

Mix the flours with the baking powder, salt, sugar, and grated orange rind in a mixing bowl. Mix the egg, milk, orange juice, and oil together, then add to the dry ingredients and mix with a wooden spoon until almost evenly blended. Add the fruit and briefly mix again – too much mixing can make the muffins tough.

Spoon the mixture into the prepared tin, dividing equally among the cups. Bake for 20–25 minutes or until a toothpick inserted into the center of a muffin comes out clean. The muffins should be golden and firm, with a distinct cracked peak. Let the muffins cool in the tin for a minute, then turn out onto a wire rack to cool for a further few minutes. Eat while still warm, with or without butter.

VARIATIONS: BLUEBERRY MUFFINS Replace the cranberries with an equal quantity of fresh or frozen blueberries. Omit the orange rind, and replace the orange juice with an equal quantity of lemon juice. You could also use blackberries or raspberries.

CHERRY MUFFINS Replace the cranberries with an equal quantity of pitted fresh cherries. Add 1 teaspoon pure vanilla extract with the orange juice.

NOTE The cups of the muffin tin should be about 2$^5/_8$ inches deep.

BURN O'VAT ROCK CAKES

INGREDIENTS

Makes about 8

1²/₃ cups (230g) self-rising flour

¹/₄ teaspoon apple-pie spice

6 tablespoons (85g) unsalted butter, chilled and diced

7 tablespoons (85g) sugar

²/₃ cup (110g) mixed dried fruit and chopped candied peel

1 egg

2 tablespoons milk

1 tablespoon raw brown sugar for sprinkling

2 baking sheets, greased

I'm very fond of good rock cakes, which should be moist, crumbly, slightly spicy, and with a fair amount of dried fruit and candied peel. I got this recipe 20 years ago from a tiny tea shop, now closed, at Burn O'Vat – a beautiful spot near Ballater in Aberdeenshire, Scotland. I always bake a batch for picnics on long car and boat trips.

Preheat the oven to 400°F.

Sift the flour and spice into a mixing bowl. Add the diced butter and rub it into the flour with your fingertips until the mixture resembles fine crumbs. Stir in the sugar and the dried fruit and peel. Mix the egg with the milk, and stir just enough into the fruit mixture to bind to a firm, stiff dough – it is important that the dough holds its shape.

Divide the dough into eight portions and spoon onto the prepared baking sheets in heaped, peaky mounds spaced well apart. Sprinkle with the raw brown sugar. Bake for 12–15 minutes or until golden brown. Transfer to a wire rack to cool completely. Eat the same day or the following day, warmed and spread with butter.

COOL THE ROCK CAKES ON A WIRE RACK.

RIGHT For many years, visitors to the Highlands of Scotland, including Queen Victoria, used to take the steam train from Aberdeen to Ballater.

CAROLL'S BROWNIES

Makes 16 squares

$^1\!/_2$ cup + 2 tablespoons (140g) unsalted butter

4 eggs

$1^2\!/_3$ cups (340g) sugar

1 teaspoon pure vanilla extract

$^1\!/_4$ teaspoon salt

$^3\!/_4$ cup (80g) unsweetened cocoa powder

1 cup (140g) all-purpose flour

1 cup (110g) walnut pieces

a 9-inch square cake pan, about 2 inches deep,
  completely lined with greased foil

After intensive research, Anthony and I have decided that this is the best recipe for brownies we have ever eaten. It is also one of the simplest. It comes from a good friend and good cook, Caroll Boltin, a food historian who lives in the Hudson Valley in New York state.

Making a good brownie — one that is moist and fudgy rather than dry and cakey — requires great self-restraint. The melted butter must be cool when it is added or it will cook the eggs. If you beat the eggs and sugar too vigorously, too much air will be incorporated and the brownies will be more like a cake. The final mixture should be gently stirred rather than beaten, or the brownies will be tough and dry. Most important of all, it is vital to avoid overcooking — Caroll's tip is to test by inserting a skewer halfway between the center and the side of the pan — the center should remain quite moist. It is also a good idea to wrap the cooled cake and keep it overnight before cutting into squares — if you can wait.

Preheat the oven to 325°F.

Very gently melt the butter and let cool. Using a wooden spoon gently beat the eggs with the sugar until well blended and creamy looking. Stir in the cooled butter and the vanilla. Sift the salt, cocoa, and flour together and add to the mixture. Stir until thoroughly blended, then fold in the nuts. Pour the mixture into the prepared pan. Bake for about 40 minutes or until a skewer inserted midway between the center and the side of the pan comes out clean.

Cool in the pan for a few minutes, then lift the cake, still in the foil, out of the pan onto a wire rack. When completely cold, remove the foil and cut into 16 squares. Very good with vanilla ice-cream.

VARIATIONS For children who can't eat nuts I make the same mixture, substituting 4oz (110g) best-quality white chocolate, coarsely chopped, for the walnuts. For parties I double the recipe and bake it in a roasting pan lined with foil.

The best brownies ever — moist and fudgy, with lots of walnuts.

BROWN SUGAR MERINGUES

INGREDIENTS

Makes 4 pairs
2 *egg whites*
a pinch of cream of tartar (optional)
½ cup packed (110g) light brown sugar, sifted

FILLING:
⅔ cup (140ml) heavy cream, chilled
¼ cup (45g) minced candied ginger

2 baking sheets, lined with parchment paper

1 BEAT THE SUGAR INTO THE EGG WHITES
TO MAKE A GLOSSY, FIRM MERINGUE.

2 USE A COUPLE OF LARGE SPOONS TO
HEAP THE MERINGUE ON BAKING SHEETS.

The rich caramel flavor of these meringues comes from using light brown sugar rather than white sugar. Although the meringue mixture is made in the usual way, it is important to sift the sugar so that pockets of melted sugar do not form during baking. Use egg whites that are several days old — or add a pinch of cream of tartar if they are very fresh — and have them at room temperature. Pairs of meringues can be sandwiched together with ginger cream, as here, or you can use the chocolate filling for the macaroons on page 24.

Preheat the oven to 250°F.

Put the egg whites and cream of tartar into a spotlessly clean, grease-free bowl (avoid plastic if possible as it is difficult to keep really clean). Beat, slowly at first and then gradually increasing the speed, until the whites form a smooth foam that will stand in soft peaks. Take care not to overbeat the meringue to stiff peaks or it will collapse during baking. Beat in the sugar a tablespoon at a time. The final meringue should form firm peaks when the beaters are lifted out.

Spoon onto the prepared baking sheets to form 8 even-sized heaps. Bake in the preheated oven for 3–4 hours or until firm, dry, and crisp. Let cool completely, then store in an airtight tin until ready to assemble — they can be kept for a week at this stage.

To finish, whip the cream until stiff and stir in the ginger. Use to sandwich pairs of meringues together. Eat immediately if you like crisp meringues — after a couple of hours they become slightly and deliciously gooey, which is how I like them.

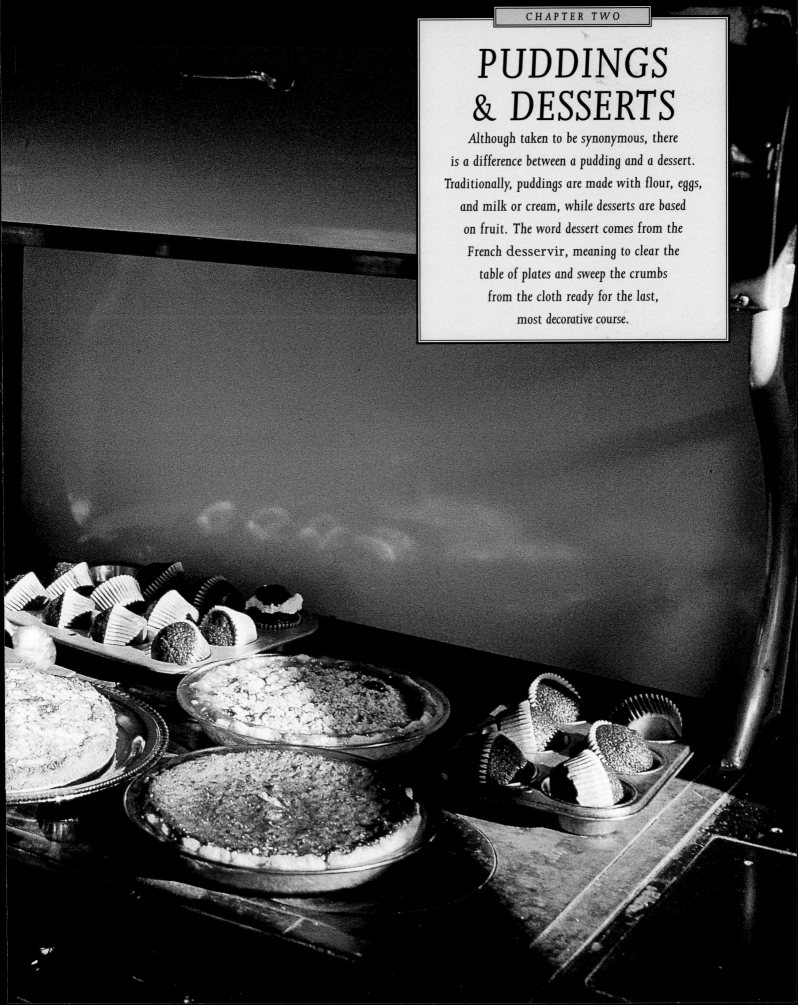

CHAPTER TWO

PUDDINGS & DESSERTS

Although taken to be synonymous, there
is a difference between a pudding and a dessert.
Traditionally, puddings are made with flour, eggs,
and milk or cream, while desserts are based
on fruit. The word dessert comes from the
French desservir, meaning to clear the
table of plates and sweep the crumbs
from the cloth ready for the last,
most decorative course.

QUEEN OF PUDDINGS

Serves 4

2 cups (85g) fresh white bread crumbs or
    spongecake crumbs

1/2 cup (100g) sugar

the grated rind of 1 large unwaxed lemon

2 cups (430ml) whole milk

3 tablespoons (45g) unsalted butter

3 extra large eggs, separated

1/4 cup strawberry preserves

4 ramekins of 1 1/4-cup capacity, greased

The best English puddings are the old-fashioned nursery favorites. I am not sure where this recipe comes from, but along with chocolate Castle Puddings (see opposite), it was one of my childhood treats. You can use any good jam or preserves, or even lemon curd (see page 129).

Preheat the oven to 325°F.

Put the crumbs and 1 tablespoon of the sugar into a mixing bowl and stir in the lemon rind. Heat the milk with the butter in a saucepan until the butter just melts, then pour the mixture over the crumbs and stir well. Let soak for 15 minutes. Stir in the egg yolks.

Divide the custard mixture among the prepared ramekins and bake in the preheated oven for 15–20 minutes or until the custards are just set and firm to the touch. Remove from the oven and spoon the jam onto the surface of the custards.

Beat the egg whites in a spotlessly clean, grease-free bowl until they form stiff peaks. Gradually beat in the remaining sugar to make a stiff, glossy meringue. Spoon the meringue on top of the jam. Return the ramekins to the oven and bake for about 10 minutes or until the meringue topping is lightly browned.

Serve warm or at room temperature, with cream or crème fraîche.

BAKE QUEEN OF PUDDINGS JUST UNTIL THE MERINGUE TOPPING IS LIGHTLY BROWNED.

PREVIOUS PAGE At the end of an afternoon of baking, Dee Dee Meyer finishes icing a raspberry torte.

CASTLE PUDDINGS

Makes 8

SPONGE PUDDINGS:

1/2 cup (110g) unsalted butter, at room
   temperature

1/2 cup + 1 tablespoon (110g) sugar

2 eggs, beaten

1/2 cup + 2 tablespoons (85g) self-rising flour

1/2 teaspoon baking powder

1/3 cup (30g) ground almonds

3 tablespoons (15g) unsweetened cocoa powder

1 tablespoon milk

SAUCE:

2 cups (430ml) whole milk

1/4 cup (20g) unsweetened cocoa powder

5 tablespoons (60g) sugar

2 tablespoons (15g) cornstarch

2 egg yolks

8 dariole molds of about 3-fl oz capacity, greased

These are chocolate and almond sponge puddings, baked in dariole molds, then turned out and served with chocolate custard sauce. When I was small, I pretended they were Saracen castles surrounded by moats; like any good Crusader I demolished them completely.

Preheat the oven to 350°F.

To make the puddings, beat the butter until creamy, using a wooden spoon or electric mixer. Gradually beat in the sugar. When the mixture is very light and fluffy, beat in the eggs a tablespoon at a time, beating well after each addition. Sift the flour with the baking powder, ground almonds, and cocoa powder, then fold into the beaten mixture with the milk, using a large metal spoon.

Spoon the mixture into the prepared molds, which should be two-thirds full. Stand the molds in a bain-marie – a roasting pan half-filled with very hot water. Cover the whole thing with foil, then bake in the preheated oven for about 30 minutes or until firm.

Meanwhile, make the sauce. Heat the milk in a heavy saucepan until scalding hot. Sift the cocoa, sugar, and cornstarch into a mixing bowl. Stir in the egg yolks to make a smooth, thick paste, then stir in the hot milk. When thoroughly blended, pour the mixture into the saucepan and stir over low heat until thickened – do not let the sauce boil.

To serve, carefully loosen the puddings with a small metal spatula or round-bladed knife, and unmold onto a deep dish or individual plates. Spoon the sauce around the base of the puddings and eat immediately. Allow two puddings per adult, one for a child.

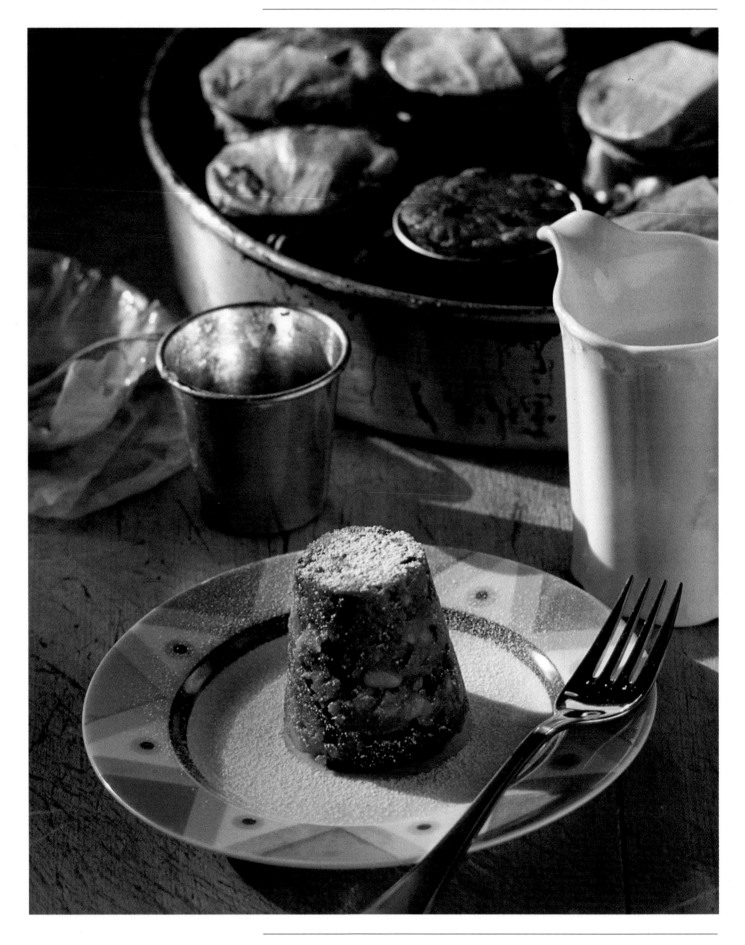

LITTLE HONEY-NUT PUDDINGS

INGREDIENTS

Makes about 12

4 tablespoons (60g) unsalted butter, at room
    temperature

3 tablespoons (60g) honey

2 eggs, beaten

²/₃ cup (110g) chopped dried figs

1 cup (110g) chopped blanched almonds

¹/₂ cup (60g) pine nuts

¹/₂ heaped cup (60g) currants

²/₃ cup (110g) raisins

¹/₂ heaped cup (60g) golden raisins

1 small apple, such as a McIntosh,
    peeled, cored, and grated

¹/₂ teaspoon apple-pie spice

¹/₄ cup packed (60g) dark brown sugar

2¹/₂ cups (110g) fresh white bread crumbs

¹/₃ cup (60g) minced mixed candied peel

a pinch of salt

the grated rind and juice of 1 small, or ¹/₂ large,
    unwaxed lemon

12 dariole molds of about 3-fl oz capacity, greased

As I discovered, by accident, these individual honey-nut puddings can be baked rather than steamed. The recipe is wonderfully odd: it contains no flour, just bread crumbs, and has no suet, just butter. It also contains plenty of nuts, almonds, and pine nuts, honey as well as dark brown sugar, and figs along with the other dried fruits. It is so good that I now make this at Christmas rather than the traditional sticky-rich plum pudding. Once the ingredients are assembled, the pudding is quick and simple enough to make for a winter Sunday lunch. Serve with brandy butter, cream, or ice-cream.

Preheat the oven to 325°F.

  Put the butter into a large mixing bowl and beat until creamy, using a wooden spoon or electric mixer. Beat in the honey. Gradually beat in the eggs, a tablespoon at a time. The mixture will resemble scrambled eggs at this point. Put all the other ingredients into another bowl and mix well. Stir into the butter mixture. When thoroughly blended, spoon into the prepared dariole molds – they should be seven-eighths full. Cover each mold with a piece of greased parchment paper, pleated in the middle, then tie it on with string.

  Set the molds in a bain-marie – a roasting pan half-filled with very hot water. Cover the whole thing with foil and bake in the preheated oven for about 1 hour or until the puddings are firm to the touch and have shrunk slightly from the sides of the molds.

  Carefully loosen the puddings using a small metal spatula, then unmold onto individual serving plates and serve hot.

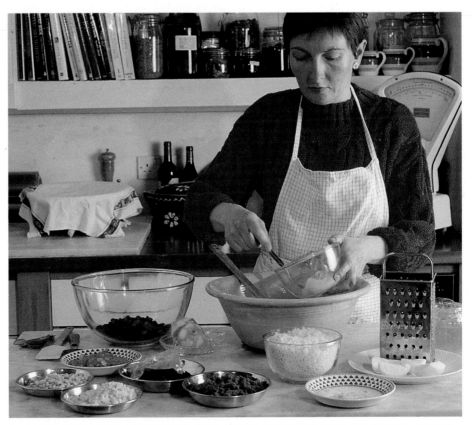

LEFT Serve Little Honey-Nut Puddings hot, dusted with confectioners' sugar.

BEAT THE EGGS WITH A FORK UNTIL WELL MIXED, THEN BEAT INTO THE HONEY MIXTURE.

DOTTY'S BAKED OATMEAL

INGREDIENTS

Serves 6

¹/₂ cup (115ml) soybean or sunflower oil

2 eggs, beaten

1 cup (170g) sugar

3¹/₂ cups (280g) quick-cooking oats

2 teaspoons baking powder

¹/₂ teaspoon salt

1 cup (230ml) whole milk

TO SERVE:

chopped fresh peaches or strawberries

cream

a deep baking dish or soufflé dish, about 8 inches
   in diameter, greased

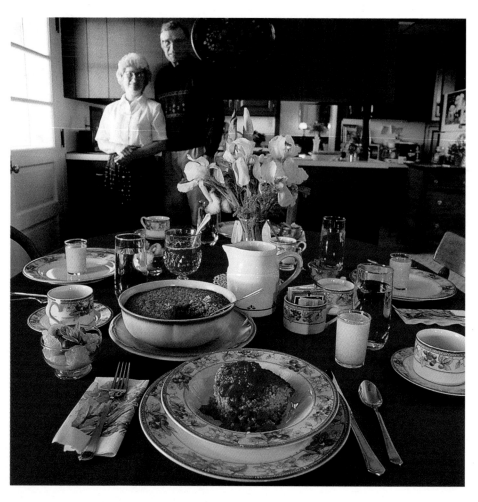

RIGHT Dottie and Andy Hess serve their guests a
hearty farmhouse breakfast, which usually
includes Baked Oatmeal with a fresh fruit
compote.

Dotty and Andy Hess have a 170-acre family farm, mainly cattle, pigs, and corn, in Mount Joy, in Lancaster County, Pennsylvania. Since their seven children have now left home, Dotty has converted the bedrooms of their pretty farmhouse to take in bed-and-breakfast guests.

Staying with the Hess family was a real treat for us: the rooms are charmingly decorated and exquisitely comfortable, with a candlelight in each window in the local Mennonite style. The highlight of each day was a hearty farmhouse breakfast made almost entirely with home-grown ingredients. One morning Dotty greeted us with glee — she had just cut the first asparagus spears of the season and was about to cook them with the breakfast eggs.

To whet our appetite — as if she needed to — she gave us baked oatmeal. It is nothing like porridge, but rather resembles an oatmeal muffin. It was accompanied by a compote of peaches that had been grown in the back garden. The dish was so good that Dotty made it for us again the next morning, this time with her strawberries. This is her recipe, which I like to make for family lunches — it has become a favorite.

Preheat the oven to 350°F.

Mix the oil with the eggs and sugar. When thoroughly blended, stir in the oats, baking powder, and salt followed by the milk. Mix well, then pour into the prepared baking dish.

Bake for 35–40 minutes or until golden and firm to the touch. Serve warm, with the fresh fruit and cream.

VARIATION Dotty sometimes adds grated raw apples, ground cinnamon, and chopped walnuts or pecans to the mixture before pouring it into the baking dish.

CHERRY CLAFOUTIS

INGREDIENTS

Makes an 8-inch tart, to serve 4—6
PASTRY:

1¼ cups (170g) self-rising flour

a pinch of salt

2 tablespoons sugar

6 tablespoons (85g) unsalted butter, chilled and diced

1 egg yolk, mixed with 2 tablespoons ice water

FILLING:

1 lb (450g) ripe cherries, pitted, or a 14-oz (411-g) can pitted black cherries, drained

6 tablespoons (85ml) cream

2 extra large eggs, beaten

3 tablespoons ground almonds

1 tablespoon kirsch or brandy

1½ tablespoons (20g) unsalted butter, melted

an 8-inch loose-based tart pan

a baking sheet

The classic French clafoutis is a cross between an egg custard and a popover, studded with fruit. This is a version of French chef Roger Vergé's very rich, very light clafoutis with a pastry base. Fresh cherries work best, but frozen or canned cherries are good too, as are fresh or plump dried apricots, or juicy prunes.

To make the pastry, put the flour, salt, and sugar into the bowl of a food processor and briefly mix. Add the diced butter and process until the mixture resembles fine crumbs. With the machine running, add the yolk mixture through the feed tube. As soon as the dough comes together, stop the machine – the dough should be soft but not sticky. Alternatively, the dough can be made by hand (see page 132). Wrap and chill for 10 minutes.

Preheat the oven to 400°F. Put a baking sheet in the oven to heat up.

Roll out the pastry dough on a lightly floured work surface to a round about 10 inches in diameter. Using the rolling pin as a support, lift the dough and drape it over the tart pan. Gently press the dough into the pan to line the sides and bottom. Trim off any excess dough, and prick the bottom all over with a fork. Chill for 10 minutes.

Line the pastry shell with a piece of wax paper and fill with pie weights. Set the tart pan on the preheated baking sheet and bake the pastry shell for 10 minutes. Carefully remove the paper and weights – the pastry will still be soft. Return the tart shell to the oven and bake for a further 5 minutes or until firm and lightly golden. Remove the pan from the oven, leaving the baking sheet inside. Do not unmold the tart shell.

Make sure the cherries – both fresh and canned – are thoroughly drained. Put the cream, eggs, ground almonds, and kirsch or brandy in a bowl and mix thoroughly, then mix in the melted butter. Arrange the cherries in the tart shell, then slowly pour the custard mixture over them. Set the tart pan on the hot baking sheet again and bake for 15–20 minutes or until the filling is golden and set. Carefully remove the clafoutis from the tart pan and serve warm, with whipped cream.

Above CAREFULLY POUR THE RICH EGG CUSTARD MIXTURE OVER THE FRUIT IN THE BAKED PASTRY SHELL.

DEE DEE'S RASPBERRY TORTE

INGREDIENTS

Serves 8
BASE:
1¹/₃ cups (200g) all-purpose flour
1 teaspoon baking powder
¹/₃ cup (60g) sugar
¹/₂ cup (110g) butter, at room temperature
1 egg, beaten
¹/₄ cup (85g) raspberry jam

FILLING:
²/₃ cup (110g) sugar
¹/₂ cup (110g) butter, at room temperature
¹/₂ teaspoon pure almond extract
2 eggs, beaten
2—3 tablespoons sliced almonds for sprinkling

TOPPING:
¹/₄ cup (85g) raspberry jam
¹/₂ cup (60g) confectioners' sugar, sifted
about 2 teaspoons lemon juice

a 10- to 11-inch springform cake pan, greased

While staying with Dotty and Andy Hess we were invited to dine with a family who belong to the Old Order River Brethren. Dee Dee and Jack Meyer and their six children live near Manheim, in a house built with the help of their Amish friends. The Old Order communities — the Amish, the Mennonites, and the Brethren — came to Pennsylvania from the German part of Switzerland in the early 18th century. Jack explained that all stemmed from the Anabaptists — rebaptizers — who believe in making a conscious choice to accept God and only baptize adults.

So-called "Pennsylvania Dutch" cooking has a strong German influence. It is an oral tradition, taught from one generation to the next, and each nutritious meal is prepared from scratch. The dishes are hearty and simple — most farming families eat three full meals a day. The ingredients are those easily obtainable from local farms: beef, chicken, and pork; potatoes, corn, and cucumbers; milk and eggs; grains and beans; apples and soft fruits. Fruit and vegetables are preserved by canning and pickling.

Dinner at the Meyers was memorable. Dee Dee and a friend spent most of the afternoon cooking for the eight members of the family and fourteen guests. As the children arrived home from school, even the smallest were given tasks. We all dined at one long table, lit by oil lamps, and Jack explained that they enjoyed the opportunity to entertain paying guests: "It is good for other people to see how we live, to share a meal with us, to ask questions." To go hungry is to ignore the bounty of the earth, and the Old Order Communities take advantage of every occasion — weddings, barn raisings, Sabbath dinners — to enjoy a delicious meal together.

To make the base, put the flour, baking powder, and sugar into a mixing bowl, and stir to combine. Add the butter and egg and work the ingredients together, using a round-bladed knife, a fork, or wooden spoon, until the mixture resembles coarse crumbs. Using your hands, press the crumbs together, then gently knead to make a shortbread-like dough.

With the heel of your hand, press the dough into the bottom of the prepared pan to make an even layer. Spread the jam over the base, then chill for 10 minutes. Meanwhile, preheat the oven to 350°F.

To make the filling, put the sugar, butter, almond extract, and eggs into a mixing bowl. Using an electric mixer, beat until very light and fluffy.

BELOW Dee Dee's children — even the youngest — help her prepare dinner for her guests.

Spoon the mixture onto the jam-covered base and spread evenly. Sprinkle with the sliced almonds.

Bake for about 40 minutes or until firm and golden. Let cool until the torte is firm enough to handle, then unclip the side of the pan and carefully remove it.

Beat the jam to soften it a little, then gently spread over the top of the torte. Mix the confectioners' sugar with enough lemon juice to make a smooth and pourable icing. Using a small spoon, drizzle the icing over the torte. Serve warm or at room temperature, within 24 hours of baking.

ABOVE The farmhouse the Meyers built near Manheim, Pennsylvania.

RIGHT Dee Dee Meyer.

BREAD AND BUTTER PUDDING

INGREDIENTS

Serves 4–6

1¼ cups (280ml) whole milk

1¼ cups (280ml) light cream

1 vanilla bean, split

a pinch of salt

4 eggs

½ cup + 1 tablespoon (110g) sugar or
    vanilla-flavored sugar

5 thin slices, about 6oz (170g), tea bread
    (page 96), white bread, or brioche (page 90)

about 3 tablespoons (45g) unsalted butter, at room
    temperature

confectioners' sugar for sprinkling

a shallow baking dish of about 1-quart capacity,
    buttered

The basic recipe for this old-fashioned but now highly fashionable pudding uses four eggs to 2½ cups (560ml) of liquid for the custard, plus some bread. The liquid can be milk, cream, or a combination. The bread can be plain white, brioche, croissant, or, as here, a fruited tea bread. The bread is usually spread with butter, but I have eaten very good puddings where the bread has been spread with marmalade or lemon curd.

Put the milk, cream, vanilla bean, and salt into a saucepan and heat slowly until scalding hot. Remove from the heat, cover, and set aside to infuse for 20 minutes.

Put the eggs and sugar into a large wide-mouthed measure or mixing bowl and lightly whisk together. Remove the vanilla bean from the milk mixture, then whisk into the egg mixture.

Butter the bread. Cut each slice in half diagonally, and cut off the crusts if desired. Arrange in the prepared baking dish so the top edges of each piece of bread are above the rim. Carefully pour the custard down the sides of the dish. Let stand for 2 hours.

When ready to cook, preheat the oven to 325°F. Stand the baking dish in a bain-marie – a roasting pan half-filled with lukewarm water – and bake for about 40 minutes or until just firm to the touch. If the custard is overcooked, it will separate and become watery.

Heat the broiler. Remove the baking dish from the bain-marie and sprinkle the top of the pudding with sifted confectioners' sugar. Put the dish under the hot broiler for a few seconds, until the sugar is golden and caramelized. Serve warm or at room temperature, with cream or ice-cream.

Above AS YOU POUR THE CUSTARD INTO THE DISH, CAREFULLY LIFT THE BREAD SO THE CUSTARD CAN MOISTEN ALL THE SLICES.

Right THE PUDDING IS COOKED WHEN IT IS JUST FIRM TO THE TOUCH IN THE CENTER.

CHOCOLATE BREAD PUDDING

Serves 4–6

6oz (170g) plain or chocolate brioche (page 90),
    challah, or milk bread

3 cups (710ml) whole milk

¹/₄ cup (50g) sugar

3 extra large eggs, beaten

²/₃ cup (110g) raisins

¹/₃ cup (40g) finely chopped toasted hazelnuts

a few drops of pure vanilla extract

4oz (110g) good semisweet chocolate, finely
    grated or melted

2 teaspoons baking powder

1 teaspoon ground cinnamon

¹/₄ teaspoon freshly grated nutmeg

4 tablespoons (60g) unsalted butter

a baking dish of about 1-quart capacity, buttered

Above USE A LARGE KNIFE TO CUT THE
BRIOCHE INTO NEAT, SMALL CUBES.

Above right TO ENSURE THAT THE PUDDING
IS MOIST, TAKE IT OUT OF THE OVEN AS
SOON AS IT IS DONE.

Kenny's restaurant serves the best Cajun and Creole food in London. It is owned and run by a Scot who's proud to be an honorary citizen of New Orleans — as a mere non-resident alien spouse of an American, I'm jealous. Kenny's puddings are served in magnificently large portions, and this is my favorite. He serves it with ice-cream or egg custard sauce flavored with bourbon.

Dice the brioche, challah, or bread, discarding the crusts. Mix the milk with the sugar and eggs in a mixing bowl. Stir in the cubes of bread and let soak for 30 minutes.

Meanwhile, preheat the oven to 325°F.

Stir the raisins, hazelnuts, vanilla, and chocolate into the bread mixture. Sift the baking powder with the spices and stir in. Spoon or pour into the prepared baking dish and dot the top with the butter.

Bake for 1–1¹/₄ hours or until just firm to the touch. Serve hot or warm, on its own or with ice-cream or custard sauce.

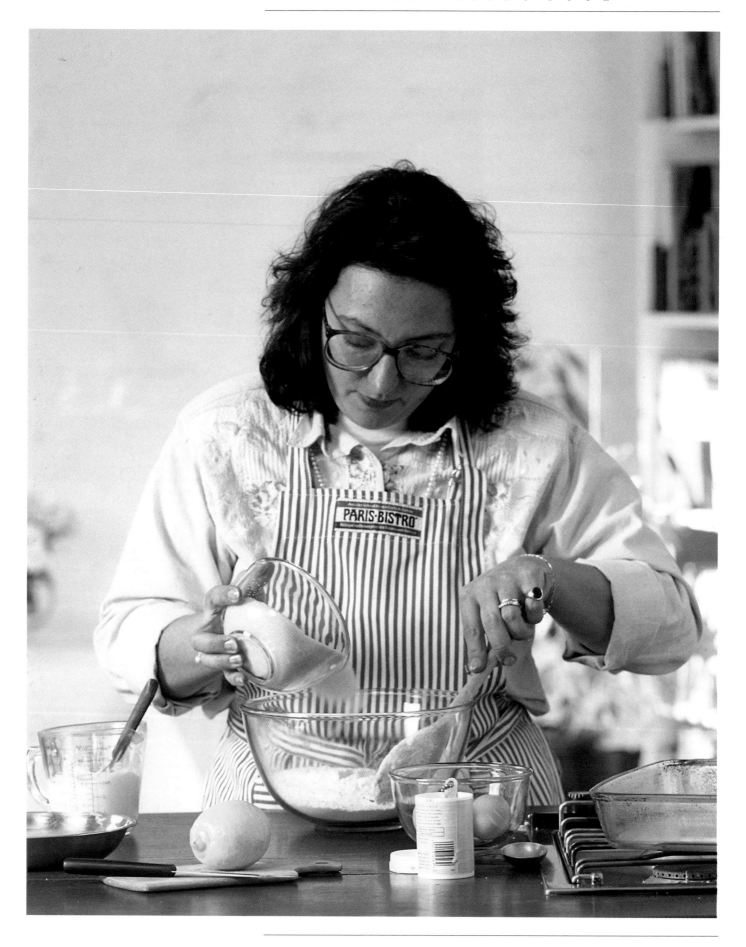

TURKISH LEMON PUDDING

INGREDIENTS

Serves 6–8

2 cups (300g) all-purpose flour

1 1/2 cups (340g) sugar

3 extra large eggs

1 cup (230ml) plain yogurt, preferably thick
 strained Turkish or Greek yogurt

1 1/2 teaspoons baking soda

the juice of 1/2 lemon

1/2 cup (115ml) boiling water

clotted or whipped cream for serving

SYRUP:

2 cups (455ml) water

2 cups (450g) sugar

the juice of 1 1/2 lemons

a baking dish, about 8 x 12 inches,
 greased

This recipe comes from my friend, Zeynep Conker Stromfelt, whose mother is pastry chef at a top Istanbul restaurant. Zeynep is a living cookbook of classic Turkish recipes, but she is especially fond of this typical family pudding: "It comes from my grandmother; it is quick and simple to prepare; and my children adore it." The unusual batter bakes to a very light sponge which is then soaked, like a baba or savarin, in a sweet, very lemony syrup. I thought it would be made with honey, but Zeynep explained that honey is not used in Turkish cooking.

Preheat the oven to 325°F.

Put the flour into a mixing bowl and stir in the sugar, then the eggs. Add the yogurt, baking soda, and lemon juice. Mix thoroughly to make a very thick, lump-free batter. Pour into the prepared baking dish and bake for 45 minutes to 1 hour or until a skewer inserted into the center comes out clean. The sponge will peak in the center.

While the sponge is baking, make the syrup. Boil the water in a medium-sized saucepan, then add the sugar and stir over low heat until dissolved. Bring back to a boil and boil for 1 minute, then remove from the heat and add the lemon juice. For an even more intense flavor you can add grated lemon rind to taste, but this is less popular with children. Keep the syrup hot.

As soon as the sponge comes out of the oven, loosen the edges and prick it all over with a skewer. Pour the boiling water over. Cover the sponge with foil and let stand for about 10 minutes or until the water has been completely absorbed.

Prick the sponge again, then slowly spoon the very hot syrup over – it will gradually be absorbed and the sponge will swell. Serve at room temperature, with clotted or whipped cream.

This pudding is best when quickly made and immediately baked, so Zeynep assembles all the ingredients before she starts work. The mixture is unusual in that it contains yogurt.

MOTHER-IN-LAW'S APPLE CRISP

When we visit my husband's family in Yarmouth, Maine, everyone gathers together for our first dinner at home. Each member of the family cooks something, and dessert is always the same — my mother-in-law's apple and blueberry crisp. Annette got this recipe from her mother-in-law, so by giving it to me she establishes a family tradition. I prefer this fruit crisp to its English cousin, the apple crumble, because the topping is lighter and crunchier. As with a crumble, you can vary the fruit filling to suit the season — peach and raspberry, blackberry and apple or pear, pear and prune, plum and orange, apricot and banana, rhubarb and red currant. The blueberries that grow wild up on the Maine coast are a delicacy — small but very juicy with a distinct tartness, which is enhanced by a little lemon rind and juice.

INGREDIENTS

Serves 4–6

6 large tart apples, such as Granny Smiths
1¹/₂ cups (230g) blueberries — fresh or frozen
(don't thaw)
the grated rind and juice of 1 small unwaxed lemon
sugar (optional)

TOPPING:
1 cup (140g) all-purpose flour
¹/₂ cup (100g) light brown sugar
110g (4oz) unsalted butter, diced
1¹/₂–2 cups (170–230g) walnut pieces

a large shallow baking dish, lightly greased

Preheat the oven to 375°F.

Peel, core, and dice the apples. Put into a bowl with the blueberries and the grated lemon rind and juice. Toss gently until thoroughly mixed. Add a little sugar (light brown or granulated) to taste if using sour or very tart fruit — Granny Smith apples usually don't need sugar. Put the fruit into the prepared baking dish in an even layer.

To make the topping, combine the flour and sugar in a mixing bowl. Add the butter and rub and squeeze into the flour mixture — it should not look like bread crumbs but rather form flakes or pea-sized lumps of dough. Stir in the nuts. Sprinkle the topping evenly over the fruit.

Bake for about 30 minutes or until the fruit is tender but not mushy, and the topping is crisp and golden. The fruit juices will probably bubble up through the topping in places, which looks very appetizing. Eat warm or at room temperature, within 24 hours of baking, with ice-cream, yogurt, crème fraîche, or whipped cream.

ABOVE Yarmouth, Maine, where my husband's family lives.

OPPOSITE My mother-in-law Annette lends me her kitchen as well as her best recipes.

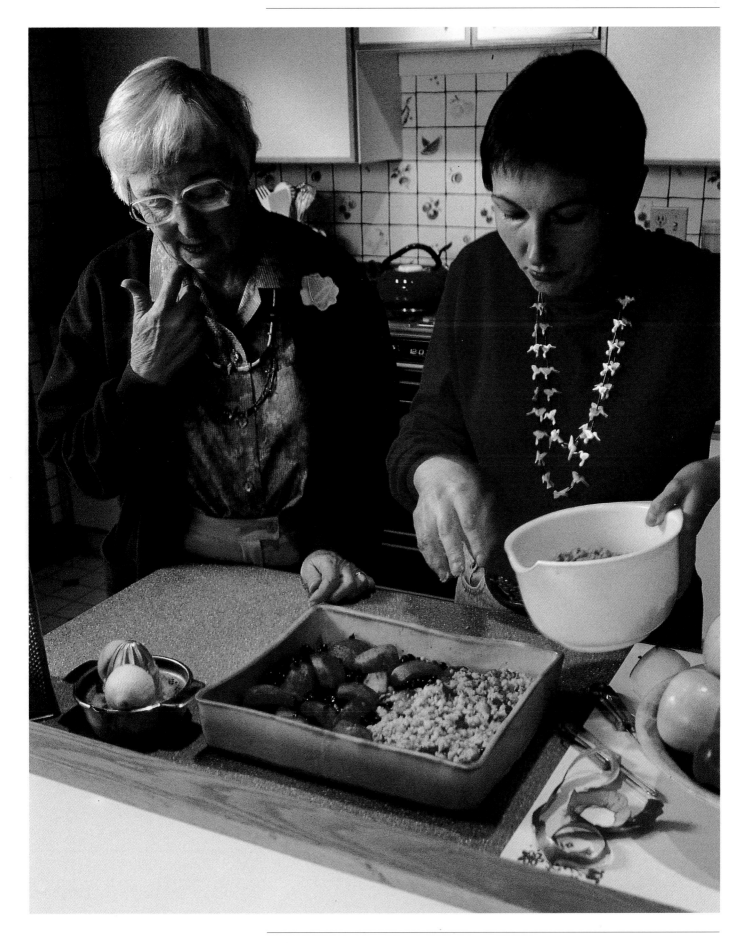

FRUIT BASKETS

INGREDIENTS

Serves 6
COOKIES:
1 extra large egg white
5 tablespoons (60g) superfine sugar
2 tablespoons (30g) unsalted butter, melted and
  cooled
3 1/2 tablespoons (30g) all-purpose flour, sifted
the grated rind of 1/2 unwaxed orange
2oz (60g) good semisweet chocolate, chopped

CREME ANGLAISE:
2/3 cup (140ml) very creamy milk or cream
3 extra large egg yolks
2 1/2 tablespoons (30g) sugar, or to taste
the grated rind of 1/2 unwaxed orange
1 tablespoon orange liqueur

FRUIT FILLING:
about 3/4lb (340g) prepared fresh fruit, such as a
  mixture of raspberries, strawberries, grapes,
  apples, currants, mango, plums, peaches –
  whatever is available
3 tablespoons orange juice or orange liqueur

several baking sheets, greased
small individual brioche molds, squat tumblers, or
  oranges, lightly greased

These delicate, crisp cookie baskets are made with a basic tuile mixture. They are dipped in chocolate, just to coat the rim, and are filled with fresh fruit salad and served with crème anglaise. The baskets are shaped by draping the just-baked cookies over an oiled brioche mold, though a small tumbler or cup, or even an orange, could be substituted. The recipe will make more cookies than you need, to allow for failures or breakages.

Preheat the oven to 350°F.

To make the cookie baskets, put the egg white into a spotlessly clean, grease-free, non-plastic bowl. Beat until stiff, then gradually beat in the sugar, followed by the cooled melted butter and, finally, the sifted flour. If using an electric mixer, do this on low speed. Gently stir in the grated orange rind.

Spoon a teaspoon of the batter onto a prepared baking sheet and spread into a thin disk about 4 inches in diameter. Bake for about 5 minutes or until a pale gold color. Remove from the oven. Using a metal spatula, immediately loosen the cookie from the baking sheet and quickly drape it over a mold or orange – it will harden very rapidly. Let cool before removing from the mold or orange. Once you have the knack of this process you can bake the cookies two at a time.

To finish the baskets, melt the chocolate on a heatproof plate set over a pan of hot but not boiling water. Turn each basket upside-down and dip the rim into the melted chocolate. Turn the right way up and let set. You will need 6 baskets.

To make the crème anglaise, heat the milk in a heavy saucepan until scalding hot. Cream the egg yolks with the sugar until thick and pale, then gradually stir in the hot milk. Stir thoroughly, then pour into the rinsed-out milk pan. Cook over very low heat, stirring constantly with a wooden spoon, until the custard thickens enough to coat the back of the spoon. This can take as much as 5 minutes. Do not be tempted to hurry the process; if the custard boils it will curdle and cannot be used. Strain the thickened custard into a measure and stir in the orange rind and liqueur. Sprinkle the surface of the custard with a little sugar to prevent a skin from forming. Let cool, then cover and chill.

When ready to serve, set a basket on each dessert plate. Toss the prepared fruit with the juice or liqueur, then spoon into the baskets. Spoon a little crème anglaise around the base of each basket. Eat immediately.

RICH CHOCOLATE SOUFFLÉ

Serves 4

6oz (170g) good semisweet chocolate, chopped

²/₃ cup (140ml) heavy cream

3 eggs, separated

2 tablespoons brandy

2 egg whites

3 tablespoons superfine sugar

confectioners' sugar for sprinkling

4 ramekins of 1¹/₄-cup capacity, buttered and
   sugared (see recipe)

This exceedingly rich, classic French soufflé is like a hot chocolate mousse. It is made without flour, and has a light, meltingly soft texture. For the best taste you should use the finest semisweet chocolate you can find – with a high proportion of chocolate liquor. The method is quick and straightforward – if you can make meringue, you can make this soufflé.

Preheat the oven to 425°F.

Brush the ramekins with melted butter, then sprinkle with sugar to make an even coating on the bottom and sides. This will help the soufflé mixture to rise well and evenly, as well as giving a nice crunchy, thin crust. Stand the prepared ramekins on a baking sheet or in a roasting pan.

Put the chocolate into a heavy-based pan with the cream. Set over very low heat and stir occasionally until melted. Remove from the heat and stir until smooth. Gently stir in the egg yolks, one at a time, and then the brandy. Set aside.

Put the 5 egg whites into a spotlessly clean, grease-free bowl and beat until stiff peaks form. Sprinkle with the sugar and briefly beat again to make a smooth, stiff meringue. If you overbeat the meringue at this stage (it will start to look grainy), it will do more harm than good, and the end result will be less smooth.

The chocolate mixture should be just warm, so gently reheat it if necessary. Using a large metal spoon, add a little of the meringue to the chocolate mixture and mix until thoroughly combined. This "softens" the chocolate – loosens the consistency – to make it easier to combine with the meringue. Pour the chocolate mixture on top of the remaining meringue in the bowl and gently fold the two mixtures together until thoroughly combined but not over-mixed.

Spoon or pour into the prepared ramekins: the soufflé mixture should come to just below the rim. Bake at once, for 8–10 minutes. Remove from the oven when they are barely set: the centers should be soft and wobble when gently shaken. Sprinkle with confectioners' sugar and eat immediately.

1 COMBINE THE HEAVY CREAM AND PIECES OF CHOCOLATE IN A SAUCEPAN.

2 HEAT GENTLY UNTIL MELTED. REMOVE FROM THE HEAT AND STIR UNTIL SMOOTH.

3 ADD THE EGG YOLKS TO THE CHOCOLATE MIXTURE, ONE AT A TIME, STIRRING.

4 ADD THE BRANDY AND STIR UNTIL IT HAS BEEN COMPLETELY BLENDED IN.

5 THE CHOCOLATE MIXTURE SHOULD BE VERY SMOOTH AND GLOSSY. SET IT ASIDE.

6 BEAT THE EGG WHITES UNTIL STIFF, THEN ADD THE SUGAR AND BEAT BRIEFLY.

7 ADD A SPOONFUL OF THE MERINGUE TO THE WARM CHOCOLATE MIXTURE.

8 POUR THE CHOCOLATE MIXTURE ONTO THE REMAINING MERINGUE IN THE BOWL.

9 GENTLY FOLD THE TWO MIXTURES TOGETHER UNTIL EVENLY COMBINED.

10 DIVIDE THE SOUFFLÉ MIXTURE AMONG THE RAMEKIN DISHES AND BAKE AT ONCE.

ALMOND AND APPLE SLICE

In this Swiss recipe, rich, crisp sweet pastry is covered with fried almonds, topped with a mound of apples, and finished with a marzipan lattice. It is substantial but not too rich, and can be made several hours before serving.

To make the pastry, put the flour, salt, and sugar into the bowl of a food processor and mix briefly. Add the butter and process until the mixture resembles coarse crumbs. With the machine running, add the egg yolks through the feed tube, and process until the mixture forms large clumps. Do not overprocess or the dough will be greasy and heavy. Turn the dough onto the work surface and gather into a ball. Wrap and chill until firm – about 45 minutes. Meanwhile, heat the oven to 375°F.

Roll out the pastry dough on a lightly floured work surface to a 4¹/₂- x 12-inch rectangle that is about ¹/₄ inch thick. Roll the rectangle around the rolling pin and transfer it to the prepared baking sheet. If necessary neaten the edges, either by trimming with a large sharp knife or by gently shaping with your hands. Flute the edges with your fingers, and prick the pastry rectangle well all over with a fork. Chill for about 15 minutes or until firm.

Bake for 10–12 minutes or until golden and firm. Cool for a minute, then loosen the underside with a large spatula. Let cool on the baking sheet. Increase the oven temperature to 425°F.

While the pastry base is cooling, make the filling. Mix the golden raisins with the rum and set aside to soak. Peel, core, and thickly slice the apples. Mix with the raisins and any soaking liquid left. Add the cinnamon. Toss well, then tip into a baking dish or roasting pan. Bake for 15 minutes or until the apples are barely tender. Let cool in the dish.

Melt the butter in a small heavy pan. Add the chopped almonds and apple-pie spice and cook gently, stirring frequently, for 5 minutes or until golden. Let cool.

To make the topping, put the egg white and flour in a food processor.

DECORATE THE EDGE OF THE PASTRY RECTANGLE BY FLUTING WITH YOUR FINGERS.

OPEN OUT THE PASTRY BAG AND STAND IT UPRIGHT IN A MEASURE FOR SUPPORT, THEN SPOON IN THE MARZIPAN MIXTURE.

PIPE THE MARZIPAN MIXTURE OVER THE APPLE TOPPING TO MAKE A ZIGZAG LATTICE PATTERN.

Break up the marzipan with your hands and add to the processor. Process until smooth. If it is a very hot day and the mixture seems too difficult and runny to pipe, put it in the fridge to chill for 30 minutes. Spoon the mixture into the pastry bag fitted with the plain tip.

To finish the slice, preheat the oven to 450°F. Spoon the nut mixture onto the pastry base on the baking sheet. Leave a narrow border of pastry showing. Spoon the apple mixture on top, mounding it neatly and evenly with your hands. Finally, pipe on the marzipan mixture in a zigzag lattice pattern. Let stand for about 10 minutes.

Bake for 5–8 minutes or until barely golden. Let cool for 15 minutes, then brush the top with the warmed apricot jam and sprinkle with the toasted sliced almonds.

Serve at room temperature, within 24 hours of baking. Delicious with vanilla ice-cream, cream, crème anglaise (see page 58), or crème fraîche.

STRAWBERRY BABAS

Makes 12
DOUGH:
1³/₄ cups (230g) unbleached white bread flour
1 teaspoon salt
1¹/₂ tablespoons (15g) sugar
1 0.6-oz cake fresh yeast (15g)
3 tablespoons milk, lukewarm
3 eggs, beaten
the grated rind of 1 unwaxed lemon
¹/₂ cup (110g) unsalted butter, at room
    temperature

SYRUP:
2¹/₂ cups (500g) sugar
1 quart (1 liter) water
the grated rind and juice of 1 large unwaxed lemon,
    or to taste

FILLING:
1 cup (250g) mascarpone or ricotta cheese
¹/₂lb (250g) strawberries, washed and hulled
fine shreds of lemon rind for decorating (optional)

12 dariole molds of about ¹/₂-cup capacity,
    buttered (see recipe)
a baking sheet

Babas are like very light sponge cakes soaked in a flavored syrup. But, in fact, they are made from a yeast dough enriched with eggs and butter, rather than a cake batter leavened with baking powder. Popular rum babas contain rum-soaked currants, and more rum is poured over after baking. The babas here are flavored with lemon, and are filled before serving with mascarpone or ricotta and sliced strawberries. You could also sprinkle over a little brandy or kirsch.

To make the dough, mix the flour, salt, and sugar in a mixing bowl, and make a well in the center. Crumble the yeast into a small bowl and cream it to a smooth paste with the lukewarm milk. Pour into the well in the flour, then mix in the eggs. Work the flour into the liquids with your hand, to make a smooth, very thick, batter-like dough. Knead the dough, in the bowl, by beating it with your hand: tilt the bowl slightly and, using your hand like a spoon, lift the dough and throw it back into the bowl with a slapping motion. Continue for 5 minutes or until the dough becomes very elastic, smooth, and slightly stiff. Cover the bowl with a damp dish towel and let rise in a warm place for 45 minutes to 1 hour or until the dough has doubled in bulk.

Butter the molds thoroughly. Chill them in the freezer for 10 minutes and then butter them again – this double buttering helps prevent the delicate dough from sticking to the molds and makes unmolding the soft-crusted babas very easy. The butter sets, so it will not be absorbed by the dough as it rises.

Punch down the risen dough with your knuckles, then using your hand as before, beat in the grated lemon rind and the soft butter. When the mixture is very smooth, with no streaks, use two spoons to divide it among the prepared molds. They should be just under half full. Arrange the molds on the baking sheet, cover with a damp dish towel, and let rise at normal to warm room temperature until the dough reaches almost to the top of the molds. This will take about 45 minutes – check to make sure the dough is not sticking to the dish towel.

1 *WHEN THOROUGHLY BEATEN, THE DOUGH WILL BE ELASTIC.*

2 *USE A PASTRY BRUSH TO COAT THE INSIDES OF THE MOLDS WITH SOFT BUTTER. CHILL AND BUTTER AGAIN.*

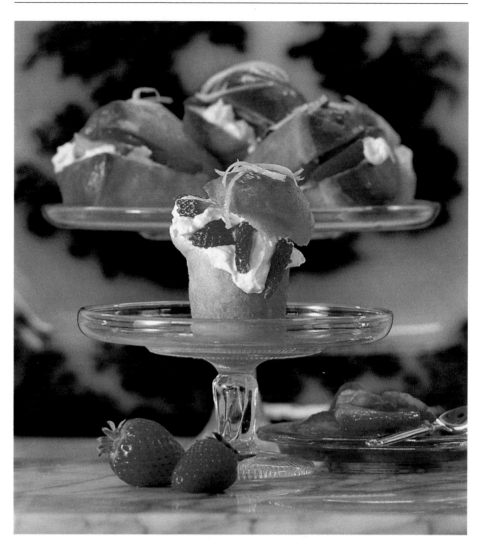

RIGHT The babas can be split horizontally or vertically before filling generously with creamy mascarpone and fruit.

Preheat the oven to 400°F.

Bake the babas for 15–20 minutes or until golden brown and beginning to shrink away from the sides of the molds. Turn out very carefully onto a wire rack and let cool.

To make the syrup, stir the sugar and water in a saucepan over low heat until dissolved. Then bring to a boil and boil, without stirring, for 2–3 minutes or until the syrup clears. Stir in the lemon rind and juice.

Remove the pan from the heat. Add the babas, a couple at a time, to the hot syrup and let them soak for a minute or so, turning them over. Lift them out with a slotted spoon onto a serving plate. When cool, keep covered until ready to serve.

To make the filling, beat the mascarpone or ricotta until fluffy. Slice the strawberries and sweeten with a little sugar if necessary.

Slice off the top of each baba at an angle. Spoon a little mascarpone or ricotta onto the cut surface of each baba, then top with strawberries and replace the cut-off top. Sprinkle with liqueur, if using, and shreds of lemon rind and serve as soon as possible.

NOTE You can use 1 package (¹/₄oz/7g) active dry yeast instead of fresh yeast. For rapid-rise dry yeast, add it to the flour, salt, and sugar. Proceed with the recipe, adding the lukewarm milk with the eggs.

APRICOT ALMOND BRAID

Ideal for picnics and alfresco meals, this is a moist and fruity, well-flavored cake made from sweet yeast dough. It is filled with chopped dried apricots and ground and chopped almonds.

INGREDIENTS

Cuts into about 8 slices
DOUGH:
1³⁄₄ cups (230g) unbleached white bread flour
¹⁄₂ teaspoon salt
3 tablespoons (40g) unsalted butter, chilled and diced
²⁄₃ 0.6-oz cake fresh yeast (10g)
5 tablespoons (70ml) milk, at room temperature
1 egg, beaten

FILLING:
³⁄₄ cup (110g) roughly chopped dried apricots
²⁄₃ cup (140ml) orange juice
6 tablespoons (85g) unsalted butter, at room temperature
¹⁄₂ cup (60g) light brown sugar
¹⁄₃ cup (30g) ground almonds
6 tablespoons (60g) golden raisins
¹⁄₄ cup (60g) toasted and roughly chopped blanched almonds
the grated rind of 1 unwaxed orange

TO FINISH:
¹⁄₃ cup (30g) toasted sliced almonds for sprinkling

a large baking sheet, greased

NOTE You can use 2 teaspoons active dry yeast instead of fresh yeast, dissolving it in warm milk. For rapid-rise dry yeast mix it with the flour and salt, then proceed with the recipe.

To make the filling, put the apricots and orange juice into a small pan. Bring to a boil, then remove from the heat and let soak while making and rising the sweet yeast dough.

Mix the flour and salt in a large mixing bowl. Rub in the butter to make fine crumbs. Make a well in the center. Crumble the yeast into a small bowl and cream it to a smooth liquid with the milk. Stir in the egg. Pour the yeast mixture into the well in the flour. Gradually work the flour into the liquid to make a soft but not sticky dough. Turn the dough onto a lightly floured work surface and knead for 10 minutes or until very smooth and elastic. Return the dough to the bowl, cover with a damp dish towel, and let rise at normal room temperature for about 1 hour or until the dough has doubled in bulk.

Meanwhile, prepare the filling. Drain the soaked apricots, reserving the liquid to glaze the baked braid. Beat the butter with the sugar until fluffy, then work in the ground almonds followed by the drained apricots, golden raisins, chopped almonds, and orange rind.

Punch down the risen dough with your knuckles, then turn onto a lightly floured work surface. Roll out to a rectangle about 10 x 12 inches. Spread the filling evenly over the dough, then roll up fairly tightly from one long side, like a jelly roll. Using your hands, gently roll the cylinder on the work surface to make it longer and thinner – it should be about 18 inches long. Lift it onto the prepared baking sheet.

Using a large, very sharp knife, cut the roll lengthwise into three equal strips, leaving them joined at one end. Working with the cut sides facing upward as much as possible, braid the three strips together. Pinch the ends together and tuck under neatly. Cover loosely with a damp dish towel and let rise at normal room temperature for about 1 hour or until the braid has doubled in size.

Preheat the oven to 400°F.

Bake the risen braid for about 25 minutes or until golden brown and firm. Remove from the oven. Heat the reserved orange juice and brush over the hot braid. Sprinkle with the sliced almonds and transfer to a wire rack to cool. Serve warm, with cream. Eat within 2 days. To reheat the braid, wrap in foil and heat for about 10 minutes at 350°F.

1 AFTER SPREADING WITH THE APRICOT FILLING, ROLL UP THE DOUGH QUITE TIGHTLY.

2 CUT THE ROLL DOWN ITS LENGTH INTO THREE STRIPS, THEN BRAID THESE TOGETHER.

RED FRUIT SLUMP

INGREDIENTS

Serves 4
1-1¼lb (500g) fresh or frozen red fruits
3–4 tablespoons sugar, to taste
2 tablespoons water or crème de cassis

DUMPLINGS:
7 tablespoons (60g) self-rising flour
2 tablespoons (30g) unsalted butter, chilled and diced
1½ tablespoons (15g) sugar
a pinch of ground cinnamon
2 tablespoons milk

a baking dish of about 1-quart capacity

This is another German dessert from Brigitte Friis (see her divine Almond Squares on page 23). A mixture of red fruits is cooked until the juices just start to run, then tiny pastry dumplings are added, and the dessert is baked until the fruit is just tender and the dumplings are cooked and feather-light. Brigitte freezes fruit from her garden — cherries, raspberries, blackberries, loganberries, strawberries, and currants — to make this dessert, but frozen mixed red fruits, sold in bags, and fresh fruit both work just as well.

Preheat the oven to 375°F.

Put the fruit (there is no need to thaw frozen fruit) in the baking dish and sprinkle over the sugar and the water or cassis. Cover with a lid or foil and bake in the preheated oven for 10–12 minutes or until the juices start to run — the time will depend on the type and ripeness of the fruit, and whether it is fresh or frozen.

Meanwhile, make the pastry dumplings. Sift the flour into a small mixing bowl, add the diced butter, and rub in using the tips of your fingers until the mixture resembles fine crumbs. Stir in the sugar and cinnamon, and bind to a soft but not sticky dough with the milk. Using your hands, roll the mixture into 12 small balls.

Remove the baking dish from the oven, uncover, and stir the fruit gently. Arrange the pastry balls in the dish so they are nestling in the hot fruit juices. Cover again and bake for about 15 minutes or until the dumplings are firm to the touch. Serve hot, warm, or at room temperature, with ice-cream, cream, or crème fraîche.

CARROLL'S FUDGE PIE

INGREDIENTS

Serves 6–8

1 cup (200g) sugar

$^{1}/_{2}$ cup (110g) unsalted butter, at room
    temperature

2 eggs, separated

$2^{1}/_{2}$oz (70g) good semisweet chocolate, chopped

$^{1}/_{3}$ cup (50g) all-purpose flour

a few drops of pure vanilla extract

a pinch of salt

CHOCOLATE CREAM:

3 tablespoons unsweetened cocoa powder

$^{1}/_{3}$ cup (40g) confectioners' sugar

$^{2}/_{3}$ cup (140ml) heavy cream, chilled

a few drops of pure vanilla extract

a 9-inch pie pan, about $1^{1}/_{2}$ inches deep, or a tart
    pan (not loose-based), greased

Caroll Boltin, who makes the best brownies in the world (see the recipe on page 40), prefers this very rich chocolate pudding to Mississippi Mud Pie or Death By Chocolate. She adds that it is embarrassingly easy and quick to make for something that tastes so good. Serve in very thin slices with whipped cream, chocolate cream (recipe below), or ice-cream.

Preheat the oven to 325°F.

Beat the sugar and butter together until creamy, then beat in the egg yolks one at a time. Melt the chocolate in a heatproof bowl set over a pan of hot but not boiling water, then remove from the heat and let cool, stirring occasionally. Beat the cooled chocolate into the yolk mixture. Add the flour, vanilla, and salt and fold into the mixture, using a large metal spoon, until thoroughly combined.

In a spotlessly clean and grease-free bowl, beat the egg whites until stiff peaks form. Fold into the chocolate mixture in three batches.

Spoon into the prepared pie or tart pan and spread evenly. Bake for 30 minutes. Let cool and then chill.

To make the chocolate cream, sift the cocoa powder and sugar into the cream. Stir gently until combined, then cover and chill for 2 hours. The mixture should be quite stiff. Stir in the vanilla. If the cream isn't stiff, whip it until it holds its shape. The chocolate cream can also be used to sandwich chocolate macaroons or meringues (pages 24 and 41).

Decorate the fudge pie, if desired, with piped chocolate cream, or serve the cream separately.

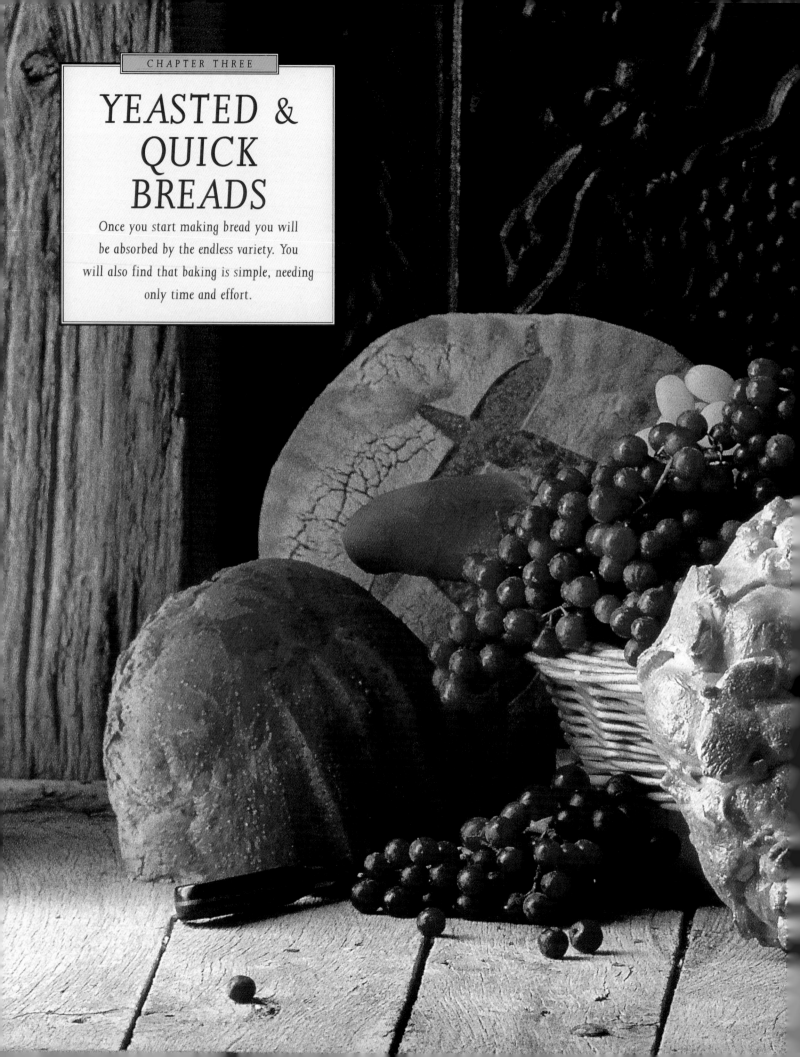

CHAPTER THREE

YEASTED & QUICK BREADS

Once you start making bread you will
be absorbed by the endless variety. You
will also find that baking is simple, needing
only time and effort.

MY FAVORITE BREAD

INGREDIENTS

Makes 1 large loaf

2¾ cups (340g) unbleached white bread flour

1⅓ cups (170g) stoneground whole-wheat bread
    flour

1¾ cups (170g) rye flour

2 tablespoons (15g) sea salt, crushed or ground

1 0.6-oz cake fresh yeast (15g)

2 cups (430ml) water from the cold tap

extra flour for dusting and sprinkling

a large baking sheet, lightly greased

Combining three flours — white, whole-wheat, and rye, all stoneground for choice — gives me the best of loaves. There is plenty of flavor, a proper crust, a good texture, and chewy crumb — especially if I use coarse-ground whole-wheat flour — and the bread keeps well. The dough is easier to knead than a loaf made only with whole-wheat flour. It is shaped into a round and simply baked on a greased baking sheet, though you can also use a large loaf pan.

Mix the flours and salt in a large mixing bowl and make a well in the center. Crumble the yeast into a small bowl and cream to a smooth liquid with 4 tablespoons of the cold water. Pour the yeast liquid and the rest of the water into the well in the flour. Using your hand draw a little flour into the liquid and mix thoroughly. Gradually draw in more flour until you have a thick, smooth batter in the well. Sprinkle this batter with a little flour to prevent a skin from forming, then cover the bowl with a damp dish towel and let "sponge" for about 20 minutes: the batter will become aerated and frothy and will expand to fill the well firm the flour. This "sponging," or proving, shows that the yeast is not only alive and kicking but starting to grow. If the batter does not show any signs of life after 30 minutes, the yeast is probably too old and you will have to replace the yeast and liquid, and start again.

Gradually mix the remaining flour into the batter to make a firm dough. Gather the dough into a ball — it should leave the sides of the bowl clean. If the dough seems sticky or wet, work in extra flour a tablespoon at a time; if there are dry crumbs at the bottom of the bowl and the dough seems stiff, work in extra water a tablespoon at a time.

1 BREAK UP THE FRESH YEAST BY CRUMBLING IT BETWEEN YOUR FINGERS.

2 MIX THE YEAST WITH A LITTLE WATER UNTIL SMOOTH, THEN ADD TO THE FLOUR.

3 ADD THE REST OF THE WATER TO THE WELL, THEN DRAW IN THE FLOUR.

4 WHEN THE FLOUR IS MIXED IN, THE DOUGH SHOULD BE FIRM BUT NOT STICKY.

LEFT My Favorite Bread and Light Rye Loaf (see recipe on page 78).

PREVIOUS PAGE (left to right) My Favorite Bread, Simple Sourdough, Harvest Wreath, a French loaf, and Light Rye Loaf.

5 IT'S IMPORTANT TO KNEAD THE DOUGH THOROUGHLY – 10 MINUTES BY HAND.

6 ROLL THE DOUGH INTO A BALL, THEN RETURN TO THE BOWL FOR THE FIRST RISE.

7 AFTER ABOUT 2 HOURS OF RISING, THE DOUGH WILL HAVE DOUBLED IN SIZE.

8 USE YOUR FIST TO FLATTEN THE DOUGH AND KNOCK OUT LARGE AIR BUBBLES.

Turn the dough onto a lightly floured work surface – use as little flour as possible – and knead it thoroughly for 10 minutes. Kneading is vital for a good even-textured loaf. It also ensures that the yeast is thoroughly distributed, so the loaf will rise and cook evenly. To knead, first stretch the dough away from you using the heel of your hand, then gather the dough back into a ball and give it a quarter turn. Continue kneading in this way by continually stretching and turning the dough; as the dough is kneaded it gradually changes texture, becoming smoother, firmer, and more elastic, and looking almost glossy.

You also use an electric mixer fitted with a dough hook to knead the dough, but as it is quite easy to over-knead using a machine – something that is almost impossible by hand – reduce the kneading time to about 7 minutes or follow the manufacturer's instructions. If the dough is over-kneaded the gluten strands that have been carefully developed and strengthened will be irretrievably broken and the dough will collapse.

I have never been able to knead a bread dough to my satisfaction in a food processor.

Shape the dough into a ball and return to the cleaned mixing bowl. (For delicate doughs I like to use a lightly greased bowl, and I turn the ball of dough over so it is covered with a thin layer of oil to prevent it from sticking or drying.) Cover the bowl with a damp dish towel, or put the bowl in a very large plastic bag that has been greased inside – a supermarket bag is ideal. It is important that the dough stays moist for the yeast to work effectively; also, if a dry crust forms it can result in hard lumps in the baked loaf.

Let the dough rise at cool to normal room temperature, in a draft-free place, for 1½–2 hours or until doubled in bulk. Most bread recipes say to put the dough in a very warm spot so it rises very quickly, but I think bread has a better flavor if the dough is left to rise at a fairly cool temperature – around 60°F.

The loaf will be heavy if not left to rise for long enough, though over-rising is more of a problem: if a dough is seriously distended by being left to rise too long, it tends to collapse in the heat of the oven. If the dough is only slightly over-risen it can usually be saved if you knead it again for a couple of minutes before shaping and rising again. When the dough has properly risen you should be able to press the tip of a finger into the center without the dough springing back.

Punch down the risen dough by flattening it with your knuckles, lightly floured. This breaks down the very large bubbles and redistributes the gases so there will be no large holes or solid pieces in the baked loaf. Turn the dough onto a floured work surface and shape it into a ball. Cup your hands, lightly floured, over the ball, then gently smooth the dough so the sides and top are nicely rounded and the ball has a good, even shape. Put the shaped loaf onto the prepared baking sheet. Cover as before and let rise for 1½–2 hours or until doubled in size.

Preheat the oven to 425°F.

Uncover the loaf. With a very sharp knife slash the top of the dough round diagonally three times. If you wish, sprinkle with a little flour to give the surface a matt finish when baked. Bake for 15 minutes or until golden, then lower the oven temperature to 375°F and bake for a further 20–25 minutes or until the loaf sounds hollow when tapped on the base. If it does not sound hollow, return it to the oven, placing it upside down directly on the oven rack, and bake for 5 minutes longer, then test again.

Transfer the bread to a wire rack to cool.

NOTE You can use 1 package (¼oz/7g) active dry yeast instead of fresh yeast; dissolve it in 4 tablespoons warm water, and proceed as for fresh yeast. For rapid-rise dry yeast, mix it into the flours when you add the salt. Mix thoroughly. Omit the sponging stage, and mix in all the liquid at once to make the dough. Then proceed with the recipe.

9 SET THE SHAPED LOAF ON THE BAKING SHEET, COVER, AND LET RISE AGAIN.

10 THE LOAF WILL RISE TO DOUBLE IN SIZE WHILE KEEPING ITS NEAT, ROUND SHAPE.

11 SLASH THE TOP OF THE LOAF WITHOUT DRAGGING THE KNIFE BLADE. BAKE.

12 HOLD THE HOT BAKED LOAF WITH A THICK CLOTH AND TAP THE UNDERSIDE.

A PLAIN WHITE LOAF

INGREDIENTS

Makes 1 large loaf
5^{1}/$_{2}$ cups (680g) unbleached white bread flour,
    preferably stoneground
2 tablespoons (15g) sea salt, crushed or ground
1 0.6-oz cake fresh yeast (15g)
2 cups (430ml) water from the cold tap
extra flour for dusting

a large loaf pan, about 9 x 5 x 3 inches, greased

You can use this basic recipe to make a pan loaf, a large oval loaf, a big round or braided loaf, or even rolls. You can also experiment with different toppings, as well as additions to the dough – sunflower or sesame seeds, chopped herbs, dried fruit, and nuts, for example.

Make the dough with the flour, salt, yeast, and water and knead following the instructions on pages 73-4. Cover and let rise until doubled in bulk.

Punch down the risen dough and turn onto a lightly floured work surface. Pat out to a rectangular shape about 1 inch thick and the length of the pan. Roll up the dough from one short end. Pinch the seam together with your fingers, then put the dough into the prepared pan seam-side down, tucking the ends underneath. The pan should be half filled. Cover the pan with a damp dish towel and let rise until doubled in size – about 1 hour at normal room temperature and 1^{1}/$_{2}$ hours in a cool room.

Preheat the oven to 450°F.

Uncover the loaf and sprinkle the top with a little flour. Using a very sharp knife, make one deep slash down the center of the loaf. Bake for 15 minutes, then lower the oven temperature to 400°F and bake for a further 20–30 minutes or until the loaf sounds hollow when tipped out of the pan and tapped on the base. Turn out onto a wire rack to cool.

NOTE You can use 1 package (^{1}/$_{4}$oz/7g) active dry yeast instead of fresh yeast. For rapid-rise dry yeast, add it to the flour and salt. Omit the sponging stage and add all the water at once. Proceed with the recipe.

1 ROLL UP THE DOUGH TIGHTLY SO THERE ARE NO LARGE AIR BUBBLES OR HOLES.

2 PINCH THE SEAM TOGETHER AND PUT INTO THE PAN, TUCKING THE ENDS UNDER.

TO SHAPE COTTAGE LOAF ROLLS (TOP), PUSH YOUR FLOURED LITTLE FINGER THROUGH THE TWO BALLS OF DOUGH. FOR OVAL ROLLS, MAKE A DEEP CREASE DOWN THE CENTER WITH THE SIDE OF YOUR FINGER (ABOVE).

VARIATION: BREAD ROLLS Punch down the risen dough, then divide it into 2oz (60g) portions (or about half the size the finished rolls will be). For a *round smooth roll*, take a portion of dough and shape it into a rough ball. Cup the dough in your palm and, using the fingers of your other hand, pull the outer edge of the dough outward then push back in toward the center. Turn the dough and repeat until the ball is smooth and neat underneath. Another method is to put the rough ball of dough on the work surface, cup your hand over the ball so your fingertips and wrist touch the work surface, and gently rotate your hand so the dough underneath is rolled around and smoothed into a neat roll. For a *cottage loaf shape*, take a portion of dough and cut off a third. Roll each piece into a neat ball. Slightly flatten the larger ball, put the smaller ball on top, and secure together by pushing a finger down through the center. To make a *braid*, take a portion of dough and roll it into a sausage shape about 3 inches long. Cut into three lengthwise, leaving the three strands attached at one end, then braid them together. To make *wedges*, take three portions of dough and knead them together until smooth. Form into a disk about 1 inch thick and cut this into three wedges as if cutting a cake. To make *oval rolls*, take a portion of dough and shape into a ball. Flatten slightly and mold to an oval with your hands, then make a crease down the center using the side of your little finger.

Arrange the rolls on greased baking sheets, placing them well apart. Cover with a damp dish towel and let rise until doubled in size – 30–40 minutes at normal room temperature. Preheat the oven to 425°F. Remove the dish towel and lightly glaze the rolls with beaten egg or milk. Or they can be sprinkled with flour, cornmeal, sea salt, poppy seeds, rye or wheat flakes, cracked wheat, or sesame seeds. Bake for 18–20 minutes or until the rolls are golden brown and sound hollow when tapped on the base.

LIGHT RYE LOAF

INGREDIENTS

Makes 1 large loaf
3¾ cups (450g) unbleached white bread flour
2 cups (230g) rye flour, stoneground if possible
1 tablespoon caraway seeds
1 tablespoon (5g) salt
1 0.6-oz cake fresh yeast (15g)
2 cups (430ml) water from the cold tap

a baking sheet, greased

1 MAKE A DEEP CREASE IN THE CENTER OF THE LOAF WITH THE SIDE OF YOUR HAND.

2 ROLL THE LOAF OVER AND PUT ON THE BAKING SHEET, SEAM UNDERNEATH.

Many rye breads are dark, pungent, and heavy, redolent of Eastern Europe, and ideal for eating with cured fish or smoked and cured meats. They can also be light, milder, more open-textured loaves that make good toast and sandwiches. This loaf, with its high proportion of white flour, is easy to work yet has the distinct taste of rye. And, of course, caraway seeds are the perfect partner to rye.

Mix the flours, caraway seeds, and salt in a large mixing bowl and make a well in the center. Crumble the yeast into a small bowl and stir to a smooth liquid with ⅔ cup (140ml) of the water. Pour the yeast liquid and the rest of the water into the well in the flour. Gradually mix in the flour to make a soft but not sticky dough. Turn the dough onto a lightly floured work surface and knead thoroughly for 10 minutes. Return the dough to the bowl, cover with a damp dish towel, and let rise at cool to normal room temperature for about 2 hours or until doubled in bulk.

Punch down the risen dough with your knuckles, then turn it onto a lightly floured work surface. Shape into an oval by kneading it lightly. With the edge of your hand, make a good crease down the center of the dough oval, then roll the dough over to make an oval sausage. Turn the dough over on the work surface so the seam is underneath and the top looks smooth and evenly shaped. Put the shaped loaf, seam-side down, onto the prepared baking sheet. Cover and let rise until doubled in size – about 1 hour at normal room temperature.

Preheat the oven to 425°F.

Uncover the loaf and slash it several times across the top, using a very sharp knife. Bake for 15–20 minutes or until golden, then reduce the oven temperature to 375°F and bake for a further 20 minutes or until the loaf sounds hollow when tapped on the base. Cool on a wire rack. The loaf is best eaten within 4 days, and is also good toasted.

NOTE You can use 1 package (¼oz/7g) active dry yeast instead of fresh yeast, dissolving it in warm water. For rapid-rise dry yeast, mix it with the flours, caraway seeds, and salt. Then add the water and proceed.

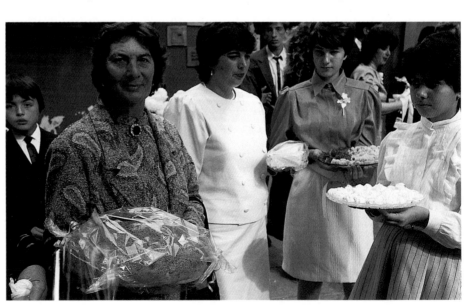

Rye breads of all sizes and shapes are baked in Eastern Europe. Here, in Old Plodiv, Bulgaria, a rye dough has been made into a decorative wedding loaf.

DANISH RYE BREAD

Makes 1 large loaf
4¹/₂ cups (450g) rye flour
³/₄ cup (100g) unbleached white bread flour
¹/₂ tablespoon sea salt, crushed or ground
1 0.6-oz cake fresh yeast (15g)
²/₃ cup (140ml) milk, at room temperature
²/₃ cup (140ml) hot water
1 tablespoon molasses
extra flour for dusting

a large loaf pan, about 9 x 5 x 3 inches, greased

David Sharland, of the Savoy Hotel in London, made this loaf for a Scandinavian festival at the hotel when he was pastry chef. He is a big fan of good rye bread, and suggests keeping this well-flavored loaf at least a day before slicing.

Mix the flours and salt together in a large mixing bowl and make a well in the center. Crumble the yeast into a small bowl and mix to a smooth liquid with the milk. Stir the hot water and molasses together until the molasses dissolves. Pour the yeast liquid into the well in the flour, then add the molasses liquid. Quickly mix the flour into the liquids to make a heavy, sticky dough. It will be difficult to work. Because rye flour has far less gluten than wheat flour the loaf will be denser and will not rise as much as one made from all wheat flour.

Turn the dough onto a floured work surface and knead for 5 minutes – it will be hard work at first but the dough should become less sticky and more pliable. (You can always knead for a few minutes, then cover the dough and take a break for 5 minutes.) Shape the dough into a loaf to fit the pan (see page 76). Put the loaf into the prepared pan seam-side down. Using a fork, prick the loaf all the way through in four or five places. Cover the pan with a damp dish towel and let rise at normal to warm room temperature for 2¹/₂–3 hours or until almost doubled in size.

Preheat the oven to 450°F.

Bake the loaf for 15 minutes, then lower the oven temperature to 400°F and bake for a further 45–50 minutes or until the loaf sounds hollow when tipped out of the pan and tapped on the base. David recommends turning the loaf out of the pan about 15 minutes before the end of the baking time, and baking the loaf on the oven shelf so it will develop a good crusty finish. Transfer the cooked loaf to a wire rack to cool completely, then wrap in wax paper and foil and keep for a day before eating. The bread keeps well for up to a week.

NOTE You can use 1 package (¹/₄oz/7g) active dry yeast instead of fresh yeast, dissolving it in warm milk. For rapid-rise yeast, mix it with the flours, then add the milk and proceed with the recipe.

SIMPLE SOURDOUGH

INGREDIENTS

Makes 1 large loaf

about 12oz (340g) bread dough (use My Favorite
Bread, page 73), risen once and kept for at least
24 hours

2 cups (430ml) water from the cold tap

2 tablespoons (15g) sea salt, crushed or ground

2¾ cups (340g) stoneground whole-wheat bread
flour

about 2¾ cups (340g) unbleached white bread
flour, stoneground if possible

a baking sheet, greased

Sourdough breads are fascinating to make – you never quite know if they will turn out or how they will taste. They are made from a starter dough, which is either made from scratch or is a lump of dough saved from the previous loaf – plus flour, salt, and water.

To make a starter from scratch, you have to make a flour and water batter and let it ferment for several days, during which time it absorbs the yeasts naturally present in the atmosphere. It is this fermentation that produces the appealing sour taste characteristic of this bread. The flavor of the final baked loaf depends on the pungency and quantity of the starter, as well as on the rising time. Because the flavor becomes more pronounced the longer the dough is left, you can tailor the recipe to suit your taste.

When I don't have the time to get a good sourdough starter going – and it can take 5 days – I just cut off a lump of dough from a normal yeast-raised loaf and store it in a covered bowl on the kitchen table (or in the fridge if it's hot) for at least 24 hours. I then use this as my starter. The flavor of the first loaf made this way will be quite mild. If you want to have a sourer loaf, keep the lump of dough for up to 5 days in the fridge.

Sourdough bread is usually left in a cloth-lined basket for its final rising, then inverted onto a sheet for baking; however, this loaf is shaped and then risen and baked on the baking sheet.

Punch down the portion of bread dough, as it will have risen even in the fridge. Put the water into a large mixing bowl, add the salt, and stir until dissolved. Add the bread dough starter and mix using your hands. When the dough has broken down to make a lumpy batter full of strands and small pieces of dough, work in the whole-wheat flour. When thoroughly combined, gradually work in enough white flour to make a soft but not sticky dough.

Turn the dough onto a lightly floured work surface and knead thoroughly for 10 minutes – the dough changes and becomes firmer as you knead it, so it is important not to knead in too much flour at the very beginning. Return the dough to the bowl, cover with a damp dish towel,

1 USE YOUR HANDS TO SQUEEZE AND MIX THE
DOUGH STARTER INTO THE SALT WATER.

2 CONTINUE MIXING VIGOROUSLY TO BREAK
DOWN THE DOUGH AND MAKE A LUMPY BATTER.

3 WORK IN THE WHOLE-WHEAT FLOUR. THE
DOUGH WILL BE SMOOTH BUT STICKY.

4 ADD ENOUGH WHITE FLOUR TO MAKE A
SOFT DOUGH THAT IS NO LONGER STICKY.

and let rise until almost doubled in bulk. In a cool room this will take around 12 hours, or 8 hours at normal room temperature.

Punch down the risen dough with your knuckles. Turn onto a lightly floured work surface and cut off a portion – about 12oz (340g) – to keep as the starter for the next loaf. Cover this starter and store in the fridge for up to 5 days. Shape the rest of the dough into a round or oval loaf (see page 75 or 78). If the dough seems at all sticky or very soft, work in a little more flour, otherwise the loaf won't hold its shape during baking.

Put the loaf onto the prepared baking sheet, then cover and let rise as before until almost doubled in size – 8 hours in a cool room, 4 hours at normal room temperature.

Preheat the oven to 450°F.

Slash the top of the loaf several times, using a very sharp knife. Bake for 20 minutes, then reduce the oven temperature to 400°F and bake for a further 15 minutes or until the loaf sounds hollow when tapped on the base. Transfer to a wire rack to cool.

The loaf will keep well for at least 5 days, and, when no longer at the peak of freshness, makes wonderful toast.

ORANGE PUMPERNICKEL BREAD

Makes 2 small loaves

2³/₄ cups (280g) rye flour, preferably coarse stoneground

1¹/₃ cups (170g) unbleached white bread flour

1 cup (110g) stoneground whole-wheat bread flour

2 teaspoons salt

1 0.6-oz cake fresh yeast (15g)

1¹/₂ cups (340ml) lukewarm water

2 tablespoons light brown sugar

¹/₄ cup (85g) molasses

1 tablespoon vegetable oil or melted butter

the grated rind of 1 unwaxed orange

¹/₂ cup (85g) raisins

two small loaf pans, about 8¹/₂ x 4¹/₂ x 2¹/₂ inches, greased

NOTE You can use 1 package (¹/₄oz/7g) active dry yeast instead of fresh yeast.

You can't buy pumpernickel flour – pumpernickel bread is made from a blend of several flours and grains. It always contains a fair proportion of rye flour, which accounts for its dense texture and strong flavor. Commercial loaves are often baked for several hours in a slightly steamy oven, which helps develop the dark rich color. This slightly sweet loaf is excellent with creamy cheeses and makes good open sandwiches – we enjoyed something very similar at the Rose Garden tea restaurant in the Huntington Botanical Gardens in Pasadena, California. Pumpernickel bread is also fine toasted and spread with butter and marmalade for breakfast.

Mix the three flours and salt together in a large mixing bowl and make a well in the center. Crumble the yeast into a small bowl and stir it to a smooth liquid with the water. Pour the yeast liquid into the well in the flour, followed by the sugar, molasses, and oil or butter. Mix together all the ingredients in the well, then work in the flour to make a soft and slightly sticky dough – it will be heavy and quite difficult to work.

1 COMBINE THE THREE FLOURS IN A BOWL, MIX TOGETHER, AND MAKE A WELL IN THE CENTER.

2 MIX THE YEAST LIQUID, SUGAR, MOLASSES, AND OIL TOGETHER IN THE WELL.

3 AFTER RISING, ADD THE RAISINS AND GRATED ORANGE RIND TO THE DOUGH AND KNEAD IN.

Turn the dough onto a lightly floured work surface and knead for 10 minutes. The dough will still be heavy but will have become firmer and more elastic. If you find the kneading hard work, cover the dough with the up-turned mixing bowl and take a breather for a few minutes before continuing. Return the kneaded dough to the bowl, cover with a damp dish towel, and let rise until doubled in bulk – about 3 hours at normal room temperature.

Punch down the risen dough with your knuckles, then turn it onto a lightly floured work surface. Sprinkle the orange rind and raisins over the dough and knead for a minute until evenly distributed. Divide the dough in half and shape each piece into a loaf to fit the pans (see page 76). Put into the prepared pans seam-side down. Cover with a damp dish towel and let rise until doubled in size: 1½–2 hours at room temperature.

Preheat the oven to 400°F.

Bake the risen loaves for 35–40 minutes or until they sound hollow when tipped out of the pan and tapped on the base. Turn out onto a wire rack to cool. When cold, wrap in wax paper, then in foil. Keep for a day before slicing.

ITALIAN SEMOLINA BREAD

Makes 1 large loaf
1 0.6-oz cake fresh yeast (15g)
½ cup (115ml) water from the cold tap
1⅔ cups (200g) unbleached white bread flour
1⅔ cups (280g) semolina flour
1 teaspoon salt
2 tablespoons (30g) butter, chilled and diced
1 tablespoon honey
1 egg, beaten
beaten egg for glazing

a baking sheet, greased

Durum wheat semolina flour, the kind used for pasta, makes a good-textured, fairly close loaf with a nice flavor. Because the flour is hard, with a higher gluten content than even bread flour, I think it is best to mix it with white or whole-wheat bread flour to prevent the loaf from being tough. Good Italian grocers and wholefood markets should stock semolina flour.

Crumble the yeast into a small bowl and mix to a smooth liquid with the water. Mix the flours and salt together in a large mixing bowl. Add the diced butter and rub in using the tips of your fingers to make fine crumbs. Stir the honey and egg into the yeast liquid, then add to the flour mixture and mix to a soft but not sticky dough. Turn onto a lightly floured work surface and knead thoroughly for 10 minutes. Shape the dough into a ball, return it to the bowl, and cover. Let it rise at normal room temperature for 1–1½ hours or until the dough has doubled in bulk.

Punch down the risen dough with your knuckles and turn it onto a very lightly floured work surface. Shape the dough into an oval (see page 78) and place on the prepared baking sheet. Cover with a damp dish towel and let rise as before until doubled in size – about 1 hour.

Preheat the oven to 375°F.

Brush the risen loaf with beaten egg to glaze, then bake for 30–35 minutes or until the bread sounds hollow when tapped on the base. Transfer to a wire rack to cool. Eat within 24 hours, or toast, or freeze for up to 3 months.

NOTE You can use 1 package (¼oz/7g) active dry yeast instead of fresh yeast, dissolving it in warm water. For rapid-rise dry yeast, mix it with the flours and salt. Rub in the butter. Mix the water with the honey and egg, then proceed with the recipe.

OPPOSITE *Eating al fresco in Paghezzana, Italy.*

EASTER BRAID

INGREDIENTS

Makes 1 large loaf

5½ cups (680g) unbleached white bread flour

5 tablespoons (60g) sugar

2 teaspoons salt

1 tablespoon apple-pie spice

1 0.6-oz cake fresh yeast (15g)

2 cups (430ml) lukewarm milk

6 tablespoons (85g) unsalted butter, chilled and diced

1 egg, beaten

⅔ cup (110g) currants

3 tablespoons finely chopped mixed candied peel

GLAZE:

beaten egg for brushing

about 3 tablespoons honey, warmed

a large baking sheet, lightly greased

Here the dough traditionally used for Hot Cross Buns — rich with butter, spice, and fruit — is braided into an attractive loaf and glazed with honey. To keep its shape, the dough should not be too soft, and should not be left to rise in a warm spot. Leftover Braid is excellent toasted or used for Bread and Butter Pudding (see page 52).

Put 1⅓ cups (170g) of the flour into a small mixing bowl with the sugar, and make a well in the center. Sift the remaining flour with the salt and spice into a large mixing bowl. Crumble the yeast into the well in the smaller bowl. Pour the lukewarm milk onto the yeast and mix until combined. Work the flour and sugar into the yeast liquid to make a smooth batter. Cover and let "sponge" for about 20 minutes — the batter will become bubbly as the yeast begins to grow.

Add the diced butter to the flour mixture in the larger bowl and rub in, using your fingertips until the mixture looks like coarse crumbs. Stir the egg into the frothy yeast batter and add to the flour. Mix together to form a fairly firm, rather than soft or sticky, dough. Turn the dough onto a lightly floured work surface and knead for 10 minutes or until quite firm, silky smooth, and elastic. Put the dough back into the bowl, cover with a damp dish towel, and let rise at cool to normal room temperature for 1–1½ hours or until doubled in bulk.

Turn the risen dough onto a lightly floured work surface and punch down with your knuckles. Sprinkle over the currants and peel, and gently but thoroughly knead into the dough until evenly distributed. The dough should be quite pliable but not soft, and it should hold its shape well. If not, work in a little more flour. Divide the dough into three equal pieces (ideally, weigh the dough on kitchen scales).

Using your hands, roll each piece into a sausage shape about 16 inches long. Lay the three pieces of dough parallel to each other on the prepared baking sheet, then braid them together neatly but not too tightly. Take care not to stretch the dough unduly. Tuck the ends under. Cover with a damp dish towel and let rise at cool to normal room temperature for about 1 hour or until almost doubled in size.

Preheat the oven to 425°F.

1 ROLL EACH OF THE THREE PIECES OF DOUGH INTO A LONG, EVEN SAUSAGE SHAPE.

2 LAY THE PIECES ON THE BAKING SHEET AND BRAID WITHOUT STRETCHING THEM.

3 TUCK UNDER THE ENDS OF THE FINISHED BRAID, THEN LET RISE BEFORE BAKING.

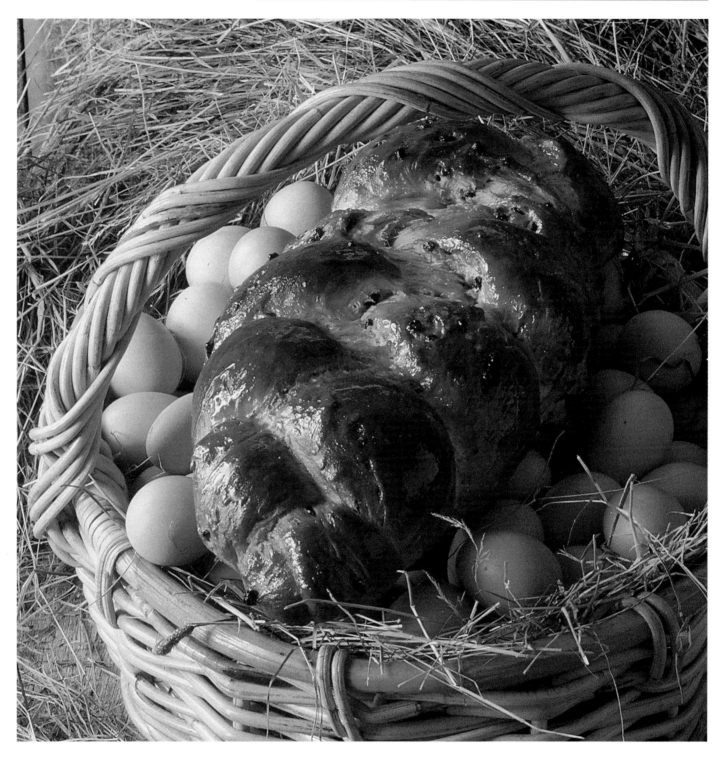

Carefully brush the loaf with the beaten egg, then bake for 15–20 minutes or until golden. Lower the oven temperature to 400°F and bake for a further 20 minutes or until the loaf sounds hollow when tapped on the base. Transfer to a wire rack, brush with the warm honey, and cool.

NOTE You can use 1 package (¼oz/7g) active dry yeast instead of fresh yeast. For rapid-rise dry yeast, add it to the 1⅓ cups (170g) flour and sugar. Pour the measured lukewarm milk into the well in the dry ingredients and proceed with the recipe.

HARVEST WREATH

INGREDIENTS

Makes 1 large wreath

7¼ cups (900g) unbleached white bread flour, preferably stoneground

1½ tablespoons salt

1 0.6-oz cake fresh yeast (15g)

2⅓ cups (570ml) water from the cold tap

1 egg, beaten with a large pinch of salt, for glazing

a large baking sheet, greased

As Anthony and I traveled though Europe, we came across many extremely attractive loaves baked to celebrate the harvest. This elaborately decorated loaf was made to eat at a party in a Burgundy vineyard at the end of the vendange, or grape-picking. There is a fair amount of salt in the dough, which enables it to maintain its shape. As with the Easter Braid on page 86, it is important that the dough be smooth but not soft and that it is left to rise in a fairly cool spot.

Put the flour and salt into a large mixing bowl and make a well in the center. Crumble the yeast into a small bowl, add a quarter of the water, and mix to a smooth liquid. Pour into the well in the flour, then add the rest of the water. Gradually mix the flour into the liquid to make a fairly firm dough. Turn the dough onto a lightly floured work surface and knead thoroughly for 10 minutes – the dough must be smooth and pliable. If it is at all sticky, knead in extra flour a tablespoon at a time. Put the dough back into the bowl, cover with a damp dish towel, and let rise at cool to normal room temperature for 1½–2 hours or until doubled in bulk.

Punch down the risen dough with your knuckles. Divide the dough into four equal portions. Cover and set aside one portion of the dough to be used for decoration. Using your hands, roll each of the remaining three portions into a sausage shape about 2 feet long. Lay the three sausages parallel to each other on the work surface and hold one end of each together in one hand. With the other hand lift and twist the three strands together. Carefully join both ends of the twisted dough together to make a neat wreath. Transfer to the prepared baking sheet.

1 USE BOTH HANDS TO TWIST THE STRANDS OF DOUGH TOGETHER WITHOUT STRETCHING.

2 JOIN THE ENDS TO MAKE A RING, LIFT IT ONTO THE SHEET, AND NEATEN THE EDGES.

3 ROLL OUT THE REST OF THE DOUGH THINLY AND CUT OUT 9 LEAF SHAPES WITH A KNIFE.

4 TO MAKE THE GRAPES, ROLL THE LEFTOVER DOUGH INTO BALLS OF DIFFERENT SIZES.

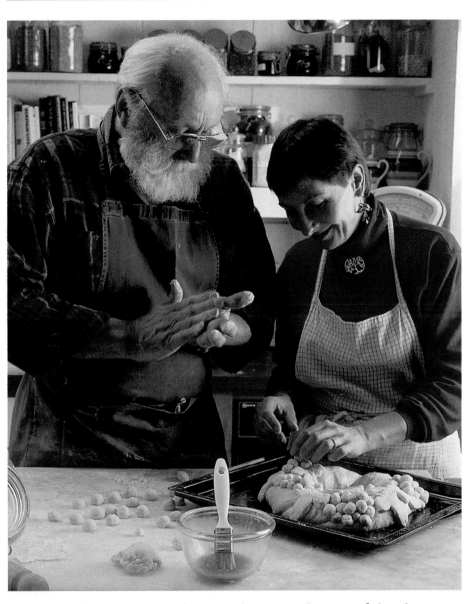

Decorating the Harvest Wreath takes time, and a second pair of hands will be welcome. Here Anthony and I present our loaf, ready for baking.

Preheat the oven to 425°F. Turn the reserved piece of dough onto a lightly floured work surface and punch down with your knuckles. Roll it out about ¼ inch thick. Then, using a very sharp knife and a real vine leaf or a paper pattern as a guide, cut out nine vine leaves. Use the leftover dough to make grapes the size of hazelnuts and small peas.

Attach the vine leaves and grapes in bunches to the wreath, using the egg glaze as a glue. Brush the decorated wreath all over with more egg glaze, then bake immediately in the preheated oven for 30–40 minutes or until the bread sounds hollow when tapped on the base. If the wreath seems to be browning very rapidly, reduce the oven temperature to 400°F. Check the wreath several times during baking to ensure that it is browning evenly, and turn it as necessary. To make sure the decorations remain in place, you may need to stick them back with more egg glaze during baking. Cool the wreath on a wire rack, and eat within 24 hours.

NOTE You can use 1 package (¼oz/7g) active dry yeast instead of fresh yeast, dissolving it in warm water. For rapid-rise dry yeast, mix it with the flour. Add all the water and proceed with the recipe.

BRIOCHE

Makes 1 large or 2 medium brioches or
   20 small brioches

1 0.6-oz cake fresh yeast (15g)

4 tablespoons lukewarm milk

1¹/₂ teaspoons salt

3¹/₂ cups (500g) unbleached white bread flour

5 eggs, beaten

1 cup (250g) unsalted butter, at room temperature

2 tablespoons (60g) sugar

²/₃ cup (110g) raisins, or good semisweet chocolate,
   chopped (optional)

1 egg, lightly beaten, for glazing

a large brioche mold, 9¹/₂ inches wide at the
   top, or a large loaf pan, about 9 x 5 x 3 inches,
   greased (see recipe) OR two medium brioche
   molds, 6¹/₂ inches wide at the top, or small loaf
   pans, about 8¹/₂ x 4¹/₂ x 2¹/₂ inches, greased
   OR 20 small brioche molds
   3¹/₂ inches wide at the top, greased

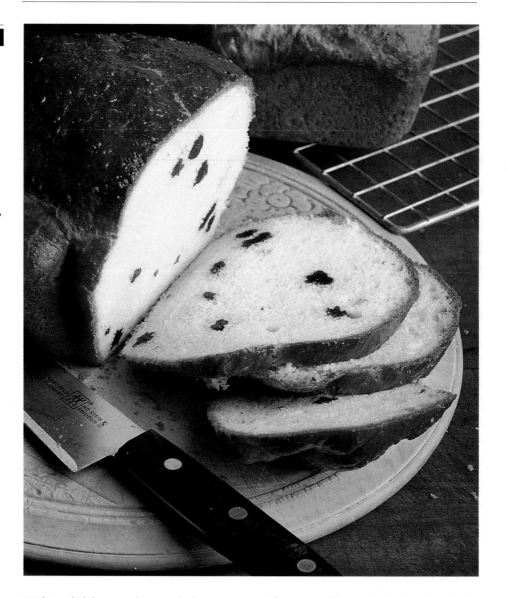

With its slightly sweet, luxuriously buttery taste and fine sponge-like crumb, the brioche is half-way between bread and cake. It is delicious eaten warm with butter for breakfast or tea. The fine texture of the crumb is achieved by using good fresh unsalted butter and by giving the dough three risings. Two of these should be at normal room temperature — too warm and the butter will melt and ooze out of the dough; the other rising is in the fridge to make the soft, rich dough firm enough to maintain its shape. The dough can be left plain, or flavored with raisins and grated orange rind or with chunks of chocolate.

   Here I've adapted the best recipe I know for brioche: it comes from the Michelin Three-Star chef, Michel Roux, and uses an electric mixer to cut out the hard work.

Crumble the yeast into the warm milk and pour into the bowl of an electric mixer fitted with a dough hook. Add the salt, flour, and eggs, and mix to a soft dough. Then knead, still using the dough hook, for about 10 minutes or until the dough is smooth and elastic. Alternatively, you can combine all the ingredients in a large mixing bowl and knead the dough

1 MIX THE YEAST LIQUID, SALT, FLOUR, AND BEATEN EGGS INTO A SOFT DOUGH.

2 AFTER BEATING IN THE BUTTER AND SUGAR, THE DOUGH WILL BE GLOSSY AND ELASTIC.

3 FLOUR YOUR KNUCKLES AND PUNCH THE CENTER OF THE RISEN DOUGH.

4 MAKE A HOLE IN THE CENTER OF THE DOUGH BALL TO HOLD THE SHAPED "TOPKNOT."

5 AFTER THE SECOND RISE, GLAZE THE BRIOCHE WITH BEATEN EGG AND THEN BAKE.

by hand, by beating and slapping the dough up and down in the bowl. This will take 15–20 minutes – the dough is ready when it comes away from the sides of the bowl in one piece.

In another bowl, beat the soft butter and sugar together until light and fluffy. With the electric mixer on low speed, add the butter mixture to the dough a little at a time, making sure each addition is completely amalgamated before adding more. If you are working by hand, squeeze the butter into the dough. Continue to beat for a couple of minutes in the mixer, or 5 minutes by hand, until the dough is smooth, glossy, and elastic. Cover the bowl with a damp dish towel and let rise at normal to warm room temperature (no more than 72°F) for about 2 hours or until doubled in bulk.

Punch down the risen dough in the bowl, using floured knuckles, then cover as before and put into the refrigerator. Let rise in the fridge for several hours but not more than a day.

Turn the dough onto a lightly floured work surface. Sprinkle over the raisins or chopped chocolate, if using, and briefly and gently knead in until evenly distributed. Shape the dough into a large ball.

Prepare the molds or pans: brush with a thin layer of melted butter, then chill until the butter hardens. Brush with a second coat of melted butter and chill briefly. By greasing the mold in this way the butter will not be absorbed by the dough, but it will help to prevent the brioche from sticking during baking.

To make a large brioche in the brioche mold, cut off a quarter of the dough for the top and set aside. Shape the larger piece of dough into a ball and place it in the prepared mold. Make a hole in the center with your fingertips. Roll the small piece of dough into an elongated egg shape with your hand held at an angle against the work surface. Using floured fingertips, gently press the narrow end of the dough "egg" into the hole in the large ball. If you are using a loaf pan, shape the dough following the method on page 76.

If making two medium brioches, divide the dough into two equal portions, then shape each as for the large brioche. For small individual brioches, divide the dough into 20 equal portions and shape each as for the large brioche.

Place the mold(s) or pan(s) in a large plastic bag that has been lightly greased inside, and fasten. Let rise at normal room temperature for 1–1½ hours or until almost doubled in size.

Preheat the oven to 425°F.

Lightly brush the top of the brioche(s) with the egg glaze, working from the outside inward. Take care not to let any glaze run into the crack between the large ball of dough and the top or onto the edges of the mold as this would prevent the dough from rising properly. Bake the brioche(s) in the preheated oven until golden brown and they sound hollow when tipped out of the mold or pan and tapped on the base. The large brioche will take 40–45 minutes; the medium brioches will take 25–30 minutes; and the small brioches 8–10 minutes. Unmold immediately onto a wire rack and let cool.

NOTE You can use 1 package (¼oz/7g) active dry yeast instead of fresh yeast. For rapid-rise dry yeast, add it to the flour and proceed with the recipe, adding the milk with the eggs.

TIPSY PRUNE FRIENDSHIP CAKE

Makes 1 large loaf
STARTER:
2 cups (280g) unbleached all-purpose flour
1 0.6-oz cake fresh yeast (15g)
2 cups (455ml) water, at room temperature

FOR DAY 1:
1 cup (200g) sugar
1 cup (140g) all-purpose flour
1 cup (230ml) milk, at room temperature

FOR DAY 5:
1 cup (200g) sugar
1 cup (140g) all-purpose flour
1 cup (230ml) milk, at room temperature

FOR DAY 10, FINISHING THE LOAF:
2 cups (250g) roughly chopped prunes
the grated rind and juice of 1 unwaxed orange
1½ tablespoons orange liqueur
1 cup packed (200g) light brown sugar
2 cups (280g) all-purpose flour
½ cup (115ml) vegetable oil
¼ teaspoon salt
2 teaspoons baking powder
2 eggs, beaten

TOPPING:
6 tablespoons (85g) dark brown sugar
2 tablespoons (30g) unsalted butter, at room
  temperature

a 9- x 13-inch cake pan or roasting pan, greased

NOTE You can use 1 package (¼oz/7g) active dry yeast instead of fresh yeast, dissolving it in warm water.

This is such an odd recipe — a fruit-filled sourdough loaf cake — but one I'm always asked for when I do demonstrations or radio phone-in programs. I believe the recipe originated in Germany, in the days before cakes were made with baking powder. I've eaten it in Amish and German communities in America, and at church suppers in Britain. It is simple to make but takes 13 days for the dough to ferment. However, you will eventually have enough starter to bake your cake plus one to keep for your next cake and two portions to give away. A couple of years ago I gave a portion of starter to Joy Skipper, who assisted on this and The Bread Book, and she has made a friendship cake every other week since, experimenting with different fillings. This is her favorite.

To make the starter, put the flour in a large, non-metallic bowl and make a well in the center. Crumble the fresh yeast into the well, then pour in the water and stir using a wooden spoon until the yeast has mixed smoothly with the liquid. Gradually stir in the flour to make a sticky batter. Cover the bowl with a damp dish towel. Leave it on the kitchen table or work surface so the batter can absorb extra yeasts from the air. It's a good idea to make a note of the day or date because it is only too easy to lose your place in the recipe. Stir the batter once a day for each of the next 3 days, and re-dampen the towel each day. At the end of this time, the starter will be ready to use.

To make the dough, stir the starter you have made, or any starter you have been given, and proceed as follows:
DAY 1: Stir the starter and add the sugar, flour, and milk. Stir well to mix, cover with a damp dish towel, and leave overnight at room temperature.
DAY 2: Stir well and re-cover with a damp dish towel.
DAYS 3 and 4: Do nothing but re-dampen the towel each day.
DAY 5: Stir well and add the sugar, flour, and milk. Stir well again, cover with a damp dish towel, and leave overnight at room temperature.
DAY 6: Stir well and re-cover with a damp dish towel.
DAYS 7, 8, and 9: Do nothing but re-dampen the towel each day.
DAY 10: Stir well, then divide the starter dough into four equal portions. Give two portions to friends, with instructions, keep one portion for your next batch (see below), and use one portion to make the loaf.

To make the loaf, put the chopped prunes into a mixing bowl with the grated orange rind and juice and the liqueur. Cover tightly and let soak for several hours or overnight.
Preheat the oven to 350°F.
Add the portion of starter dough to the prunes, together with the sugar, flour, oil, salt, baking powder, and eggs. Using a wooden spoon, mix until thoroughly combined. Spoon into the prepared pan and level the surface. Sprinkle the dark brown sugar over the top and dot with small flakes of the butter. Bake for 30–40 minutes or until a skewer inserted into the center comes out clean. Turn out onto a wire rack to cool.
Serve cut into squares or fingers. The cake is also good eaten warm with custard sauce as a pudding. Eat within 3 days of baking.

NOTE To keep the portion of starter for your next cake, add 1 teaspoon of sugar and stir well, then store in a covered container in the fridge for up to 1 week. To make a fresh cake, begin at Day 1 using this starter.

VARIATION Put the portion of starter into a bowl and mix in 1 cup packed (200g) light brown sugar, ¹/₂ cup (85g) golden raisins, 2 cups (280g) all-purpose flour, ¹/₂ cup (110ml) vegetable oil, ¹/₂ cup (60g) walnut halves, ¹/₂ teaspoon salt, 2 teaspoons each ground cinnamon and baking powder, 2 eggs, and 2 apples, peeled, cored, and diced. Put the dough into the prepared pan and add the topping as given. Bake as above.

KULICH

Makes 1 loaf

¹/₂ cup (85g) *golden raisins*

1 tablespoon *rum*

¹/₈ teaspoon *saffron threads*

1 cup (230ml) *milk, heated to boiling*

²/₃ cup (85g) *whole blanched almonds*

¹/₃ cup (60g) *minced mixed candied orange and
    lemon peel*

1 teaspoon *all-purpose flour*

¹/₂ cup + 2 tablespoons (140g) *unsalted butter, at
    room temperature*

1 cup (110g) *confectioners' sugar, sifted*

6 *egg yolks*

¹/₂ teaspoon *salt*

2 0.6-oz cakes *fresh yeast (30g)*

3³/₄ cups (450g) *unbleached white bread flour*

*a 6-inch round deep cake pan, greased and
    prepared with foil and wax paper (see recipe)*

a baking sheet

This light fruit loaf is made in Russia to celebrate Easter, and contains all the eggs and butter prohibited during Lent. In some parts of Russia, the loaf is covered with a thin, lemony glacé icing and decorated with glacé fruits, but I have left this version plain. Kulich is traditionally eaten with paskha, a sweetened and decorated fruit, nut, and curd cheese dessert made in a similar tall mold. As tall narrow molds are hard to find, some cooks use coffee cans or well-seasoned flowerpots; however, I find these more trouble than they are worth and instead use a small, deep cake pan with a stiff foil collar to extend the depth.

To prepare the pan, wrap a doubled strip of foil around the outside of the greased pan to extend about 4 inches above the rim. Tie on the foil collar securely. Butter a strip of wax paper and use to line the inside of the pan sides and the foil collar.

Preheat the oven to 400°F.

Put the raisins to soak in the rum. Crumble the saffron into a small mixing bowl and pour over the boiling milk. Let infuse for 30 minutes — longer if possible. Put the almonds in a small mixing bowl, add enough hot water to cover, and let soak for 5 minutes. Then drain and cut lengthwise into slivers. Arrange the almonds in a single layer on the baking sheet and toast in the oven for 5–10 minutes or until lightly browned. Let cool. Toss the candied peel with the teaspoon of flour.

Cream the butter with the sugar in a large mixing bowl, using an electric mixer or wooden spoon. When the mixture is light and fluffy, beat in the egg yolks one at a time followed by the salt. If necessary, gently warm the saffron milk until it is just lukewarm, then crumble in the yeast and stir until smooth. Add the flour to the creamed mixture and stir until just combined, then pour in the yeast liquid. Beat with your hand for about 8 minutes or until the mixture comes together to make a very soft, smooth, batter-like dough. Cover the bowl with a damp dish towel and let rise at normal to warm room temperature for about 2 hours or until doubled in bulk.

Punch down the risen dough. Sprinkle it with the soaked raisins, the candied peel, and the toasted almonds. Gently work them into the dough with your hands until evenly distributed. Spoon the dough into the prepared pan; it will be about half full. Cover with a damp dish towel and let rise at normal to warm room temperature for about 1½ hours or until risen almost to the top of the foil and paper collar.

Preheat the oven to 400°F again.

Bake the kulich for 20 minutes or until starting to color, then reduce the oven temperature to 350°F and bake for a further 45–55 minutes or until a skewer inserted into the center comes out clean. If the loaf starts to turn dark brown, cover with a sheet of foil or parchment paper. Put the pan on a wire rack and let cool for 10–15 minutes or until the kulich is firm enough to unmold, then turn it out onto a wire rack to cool completely. Best eaten within 3 days.

NOTE You can use 2 packages (¼oz/7g each) active dry yeast instead of fresh yeast. For rapid-rise dry yeast, mix it with the flour.

1 *AFTER ADDING THE FLOUR TO THE CREAMED MIXTURE, POUR IN THE WARM YEAST LIQUID.*

2 *BEAT THE MIXTURE WITH YOUR HAND, LIFTING IT AND SLAPPING IT DOWN.*

3 *AFTER RISING, ADD THE FRUIT, PEEL, AND NUTS TO THE DOUGH AND WORK IN.*

4 *TRANSFER THE DOUGH TO THE PAN, PREPARED WITH A STIFF FOIL COLLAR.*

TEA BREAD

This is an old-fashioned recipe where the dried fruit is soaked in strong tea before it is mixed into a sweet and spicy yeasted bread dough. I am very fond of this bread, sliced and buttered, with afternoon tea in summer, and toasted on an open fire in winter. It also makes a jolly good Bread and Butter Pudding (see page 52).

INGREDIENTS

Makes 1 large loaf

²/₃ cup (110g) mixed dried fruit and chopped candied peel

²/₃ cup (140ml) strong hot tea, strained

about ³/₄ cup (170ml) milk, at room temperature

1 0.6-oz cake fresh yeast (15g)

3³/₄ cups (450g) unbleached white bread flour

1 teaspoon salt

1 teaspoon apple-pie spice

2¹/₂ tablespoons (30g) sugar

4 tablespoons (60g) butter, chilled and diced

milk for brushing

a large loaf pan, about 9 x 5 x 3 inches, greased

NOTE You can use 1 package (¹/₄oz/7g) active dry yeast instead of fresh yeast, warming the liquid before dissolving it. For rapid-rise dry yeast, mix it into the flour with the sugar, salt, and spice. Proceed with the recipe, adding the tea and milk liquid to the well in the flour.

Put the dried fruit and peel into a mixing bowl and pour the hot tea over. Mix well and let soak for 1 hour.

Drain the fruit in a strainer set over a measuring cup. Make the liquid up to 1¹/₄ cups (280ml) with the milk. Crumble the yeast into the liquid and stir until smooth and thoroughly mixed.

Mix the flour with the salt, apple-pie spice, and sugar in a large mixing bowl. Add the diced butter and rub in using the tips of your fingers until the mixture looks like fine crumbs. Stir in the drained fruit, then make a well in the center of the mixture. Pour the yeast liquid into this well. Gradually mix the flour into the liquid to make a soft dough.

Turn the dough onto a lightly floured work surface and knead for 10 minutes or until the dough is elastic and not sticky. It does not matter if the fruit bursts open – in fact it will taste better. Return the dough to the bowl, cover with a damp dish towel, and let rise at normal room temperature for about 1¹/₂ hours or until doubled in bulk.

Gently punch down the risen dough with your knuckles, then turn onto a lightly floured work surface. Shape into a loaf to fit the pan (see page 76). Put the loaf into the prepared pan, seam-side down, then cover and let rise for about 45 minutes or until doubled in size.

Preheat the oven to 400°F.

Brush the loaf with milk, then bake for 35–40 minutes or until nicely browned and the loaf sounds hollow when carefully tipped out of the pan and tapped on the base. Turn out onto a wire rack and let cool. Eat sliced and buttered or toasted.

VARIATION: STICKY FRUIT ROLLS Prepare the dough and let rise at normal room temperature as above. Punch down the risen dough, then divide into 8 equal pieces. Shape each into a ball and place them, well apart, on two greased baking sheets. Cover and let rise until doubled in size. Bake the rolls for about 20 minutes or until golden brown and puffed up. Remove from the oven and immediately brush with a hot, sticky glaze made by dissolving 3 tablespoons sugar in 3 tablespoons whole milk. Transfer the rolls to a wire rack and let cool completely.

1 TO SHAPE ROLLS, CUP A PIECE OF DOUGH IN ONE HAND AND PULL THE SIDES ONTO THE TOP.

2 PINCH THE TOP TOGETHER. TURN THE ROLL OVER SO THE SMOOTH SIDE IS UPPERMOST.

LEMON DRIZZLE LOAF

INGREDIENTS

Makes 1 large loaf

³/₄ cup (170g) unsalted butter, at room
   temperature

1¹/₄ cups (255g) sugar

1³/₄ cups (255g) self-rising flour

3 eggs, beaten

¹/₂ cup (115ml) whole milk

the grated rind of 3 unwaxed lemons

TOPPING:

the juice of 2 lemons

the grated rind of 1 unwaxed lemon

³/₄ cup (150g) sugar

a large loaf pan, about 9 x 5 x 3 inches, greased
   and lined on the bottom

*ABOVE (left to right): Tea Bread, Sticky Fruit
Rolls, and Lemon Drizzle Loaf.*

The all-in-one method of making a cake, where all the ingredients — usually flour, butter, eggs, and sugar — are dumped into a mixing bowl and beaten to a smooth, thick batter, is reckoned to be idiot-proof. Indeed, I was able to turn out something edible while only four foot high. I think this method is best reserved for loaf cakes, such as the one here, where taste and moistness are more important than lightness and volume.

If possible, use unwaxed fruit in this plain but intensely flavored loaf. If the fruit has been waxed, be sure to scrub it well with hot soapy water and then rinse thoroughly. Serve with tea or coffee, for a simple dessert with ice cream, or hot out of the oven with custard sauce.

Preheat the oven to 350°F.

Put all the ingredients, except those for the topping, into a large mixing bowl. Using an electric mixer or wooden spoon, beat until thick and fluffy with no sign of lumps or streaks of flour. Spoon into the prepared pan and smooth the surface. Bake in the preheated oven for 50–55 minutes or until a skewer or toothpick inserted into the center comes out clean.

While the loaf is baking, combine all the ingredients for the topping. As soon as the loaf is cooked, remove it from the oven but leave it in the pan. Prick it all over with a toothpick or skewer. Quickly spoon the topping mixture over the surface, then let the loaf cool completely before unmolding. Serve thickly sliced.

NUT AND RAISIN BREAD

Makes 2 medium loaves

3¹/₂ cups (450g) stoneground whole-wheat bread flour

1¹/₂ cups (230g) unbleached white bread flour

2¹/₂ teaspoons salt

1 0.6-oz cake fresh yeast (15g)

1¹/₂ cups (340ml) water from the cold tap

1¹/₂ tablespoons well-flavored honey

extra flour for dusting

1¹/₂ cups (170g) large seedless raisins

1¹/₂ cups (170g) toasted and roughly chopped walnuts, hazelnuts, or a mixture

2 baking sheets, greased

NOTE You can use 1 package (¹/₄oz/7g) active dry yeast instead of fresh yeast, dissolving it in warm water. For rapid-rise dry yeast, mix it with the flour and salt. Omit the sponging stage, adding the water all at once. Proceed with the recipe.

VARIATIONS: PECAN BREAD Use 2¹/₂ cups (340g) each stoneground whole-wheat bread flour and unbleached white bread flour, and make the dough as above. Replace the raisins and nuts with 2 cups (230g) roughly chopped but untoasted pecans, then proceed with the recipe.

WALNUT OR MIXED NUT BREAD Make the dough, then knead in either 2¹/₂ cups (230g) toasted walnut halves or toasted and roughly chopped mixed nuts such as walnuts, hazelnuts, almonds, pecans, cashews, and macadamias. Proceed with the recipe.

Lightly toasting walnuts and hazelnuts in the oven intensifies their rich taste. Combined with the largest, most luscious raisins available, they make a wonderfully flavored loaf that's good simply sliced and buttered or served with cheese.

Mix the flours and salt together in a large mixing bowl and make a well in the center. Crumble the yeast into a small bowl and cream it to a smooth liquid with half of the water and the honey. Pour the yeast liquid into the well in the flour and mix in just enough of the flour to make a thick batter. Let "sponge" for about 15 minutes – it will look bubbly.

Add the remaining cold water to the yeast batter, then gradually work in the rest of the flour to make a soft but not sticky dough. If the dough sticks to your fingers work in a little extra flour a tablespoon at a time. If dry crumbs form and the dough seems stiff and hard to bring together, work in a little extra water a tablespoon at a time.

Turn the dough onto a lightly floured work surface and knead for 10 minutes or until smooth and elastic. Sprinkle the raisins and nuts over the dough and knead them in gently until they are evenly distributed – this will take about 2 minutes.

Shape the dough into a ball and return it to the bowl. Cover with a damp dish towel and let rise at cool to normal room temperature for about 2 hours or until doubled in bulk.

Punch down the risen dough with your knuckles, then turn onto a floured work surface and knead for a minute. Divide the dough in half and shape each portion into a neat ball. Place on the prepared baking sheets, cover as before, and let rise at normal room temperature for about 1¹/₂ hours or until doubled in size.

Preheat the oven to 425°F.

Slash the top of each loaf two or three times using a very, very sharp knife. Bake for 15 minutes, then reduce the oven temperature to 375°F and bake for a further 20–25 minutes or until the loaves sound hollow when tipped off the sheets and tapped on the base. Transfer the loaves to a wire rack to cool completely.

Eat the bread within 3 days, or toast, or freeze for up to a month.

GINGERBREAD

INGREDIENTS

Makes 1 large loaf

1½ cups (230g) self-rising flour

½ teaspoon baking soda

1 tablespoon ground ginger

1 teaspoon ground cinnamon

1 teaspoon apple-pie spice

½ cup (110g) unsalted butter, chilled and diced

½ cup (110g) dark molasses

½ cup (110g) golden syrup

½ cup packed (110g) light or dark brown sugar

1 cup (280ml) milk

⅓ cup (45g) grated candied ginger

1 extra large egg, beaten

a large loaf pan, about 9 x 5 x 3 inches, greased and lined on the bottom

A lovely spicy, sticky gingerbread, nicely hot with chopped candied ginger. I like it thickly sliced and buttered, but Anthony prefers it with a slice of moist, slightly sharp cheese.

Preheat the oven to 350°F.

Sift the flour, baking soda, and all the spices into a large mixing bowl. Add the diced butter and rub in with your fingertips until the mixture resembles fine crumbs.

In a small saucepan, melt the molasses with the golden syrup, then let cool to blood heat. Meanwhile, in another small pan, dissolve the sugar in the milk over low heat, stirring occasionally.

Add the candied ginger to the flour mixture. Whisk the milk mixture into the flour mixture, then whisk in the molasses mixture followed by the egg. When thoroughly blended, you should have a thin batter.

Pour the batter into the prepared pan and bake for 45 minutes to 1 hour or until a skewer inserted into the center comes out clean. The gingerbread will rise during baking and then fall and shrink slightly as it cools. Let cool completely in the pan. Turn out and wrap first in wax paper and then in foil. Keep for a couple of days before slicing.

1 GRATE THE CANDIED GINGER INTO THE BOWL WITH THE RUBBED-IN MIXTURE.

2 WHISK IN THE SWEETENED MILK AND THEN THE MOLASSES AND SYRUP MIXTURE.

Just the way I like it: thick slices of Gingerbread spread with unsalted butter.

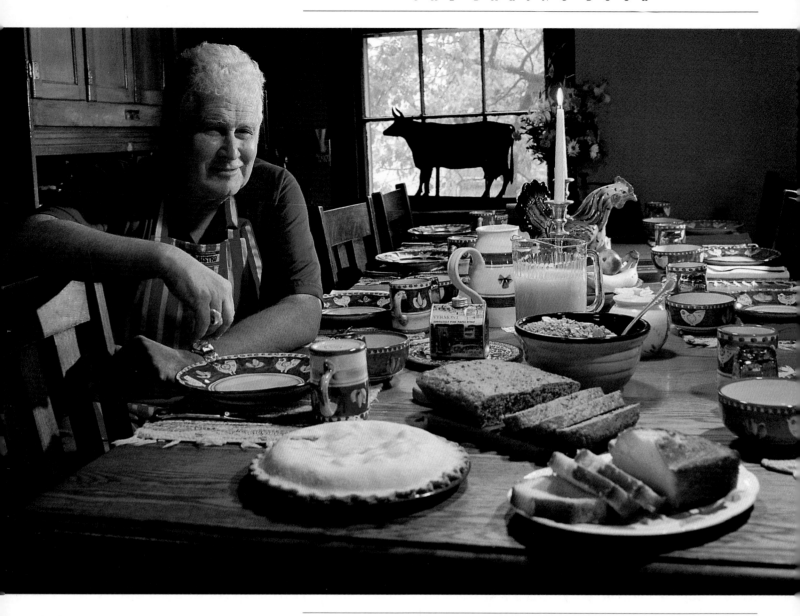

Jim Friedlander loves to experiment and share recipes. Here are his Apple Almond Cream Pie (see recipe on page 188), Bayberry Bread, and Granny Glyn's Lemon Loaf.

BAYBERRY BREAD

Anthony met Jim and Glynrose Friedlander when he stayed at their Federal-style farmhouse in Freeport, Maine. They describe the Isaac Randall House, built in 1823, as a B and B, "though not as utilitarian as the ones in Britain." And it is quite out of the ordinary: the kitchen-dining room has a hand-painted floor, an old wood stove (now converted to gas) for cooking, and copper pans and utensils everywhere. The eight bedrooms are furnished with lovely old quilts, oriental rugs, working fireplaces, and oil lamps, to give a charming, homey atmosphere.

But the decor is eclipsed by the enormous breakfasts Jim prepares each day. After homemade muesli and fresh fruit salad, he cooks pancakes, french toast (pain perdu), and bacon and eggs to order. To follow there are always a couple of specialty quick breads, and even the odd fruit pie (see Apple Almond Cream Pie on page 188).

As Jim says: "We like to eat, and we like to experiment with recipes we pick up when we travel. Then we like to share them."

Thank you, Jim, and see you soon. Bayberry, by the way, is the local name for cranberry.

INGREDIENTS

Makes 1 medium loaf
1 cup (140g) whole-wheat bread flour
1 cup (140g) all-purpose flour
1 1/2 teaspoons baking powder
1/2 teaspoon baking soda
1/8 teaspoon salt
1/4 teaspoon ground cinnamon
1/8 teaspoon grated nutmeg
1/2 cup (100g) granulated sugar
1/2 cup packed (100g) light brown sugar
4 tablespoons (60g) unsalted butter, chilled and diced
1 1/2 teaspoons grated orange rind
3/4 cup (170ml) freshly squeezed orange juice
1 egg, beaten
1 cup (110g) dried cranberries
1/2 cup (60g) roughly chopped pecans or walnuts
1/3 cup (60g) raisins (optional)

a small loaf pan, about 8 1/2 x 4 1/2 x 2 1/2 inches, or a small roasting pan, greased

Preheat the oven to 350°F.

Put the flours, baking powder, baking soda, salt, spices, and sugars into a large mixing bowl and stir until thoroughly combined. Add the diced butter and rub in with your fingertips to make coarse crumbs. Mix the orange rind with the juice and the egg, and add to the dry mixture. Mix briefly, then fold in the cranberries, nuts, and raisins. As soon as the batter is thoroughly blended, spoon it into the prepared pan.

Bake for 1 hour or until golden and firm. A skewer inserted into the center should come out clean. Turn out onto a wire rack and let cool. Serve thickly sliced, with butter. Best when eaten within 3 days.

NOTE To vary the recipe, Jim uses fresh cranberries, blueberries in season, and dried cherries all year round.

GRANNY GLYN'S LEMON LOAF

INGREDIENTS

Makes 1 large loaf
1 1/3 cups (255g) sugar
1/2 cup + 3 tablespoons (155g) unsalted butter, at room temperature
3 eggs, beaten
the grated rind of 1 1/2 unwaxed lemons
2 cups (280g) all-purpose flour
1/4 teaspoon salt
1 1/2 teaspoons baking powder
2/3 cup (140ml) milk
2/3 cup (60g) ground pecans

TOPPING:
2/3 cup (70g) confectioners' sugar, sifted
the juice of 1 1/2 lemons

a large loaf pan, about 9 x 5 x 3 inches, greased and lined on the bottom

This is another delicious recipe from the Friedlanders of Freeport, Maine. The fresh-tasting lemon loaf cake is easily made by the creaming method. The cake is enriched and flavored with pecans that have been finely ground in a food processor. To preserve the freshness of the nuts, grind them just before making the cake batter.

Preheat the oven to 350°F.

Put the sugar and butter into a mixing bowl and beat until very light and creamy, using a wooden spoon or electric mixer. Gradually beat in the eggs. Using a large metal spoon, gently stir in the lemon rind. Sift the flour with the salt and baking powder and fold in. Gradually stir in the milk followed by the ground nuts. When the batter is thoroughly blended, spoon it into the prepared pan.

Bake for about 1 hour or until risen, golden, and firm. A toothpick inserted into the center should come out clean.

While the loaf is baking, prepare the topping by stirring the confectioners' sugar and lemon juice together until smooth.

Remove the cooked loaf from the oven, and leave it in the pan. Immediately puncture the surface all over with a toothpick or skewer and spoon the topping over the loaf. Let cool completely in the pan. The lemon loaf is best eaten within 3 days of baking.

VARIATION Use freshly ground walnuts instead of pecans.

CHAPTER FOUR

FAMILY &
CELEBRATION
CAKES

From the seemingly plain but luxurious
Quatre-quarts to the richest, most seductive of
chocolate cakes, here are recipes for coffee time
and afternoon tea as well as dessert.

QUATRE-QUARTS OR POUND CAKE

INGREDIENTS

Makes 1 large loaf-shaped cake

4 eggs

about 1 cup (250g) unsalted butter, at room
   temperature

about 1¼ cups (250g) sugar

a pinch of salt

½ teaspoon pure vanilla extract

about 1¾ cups (250g) self-rising flour

6 tablespoons (60g) chopped crystallized fruit,
   soaked in 2 tablespoons rum overnight

a large loaf pan, about 9 x 5 x 3 inches, lined with
   a double thickness of greased parchment paper

*Quatre-quarts was just a rich sponge cake to me until we visited la Maison Bernachon in Lyons,
France. Called the best little chocolate shop in the world, it owes its reputation to father and son
perfectionist chocolatiers and pâtissiers, Maurice and Jean-Jacques Bernachon. Beside the
divine chocolate, made by hand from scratch, are heavenly cakes and pastries. There is also a salon
de thé where you can try in miniature the miracles available in the boutique. Here Jean-Jacques
prepared for us a breakfast of coffee and large slices of moist, very rich, angelically light, vanilla
quatre-quarts studded with fruits confits macerated in rum. Of all their superlative creations
this, the simplest, was my favorite. Jean-Jacques showed us the kitchens where trays of freshly picked
local fruits were being prepared for the long process of cooking in sugar syrup, which turns them
into the luscious fruits confits. A large dish of cherries was being steeped in brandy. The attention
to detail is fanatical; there are no short cuts to perfection.*

Jean-Jacques explained the intricacies of the seemingly simple quatre-quarts: the eggs must be
weighed first and then the same quantity weighed in flour, the finest butter, and sugar. The cake can
be made in two ways. In the first, the butter is beaten until very creamy; the sugar is gradually
beaten in to make a very light and fluffy mixture; the eggs are added a tablespoon at a time while
beating vigorously; and, finally, the flour is gently folded in. In the second, the egg yolks and sugar
are beaten to a thick foam; the butter is melted and cooled, then folded in, followed by the flour and,
finally, the beaten egg whites. This latter method, favored by the French, makes a lighter, more
tender cake, but it tends to be dry, while the former can be heavy and tough if not well made. I tried
both ways, following Jean-Jacques' instructions, and preferred the creaming method. Before you
begin, be sure that all the ingredients are at room temperature or it will be difficult to incorporate
air into the mixture.

Preheat the oven to 400°F.

Weigh the 4 eggs together – the total weight should be 8¾–9¼oz
(250–260g). Use exactly the same weight of butter, sugar, and flour.

Put the soft butter in the bowl of an electric mixer and beat at low
speed until very creamy. Gradually beat in the sugar, then beat the mixture
at high speed until it becomes very white and light in texture. Lightly beat
the eggs with the salt, then beat into the creamed mixture a tablespoon at a
time, beating well after each addition. This will take at least 7 minutes.

*PREVIOUS PAGE Royal Scotsman Fruit Cake
(left), Walnut Cake.*

1 BEAT THE BUTTER AND SUGAR TOGETHER
UNTIL VERY WHITE AND LIGHT.

2 ADD THE FLOUR, THEN GENTLY FOLD IN
THE RUM-SOAKED FRUIT.

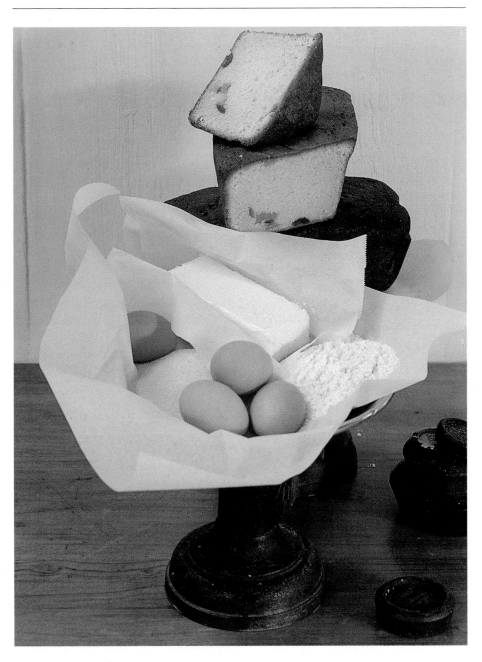

Quatre-quarts is made with equal weights of eggs, butter, sugar, and flour. The recipe here is flavored with vanilla and includes some luscious rum-soaked crystallized fruit. Alternatively, you can bake a chocolate-flavored cake and add rum-soaked golden raisins.

VARIATION: CHOCOLATE QUATRE-QUARTS Replace ⅓ cup (50g) of the weighed flour with the same amount of unsweetened cocoa powder and sift into the bowl with the flour and ½ teaspoon baking powder. Use ⅓ cup (60g) golden raisins soaked in 2 tablespoons rum instead of the crystallized fruits.

Beat in the vanilla. If the mixture starts to separate or split and slide around in the bowl, add a tablespoon of the flour with the last portions of egg. Sift the flour into the bowl and gently fold into the mixture using a large metal spoon. Try to avoid stirring or beating: cut downward through the mixture with the edge of the spoon and then fold over; give the bowl a quarter turn and repeat the cutting and folding; continue until there are no more streaks of flour. Add the fruit – it should have absorbed all the rum – and fold it in in the same way.

Spoon the batter into the prepared pan – it should be three-quarters full. Smooth the surface until level. Bake for 40–50 minutes or until a toothpick inserted into the center comes out clean. Cool in the pan for a minute, then lift the cake out of the pan, peel off the paper, and let cool completely on a wire rack. Store in an airtight tin, and eat within 5 days. The fruit will tend to settle toward the bottom during cooking, but don't worry – this is quite normal.

SEVILLE ORANGE CAKE

INGREDIENTS

Makes an 8-inch round cake

³/₄ cup (170g) unsalted butter, at room
  temperature

³/₄ cup + 2 tablespoons (170g) sugar

3 extra large eggs, beaten

1¹/₄ cups (170g) self-rising flour

¹/₂ teaspoon baking powder

7 tablespoons (140g) Seville orange marmalade,
  gently warmed

2 tablespoons milk

ICING:

1 cup (110g) confectioners' sugar, sifted

2 tablespoons warm water

an 8-inch round deep cake pan, greased and
  lined on the bottom (see pages 112-3)

OPPOSITE (from top to bottom) Seville Orange
Cake, Cinnamon Apricot Cake, February Cake
(see recipe on page 110).

Dessert oranges often lack sharpness and intense flavor, so it is hard to make a really orangey sponge cake that is not oversweet or cloying. However, good-quality Seville orange marmalade, preferably homemade with plenty of chunky peel and a slightly sharp taste, transforms a sponge batter.

Preheat the oven to 350°F.

Beat the butter until creamy, using an electric mixer or wooden spoon. Add the sugar and beat until light and fluffy. Gradually beat in the eggs, beating well after each addition. Sift the flour with the baking powder and gently fold into the mixture using a large metal spoon. When thoroughly blended, add half of the marmalade and the milk and carefully fold in.

Spoon the sponge batter into the prepared pan and spread to level the surface. Bake in the preheated oven for 45–50 minutes or until golden and firm to the touch. Turn out onto a wire rack and immediately brush with the remaining warm marmalade. Let cool completely.

To make the icing, use a wooden spoon to mix the confectioners' sugar and the warm water until smooth and lump-free; the icing should be fairly runny. Spoon over the top of the cake and let it run down the sides. Let set – about 1 hour. Store in an airtight tin, and eat within 4 days.

1 BEAT IN THE EGGS LITTLE BY LITTLE.

2 CUT AND FOLD IN THE SIFTED FLOUR.

CINNAMON APRICOT CAKE

INGREDIENTS

Makes an 8-inch round cake

¹/₂ cup + 1 tablespoon (130g) unsalted butter, at
  room temperature

²/₃ cup packed (130g) light brown sugar, sifted if
  lumpy

1¹/₄ cups (170g) self-rising flour

1 teaspoon ground cinnamon

¹/₃ cup (30g) ground almonds

3 extra large eggs, beaten

1 cup (140g) chopped dried apricots

¹/₄ cup (20g) sliced almonds

an 8-inch round deep cake pan, greased and
  lined on the bottom (see pages 112-3)

This lovely moist cake contains plenty of juicy apricots and isn't oversweet.

Preheat the oven to 325°F.

Beat the butter until creamy, using a wooden spoon or electric mixer. Add the sugar and beat until light and fluffy. Sift the flour with the cinnamon and ground almonds. Very slowly beat the eggs into the creamed mixture, beating well after each addition and adding a little of the flour mixture with the last batch. Using a metal spoon, carefully fold in the rest of the flour mixture and the apricots. When thoroughly combined, spoon into the prepared pan and level the surface. Sprinkle evenly with the sliced almonds.

Bake in the preheated oven for about 1 hour or until a skewer inserted into the center comes out clean. Let cool in the pan. Store in an airtight tin, and eat within 4 days.

WALNUT CAKE

Makes a 7-inch layer cake
³/₄ cup (170g)) unsalted butter, at room
    temperature
²/₃ cup (140g) sugar
1 tablespoon golden syrup
2 extra large eggs, beaten
¹/₂ cup (60g) roughly chopped walnuts
1¹/₄ cups (170g) self-rising flour, sifted

FILLING:
¹/₂ cup (110g) unsalted butter, at room
    temperature
1¹/₂ cups (170g) confectioners' sugar, sifted
a few drops of pure vanilla extract
2 tablespoons hot milk
¹/₄ cup (30g) very finely chopped walnuts

ICING:
2 cups (230g) confectioners' sugar, sifted
2–3 tablespoons hot water
walnut halves for decoration

two 7-inch round shallow cake pans, greased and
    lined on the bottom (see pages 112-3)

I am very fond of the old-fashioned walnut cakes I remember from childhood, but finding a good recipe has been difficult. The American-style cakes made with oil tasted fine, but the texture seemed too rubbery, while the whisked egg-and-sugar recipes popular in Europe were too tough and dry. The traditional British method of creaming the butter and sugar and then beating in the eggs made a moist but slightly heavy cake. This recipe, with golden syrup, makes a very light but moist and well-flavored cake that keeps well. The layers of nut sponge have a filling of walnut buttercream and the cake is finished with a thick glacé icing.

Preheat the oven to 350°F.

Using an electric mixer or a wooden spoon, cream the butter until light, then gradually beat in the sugar. Beat well until the mixture becomes light and fluffy, then beat in the syrup. Gradually beat in the eggs, beating well after each addition. Fold in the walnuts and the sifted flour using a large metal spoon.

Divide the batter between the prepared pans and smooth the surface. Bake in the preheated oven for 25–30 minutes or until the cakes are springy to the touch. Turn the cakes out of the pans onto a wire rack and let them cool.

To make the filling, cream the butter until soft, using an electric mixer or wooden spoon, then beat in the confectioners' sugar at slow speed to make a fluffy, smooth mixture. Beat in the vanilla, milk, and walnuts.

To make the icing, put the sifted confectioners' sugar into a mixing bowl and work in the hot water using a wooden spoon to make a very smooth, thick, spreadable icing. Cover tightly until ready to use.

To assemble, split each cake in half horizontally using a long sharp knife – the nuts will cause the crumb to tear slightly, so if possible cut the day after baking. Spread a third of the filling on half of one cake, then cover with the other piece. Spread with half the remaining filling. Put the base of the second cake on top and spread with the remaining filling. Cover with the last piece of cake. Spread the glacé icing over the top of the cake and ease it down the sides. Use as few movements as possible to avoid a lot of crumbs in the icing. Leave for an hour or so before serving, to let the icing set. Store in an airtight tin, and eat within 5 days.

1 WITH THE MACHINE RUNNING, ADD THE
GOLDEN SYRUP TO THE MIXTURE.

2 THE CAKES MUST BE COMPLETELY COLD
BEFORE YOU SPLIT THEM IN HALF.

This magnificent walnut tree (right), reputed to be one of the largest walnut trees in Britain, is planted in the grounds of Marble Hill House, Twickenham, Surrey (top).

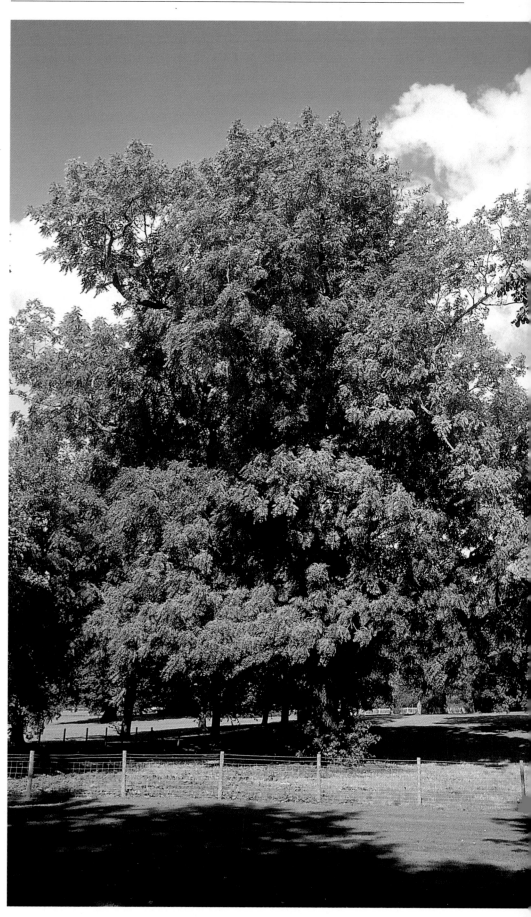

FEBRUARY CAKE

INGREDIENTS

Makes an 8-inch round cake

$^1\!/_2$ cup (110g) unsalted butter, at room
  temperature

6 tablespoons (85g) dark brown sugar, sifted if
  lumpy

2 extra large eggs, beaten

1 cup (230g) good mincemeat

1 tablespoon orange juice

$1^1\!/_4$ cups (170g) self-rising flour

a little raw brown sugar for sprinkling

an 8-inch round deep cake pan, greased and
  lined on the bottom (see pages 112-3)

I like to save a jar of homemade Christmas mincemeat (see page 137) to make this cake in February. It is usually such a dreary, wet month, and a good cake cheers us all up. This is a very quick and simple cake to make and has all the rich, spicy flavors of the well-matured mincemeat.

Preheat the oven to 325°F.

Using an electric mixer or wooden spoon, beat the butter until creamy. Add the sugar and beat until light and fluffy. Gradually beat in the eggs, beating well after each addition. Stir in the mincemeat, orange juice, and flour using a large metal spoon. When thoroughly blended, spoon the batter into the prepared pan and level the surface. Sprinkle evenly with a little raw brown sugar.

Bake in the preheated oven for 1–1$^1\!/_4$ hours or until a skewer inserted into the center comes out clean. The cake will have slight cracks. Loosen the cake and turn it out onto a wire rack to cool completely. Wrap in wax paper, put into an airtight tin, and keep for a day before cutting. Eat the cake within a week of baking.

1 AFTER THE EGGS HAVE BEEN MIXED IN, ADD THE RICH, MOIST MINCEMEAT.

2 ADD THE ORANGE JUICE FOLLOWED BY THE FLOUR AND COMBINE THOROUGHLY.

3 THE MIXTURE WILL BE QUITE STIFF. SPOON IT INTO THE CAKE PAN.

4 SMOOTH THE SURFACE, THEN SPRINKLE WITH SOME RAW BROWN SUGAR.

ROYAL SCOTSMAN FRUIT CAKE

INGREDIENTS

Makes an 8-inch round cake

1²/₃ cups (230g) all-purpose flour

1¹/₂ teaspoons baking powder

a pinch of salt

³/₄ cup (170g) unsalted butter, at room temperature

³/₄ cup packed (170g) light brown sugar

4 eggs, beaten

²/₃ cup (60g) ground almonds

2 cups (340g) mixed dried fruit and chopped candied peel

²/₃ cup (110g) candied cherries, rinsed, dried, and halved

1–2 tablespoons milk

8oz (230g) white marzipan

¹/₂ cup (45g)) sliced almonds

an 8-inch round deep cake pan, greased and lined with greased parchment paper (see pages 112-3)

ABOVE RIGHT Glen Nevis, Fort William, Scotland.

Years ago I was lucky enough to have a very short trip on the famous steam train, the Royal Scotsman. Traveling around Scotland on this train is true luxury — enjoying the glorious scenery of God's Own Country in wonderful comfort and with excellent Scottish food. This rich, moist fruit cake, with its hidden layer of marzipan, was served at tea with pistachio shortbreads. It has become a firm favorite with my family.

Preheat the oven to 350°F.

Sift the flour with the baking powder and salt, and set aside. Using an electric mixer, beat the butter until creamy, then gradually beat in the sugar. Beat until very light and fluffy. Gradually beat in the eggs, beating well after each addition. Add a tablespoon of the flour with the last two additions of egg. Using a large metal spoon, fold in the rest of the flour and the ground almonds. When thoroughly blended, fold in the fruit mixture and the cherries. Add enough milk to make a batter that just falls from the spoon when tapped.

Spoon half the batter into the prepared pan and smooth the surface. Roll out the marzipan into a disk to fit the pan and place it gently on top of the cake batter. Spoon the rest of the batter on top. Smooth the surface, then make a slight hollow in the center so the cake will rise evenly. Sprinkle with the sliced almonds.

Bake in the preheated oven for 30 minutes, then reduce the oven temperature to 325°F and bake for a further 1¹/₄–1¹/₂ hours or until a skewer inserted into the center of the cake, just down to the marzipan layer, comes out clean. (The marzipan will be soft and sticky, so if you push the skewer into it it will be hard to tell if the cake itself is cooked.) Let cool completely in the pan before turning out.

Remove the parchment paper, then wrap in wax paper and keep in an airtight tin for about 3 days before cutting.

The baked Royal Scotsman Fruit Cake, straight from the oven.

KATIE STEWART'S DUNDEE CAKE

Makes an 8-inch round cake

1¼ cups (170g) all-purpose flour

¾ cup (110g) self-rising flour

½ teaspoon salt

⅔ cup (60g) ground almonds

¾ cup (170g) butter, at room temperature

¼ cup (60g) shortening

1 cup packed (230g) light brown sugar, sifted if lumpy

4 extra large eggs, at room temperature

the finely grated rind of 1 unwaxed lemon

2 cups (340g) golden raisins

1⅓ cups (230g) currants

⅔ cup (110g) chopped mixed candied peel

about 18 blanched almond halves

an 8-inch round deep cake pan, greased and lined with greased parchment paper (see below)

a baking sheet and plenty of newspaper

1 *KATIE ALWAYS USES HER HAND TO CREAM THE FAT WITH THE SUGAR.*

2 *SHE WRAPS THICK NEWSPAPER AROUND THE PAN TO PREVENT SCORCHING.*

The *Scots* have a long tradition of baking, and Dundee has a reputation for the richest, most luxurious fruit cakes. Spices, sugar, and citrus and dried fruits arrived at the port from overseas, and fine white wheat flour was imported from England. This cake dates from the 17th century when it was a favorite at the court of Mary Queen of Scots — the royal bakers indulged the Queen's sweet tooth, her love of ostentation, and her dislike of cherries, with a cake that was packed with expensive and uncommon ingredients.

Katie Stewart has long been a heroine of mine, ever since I spent a school holiday cooking every single recipe in her Times Cookery Book. Katie, who comes from Aberdeen, has had an illustrious career. Like her mother she trained at the Domestic Science School in Aberdeen before moving down to London and Westminster College. After even more training — at the Cordon Bleu in Paris — Katie worked as a home economist for Nestlé in White Plains, New York. Back in Britain, she started writing for Woman's Mirror in 1959, then moved on to The Times and Woman's Journal, where she has been Cookery Editor for 26 years.

Katie's fruit cakes, baked to recipes handed down from her mother, are superb, and it was a great treat to watch her make them at her home in Sussex, England.

Preheat the oven to 350°F.

Sift the flours with the salt and almonds, and set aside.

In a large mixing bowl cream the fats and sugar together until soft and light, using your hand, a wooden spoon, or an electric mixer. Katie uses her hand for this — she says it is messy but quick. Mix the eggs with the grated lemon rind. Beat the egg mixture into the creamed mixture a little at a time — at least five batches — beating well after each addition. If the mixture starts to curdle or slide around in the bowl, add some of the sifted flour mixture with the last few additions of the egg mixture.

Mix a tablespoon of the flour with the fruit and peel. Using a metal spoon, lightly fold half of the remaining flour into the creamed mixture, then add the fruit mixture and, finally, the rest of the flour. Gently mix to make a medium soft consistency: the batter should drop off the spoon when it is given a gentle shake.

Spoon the batter into the prepared pan and spread level with a spoon, gently pressing the batter down. Lightly moisten the top of the cake with wet knuckles; this will prevent a hard, dry crust from forming before the cake has set. Place the almond halves on top in a neat circle. Tie newspaper, folded into four thicknesses, around the pan to prevent scorched or dry sides. Put a tray of water on the floor of the oven — this helps to keep the cake moist.

Set the cake pan on a thick pad of newspaper on a baking sheet and bake in the center of the preheated oven for 45 minutes. Lower the oven temperature to 325°F and bake for a further 1¾ hours — giving a total cooking time of 2½ hours. Let the cake cool in the pan overnight before turning out. When the cake is quite cold — 24 hours after baking — wrap it in wax paper and store in an airtight tin for a week before cutting.

LINING A ROUND CAKE PAN

Many cakes need only to have the bottom of the pan lined, but when baking a fruit-rich cake, all pans — even non-stick ones — should be lined

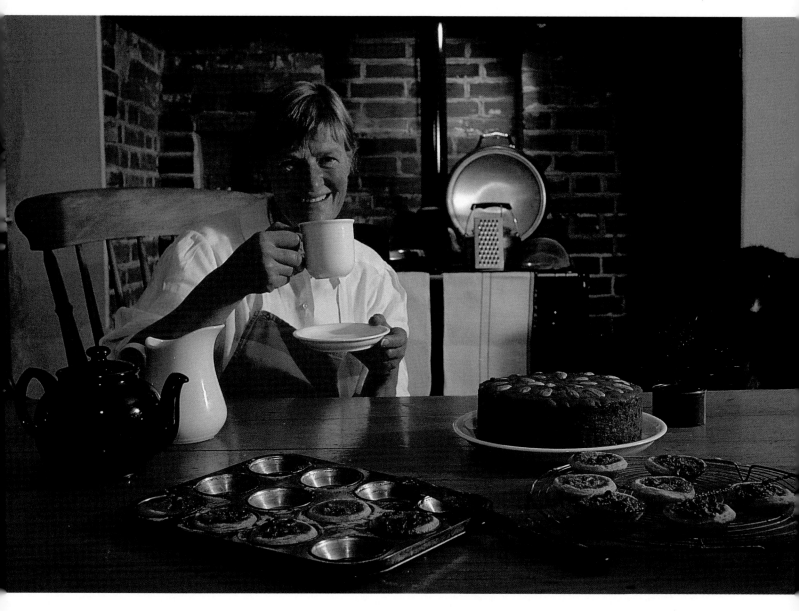

Katie in her kitchen with Charlie, the dog. On the table are freshly baked Queen Mary Tartlets (see recipe on page 140) and Dundee Cake.

on the bottom and around the sides, using heavy wax paper or non-stick parchment paper. The lining prevents the cake from sticking to the pan. For fruit cakes with a long baking period, the lining on the bottom and sides also helps prevent the cake from scorching and drying out.

First, brush the inside of the pan with melted butter so the paper will adhere – for good smooth sides it is important the paper does not become wrinkled. Cut out a disk of parchment paper to fit the bottom of the pan: set the pan on a sheet of paper and draw around the base. If only lining the bottom of the pan, put the disk of paper in place. If lining the sides as well, first measure the circumference and depth of the pan; cut a strip of paper the same length as the circumference and three times as wide as the depth of the pan. Fold the paper strip in half lengthwise. Turn up the folded edge 1 inch and snip this, up to the turned-up fold, at 1-inch intervals. Brush the paper above the snipped edge with melted butter, then fit the paper strip inside the pan so the snipped edge lies flat on the bottom and the rest smoothly lines the side. Put the disk into the pan to cover the bottom and the snipped paper edge.

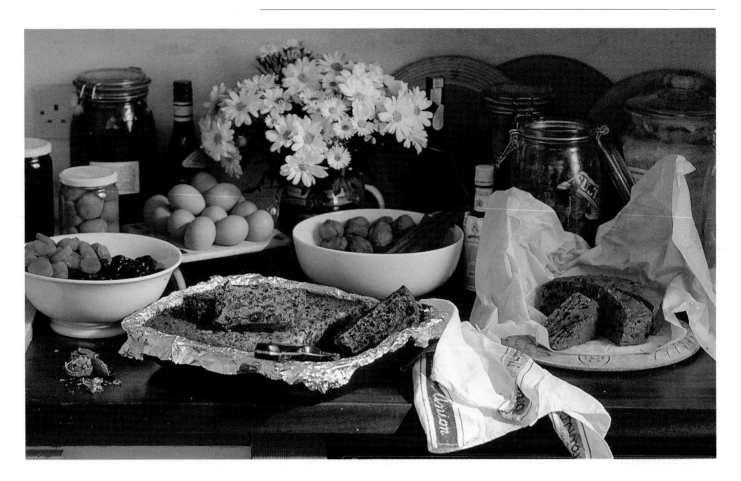

Gâteau Noir (left) and Stout Cake.

STOUT CAKE

INGREDIENTS

Makes an 8-inch round cake

1¼ cups (170g) best-quality large seedless raisins

1¼ cups (170g) best-quality golden raisins

7 tablespoons stout or dark beer

¾ cup (170g) unsalted butter, at room temperature

¾ cup packed (170g) dark brown sugar, sifted

3 eggs, beaten

1⅔ cups (230g) all-purpose flour

1½ teaspoons apple-spice spice

⅓ cup (60g) chopped mixed candied peel

¾ cup (85g) walnut pieces

an 8-inch round deep cake pan, greased and lined with greased parchment paper (see pages 112-3)

This is a dark, spiced fruit cake made with lots of raisins soaked in stout, plus walnuts for extra crunch. Made with the best fruit, it will be a good keeper, and can be covered with marzipan and royal icing, for a traditional finish.

Put all the raisins in a bowl and pour over the stout. Mix well, then cover tightly and let soak overnight.

Next day, preheat the oven to 325°F.

Beat the butter until light, using an electric mixer or wooden spoon. Gradually beat in the sifted sugar, then continue beating until the mixture becomes lighter and fluffy in texture. Gradually beat in the eggs, beating well after each addition. Sift the flour and the apple-pie spice into the bowl, and carefully fold in using a large metal spoon. Add the soaked fruit and any liquid left in the bowl, followed by the mixed peel and the walnuts. When thoroughly blended, spoon into the prepared pan and smooth the surface level.

Bake in the preheated oven for 1½ hours or until a skewer inserted into the center comes out clean. If the top of the cake looks as if it is becoming too brown, cover with a double sheet of parchment paper. Let cool in the pan, then turn out. Remove the lining paper and wrap in wax paper. Store in an airtight tin for 3–5 days before cutting.

114

GÂTEAU NOIR

INGREDIENTS

Makes 1 very large cake

²/₃ cup (140ml) each rum, port, brandy, cherry
   brandy, and water

2 teaspoons Angostura bitters

1 teaspoon ground cinnamon

1 cinnamon stick

1 teaspoon freshly grated nutmeg

¹/₂ teaspoon ground cloves

¹/₂ teaspoon ground allspice

¹/₂ teaspoon salt

2 tablespoons dark brown sugar

4¹/₂lb (2kg) mixed dried and candied fruit
   and peel (about 12 cups)

2 cups (450g) unsalted butter, at room
   temperature

3 cups (450g) raw brown sugar

8 extra large eggs, beaten

3 cups (450g) self-rising flour, sifted

1 cup (110g) chopped mixed nuts — pecans and
   almonds for choice

2 teaspoons pure vanilla extract

a roasting pan, about 13¹/₂ x 11¹/₂ inches, lined
   with greased foil

The legendary Creole Christmas cake, heavy — in every sense — with dried fruits and liquor, is not for the faint-hearted. It is very rich, and moist enough to be eaten as a dessert. I enjoy it with strong coffee. The recipe calls for a lot of ingredients, but the method is simple. I use the "luxury fruit" mixture available in 500g packets at my local supermarket, although you can use your own mixture of raisins, golden raisins, currants, mixed candied peel, chopped dried apricots and prunes, candied pineapple and cherries. The fruits are simmered with the spices and alcohols to plump them up. Then, after a few days of soaking, they are mixed with the rest of the ingredients and baked in a large roasting pan. Having tried this cake, I no longer make the traditional British Christmas cake, and my family is very happy with the change.

Put the rum, port, brandy, cherry brandy, water, bitters, ground and stick cinnamon, nutmeg, cloves, allspice, salt, brown sugar, and the fruit mixture into a large non-aluminum saucepan. Bring slowly to a boil, then simmer gently for 10 minutes, stirring frequently. The mixture will be moist, but most of the liquid will have been absorbed. Tip into a large heatproof glass or china bowl and let cool completely. Then cover and leave for 3–5 days to mature, stirring every day.

When ready to bake the cake, preheat the oven to 275°F.

Put the butter into a very large mixing bowl with the raw brown sugar and beat until fairly light, using a wooden spoon. Gradually beat in the eggs — this is quite hard work but the mixture does not need to beaten as thoroughly as a sponge cake (see Quatre-quarts, page 104). Some of the flour can be added with the last few portions of egg to prevent the mixture from curdling or splitting. Stir in the rest of the flour using a large metal spoon, then work in the fruit mixture, with any liquid left in the bowl, the nuts, and the vanilla extract. When thoroughly blended, spoon into the prepared pan and level the surface.

Cover the pan quite loosely with a double layer of parchment paper, then bake for about 3¹/₂ hours or until just cooked in the center; test with a skewer — the cake should be quite moist. Let cool completely in the pan, then turn out and peel off the foil. Wrap in wax paper and store in an airtight container for several days before cutting.

1 AFTER 3–5 DAYS OF MARINATING IN LIQUOR AND SPICES, THE FRUIT MIXTURE IS VERY MOIST AND SOFT.

2 WHEN WELL MIXED, SPOON THE HEAVY, FRUIT-DENSE CAKE BATTER INTO THE FOIL-LINED ROASTING PAN.

RHUBARB CHEESECAKE

Makes a 10-inch cake, to serve 10–12
CRUST:
1 cup (110g) graham-cracker crumbs
½ teaspoon ground ginger
2½ tablespoons (30g) sugar
4 tablespoons (60g) unsalted butter, melted

FILLING:
2lb (900g) cream cheese
the grated rind of 1 unwaxed lemon
1 teaspoon pure vanilla extract
1 cup (200g) sugar
4 extra large eggs, beaten
2 cups (455ml) sour cream

TOPPING:
½lb (250g) trimmed young rhubarb, rinsed
3 tablespoons red-currant or raspberry jelly

a 10-inch springform cake pan, greased
a baking sheet

My ideal cheesecake is deep and rich, yet light and fluffy, with plenty of flavor. My husband, who is from New York, likes the heavy, middle-European kind of cheesecake that sticks briefly to the top of your mouth and then lingers around the hips. Both types are baked rather than set with gelatin, and can be left plain or topped with fresh or poached fruit and then a glaze. This recipe is my favorite — sorry Alan — and is covered with the tender young forced rhubarb available in the spring. As this delicate fruit breaks up very readily, it is cooked slowly in the oven in red-currant or raspberry jelly and the juices are used for the glaze. Other fruit toppings could be raspberries or strawberries, poached or fresh apricots or peaches, large sweet blackberries, mixed fresh red, black, and white currants, figs, or cherries. As a glaze choose a jelly or strained jam to suit the fruit. For some reason the Philadelphia brand of cream cheese works best in this recipe — I have had disappointing results with other cream cheeses.

Preheat the oven to 300°F.

To make the crust, mix the graham-cracker crumbs with the ground ginger, sugar, and melted butter. Tip the mixture into the prepared pan, then press onto the bottom, using the back of a spoon, to make an even layer. Chill for 30 minutes while making the filling.

Put the cream cheese, grated lemon rind, vanilla, and sugar into the bowl of an electric mixer (the mixture can also be beaten by hand using a wooden spoon, but it is hard work). Beat at low speed until the mixture is very smooth, then increase the speed and gradually beat in the eggs, scraping down the sides of the bowl from time to time. When well mixed, pour in the sour cream and stir with a wooden spoon until the mixture is thoroughly combined.

3 WHEN THE CHEESE AND CREAM MIXTURE IS SMOOTH, POUR IT INTO THE PAN.

1 PRESS THE CRUMB MIXTURE FIRMLY INTO THE BOTTOM OF THE SPRINGFORM PAN.

2 THOROUGHLY WASH THE LEMON, THEN GRATE THE RIND INTO THE BOWL.

4 CUT THE RHUBARB NEATLY, THEN COOK IN A BAKING DISH WITH THE JELLY.

BRUSH THE RHUBARB WITH THE HOT,
SYRUPY COOKING JUICES TO GLAZE.

Pour the filling into the pan – it should be seven-eighths full – and set the pan on a baking sheet. Bake in the preheated oven for 1³/₄–2 hours or until just firm. The cheesecake will puff up, but it will sink on cooling and then usually cracks across the middle.

When the cheesecake is cooked, turn off the oven and open the door a few inches – wedge it, if necessary. Leave the cheesecake inside to cool slowly for 1 hour. Then remove from the oven, set the pan on a wire rack, and leave until completely cold. Cover and chill overnight before unmolding and decorating.

To make the topping, preheat the oven to 350°F. Cut the rhubarb into pieces about 1¹/₄ inches long. Spread the jelly on the bottom of a baking dish and arrange the rhubarb in a single layer on top. Cover and cook in the preheated oven for about 20 minutes or until just tender, stirring very gently from time to time. Let cool.

When ready to decorate the cheesecake, remove the rhubarb from the liquid, draining well. Spoon the rhubarb cooking juices into a small pan and bring to a boil. Simmer until syrupy. Arrange the fruit on top of the unmolded cheesecake, then brush with the hot syrup. Chill until set – about 30 minutes – before serving. Store in a covered container in the fridge, and eat within 3 days.

CHOCOLATE, THE FOOD OF THE GODS

RIGHT *Sacks of cocoa beans waiting to be mixed and roasted at the Bernachon maison du chocolat in Lyons, France.*

BELOW *After roasting for 20 minutes the cocoa beans have to be cooled before shelling.*

BOTTOM *Noël Sevre can tell whether or not the beans have been properly roasted by their smell.*

Until I went to Lyons, France, the nearest I had come to the principal ingredient of chocolate was the *Theobroma cacao* in the Princess of Wales Conservatory in Britain's Kew Gardens. This "food of the gods" tree, which grows to almost 65 feet in the wild and around 13 feet on plantations, is found in tropical America and Africa. The large, yellow-green fruits of the tree contain white juicy pulp and hard bitter seeds, and it is these seeds from which chocolate and cocoa are made.

After the fruits are harvested and the seeds removed, they are left to ferment for 4–6 days – the heat of this fermentation kills the seed's embryo and starts chemical reactions that change the initial inedibly bitter taste. Next, the seeds – now beans – are dried in the sun, and then they are put into sacks for sale.

It was a hot, sticky day when I visited the Bernachon *maison du chocolat* in Lyons. I expected to be greeted by a cloying smell, which would put me off all sweets for weeks. Instead there was merely a slightly heady, bitter aroma. The factory is, in fact, a chocolate-making *atelier* – one room containing all that is required. In one corner the ingredients are neatly arranged: sacks of beans, bags of crystal sugar, a shoe box of glossy vanilla beans, and a bowl of melted cocoa butter.

Unlike coffee, chocolate cannot be made with just one type of bean, and it is the blend of beans – up to 12 varieties here – that gives the final product its special flavor. Jean-Jacques Bernachon only buys the finest and most costly beans: chuao from Venezuela, para from Brazil, the santa-fe, sambirand, and guayaquil from Trinidad and Ecuador. He compares the beans to the *premiers grands crus* wines of Bordeaux – each variety has an individual character and adds a different quality to the blend: aroma, bitterness, depth of flavor, or richness.

The chocolate-maker, Noël Sevre, explained the process *chez* Bernachon. The almond-shaped beans are first picked over by hand to check for damage: each variety is a different color, ranging from pale coffee to a rich mahogany-brown. They are then roasted – like coffee – for 20 minutes at

350°F, which cracks the shells and releases a pleasant toasty smell. Once cooled the beans are lightly crushed to remove the shells without damaging the precious kernels. These are then ground to make a paste, and are mixed in small batches with melted cocoa butter from Holland, a little sugar – the quantity depends on how the chocolate will be used – and real vanilla from Madagascar. The resulting dryish, clay-like "dough" is mixed and put through a giant mangle three times, a process called *broyage*. The final key step is *conchage*, or conching, a long, slow operation – around 36 hours here – which gently melts and stirs or grinds the ingredients until smooth and mellow. The resulting chocolate is then set as blocks.

Cocoa beans contain roughly 50% fat and 50% meat or solids. Pressing

ABOVE After a day and a half of conchage, the finished chocolate is poured into trays and left to set into blocks.

RIGHT Jean-Jacques Bernachon and his pride and joy – the gâteau president.

ABOVE Hand-made chocolates are given the gold-leaf treatment before they are dispatched to Paul Bocuse's restaurant.

BELOW Maison Bernachon sells incomparable pâtisserie and gâteaux, as well as the famous chocolates. If you cannot wait until you reach home, you can taste everything in the tea shop/restaurant next door.

the cocoa paste releases some of the fat from the ground kernels – this is the cocoa butter. If the pressed paste is then further ground up and dried it becomes cocoa powder. Cocoa butter is added to the chocolate mixture to increase the fat content, to make it smoother, and to make it melt in the mouth as it has a low melting point. The quantity of cocoa solids – the dry cocoa paste plus the added cocoa butter – determines the quality and depth of flavor of the chocolate. *Couverture*, used for fillings and icings, is around 55%; *amer* or bitter is 65%; *super amer* or extra bitter (best for eating and making desserts and fine cakes) is around 70%; and *sans sucre* or unsweetened (used in many recipes for cakes and cookies and for sauces by the catering trade) is 100%.

Great care must be taken when melting chocolate because if it is overheated it easily scorches and becomes a hard, solid mass. The best way to melt it is to put the chopped chocolate into a heatproof bowl set over a pan of hot but not boiling water (or in a double boiler). The water should not touch the base of the bowl, nor should the chocolate come into contact with steam from the water. Stir the chocolate gently until smooth, then remove the bowl from the heat.

Sadly, the production of chocolate at Maison Bernachon is small, and Jean-Jacques will not allow it to be sold anywhere else. So a trip to Lyons or a visit to Paul Bocuse's restaurant nearby is the only way to taste chocolate perfection. Jean-Jacques is married to the great chef's daughter, Jeanne, who runs the Bernachon Passion tea shop/restaurant. Bocuse serves their hand-made chocolates, flecked with real gold leaf, and the *president gâteau*, created by Maurice, Jean-Jacques' father. This triumph of the *chocolatier* and the *pâtissier* resembles one of the British Queen Mother's Ascot hats with its ruffles and frills, except that she never wears brown.

DEVIL'S FOOD CAKE

INGREDIENTS

Makes an 8-inch layer cake

3oz (85g) good semisweet chocolate, chopped

¹/₂ cup (110g) unsalted butter

6 tablespoons (85g) dark brown sugar

1 tablespoon golden syrup

1¹/₃ cups (170g) cake flour

¹/₃ cup (30g) unsweetened cocoa powder

¹/₂ teaspoon baking soda

2 extra large eggs, beaten

6 tablespoons milk

FILLING AND FROSTING:

3 tablespoons (40g) unsalted butter, at room
    temperature

¹/₂ cup (40g) unsweetened cocoa powder

2¹/₂ cups (280g) confectioners' sugar

6 tablespoons milk

2 teaspoons strong black coffee

two 7-inch round shallow cake pans, greased and
    lined on the bottom (see pages 112-3)

Above right SPREAD THE SOFT FROSTING
THICKLY OVER THE ASSEMBLED CAKE, THEN
LEAVE OVERNIGHT BEFORE CUTTING.

It has taken me a long time to find a really good recipe for this popular cake. Most devil's food cakes look impressive but taste of little except sugar. This unorthodox recipe makes a light cake that is not too deep but has plenty of flavor. The rich chocolate fudge frosting contrasts well with the slightly bitter, double chocolate sponge. Like most chocolate cakes it is best left overnight before cutting.

Preheat the oven to 325°F.

To make the cake, put the chocolate, butter, sugar, and golden syrup in a saucepan set over low heat and melt, stirring frequently. Remove from the heat and let cool.

Sift the flour, cocoa powder, and baking soda into a mixing bowl. Make a well in the center and pour in the cooled melted chocolate mixture. Stir with the flour until well mixed, then add the eggs and milk and beat gently until the batter is thoroughly combined.

Spoon the batter into the prepared pans and spread evenly. Bake for 20–25 minutes or until firm to the touch. Let cool completely before turning out of the pans.

To make the filling and frosting mixture, beat the butter until creamy, using a wooden spoon or electric mixer. Sift the cocoa and confectioners' sugar into the bowl, and add the milk and coffee. Mix on low speed until combined, then beat vigorously until smooth and creamy. Taste and add a little more cocoa or coffee if necessary.

Spread a third of this mixture on one of the cakes and set the second cake on top. Spread the rest of the mixture evenly over the top and down the sides. Cover and leave in a cool place – but not the fridge – overnight so that the frosting can become firm and the cake can mature. The cake is best eaten within 3 days.

PECAN FUDGE CAKE

Makes a 9¹/₂-inch round cake
12oz (340g) good semisweet chocolate
³/₄ cup (170g) unsalted butter
¹/₂ cup (60g) unsweetened cocoa powder, sifted
5 extra large eggs
1¹/₄ cups (255g) sugar
1 cup (100g) roughly chopped pecans
confectioners' sugar for dusting

a 9¹/₂-inch springform cake pan, greased and lined
on the bottom (see pages 112-3)

This is a wonderfully rich and moist cake, more like a heavy mousse than a sponge because it contains no flour. The rich but not sweet taste comes from a combination of semisweet chocolate (which should have a high proportion of cocoa solids and cocoa butter) and cocoa powder. It can be served as a dessert with vanilla ice-cream or crème anglaise (see page 58).

Preheat the oven to 350°F.

Put the chocolate and butter in a heavy saucepan, or in a heatproof bowl set over a pan of hot but not boiling water, and melt very gently, stirring frequently. Remove from the heat and stir in the cocoa. Let cool

1 BEAT THE EGGS WITH THE SUGAR UNTIL THE MIXTURE IS THICK ENOUGH TO MAKE A RIBBON-LIKE TRAIL.

2 REMOVE THE BOWL FROM THE HEAT AND GENTLY FOLD IN THE COOL CHOCOLATE MIXTURE WITH A LARGE SPOON.

3 FINALLY, MIX IN THE CHOPPED PECANS. SPOON INTO THE PREPARED CAKE PAN AND BAKE IMMEDIATELY.

while beating the eggs: put the eggs into a large heatproof bowl and beat briefly. Add the sugar and set the bowl over a pan of simmering water; the water should not touch the base of the bowl. Beat, using a portable electric mixer, until the mixture is very light and fluffy and has tripled in bulk. When the beaters are lifted out of the mixture it should leave a very visible ribbon-like trail on the surface. Remove the bowl from the heat and carefully fold in the chocolate mixture, followed by the pecans. Spoon into the prepared pan and smooth the the surface.

Bake for 30–35 minutes. The top of the cake will be firm but the inside should still be moist – if this cake is overcooked it will be too dry and crumbly to slice. Let cool completely in the pan, then unmold and dust with confectioners' sugar. Store in an airtight pan, and eat within 4 days.

BELOW Devil's Food Cake (see recipe on page 121), Pecan Fudge Cake.

THE BEST CHOCOLATE CAKE

Makes 1 heart-shaped cake

4oz (110g) good semisweet chocolate, chopped

½ cup (110g) unsalted butter, at room temperature

7 tablespoons (85g) sugar

4 extra large eggs, separated

1⅓ cups (110g) ground almonds

a pinch of salt

GANACHE FROSTING:

½ cup (115 ml) heavy cream

4 oz (110g) good semisweet chocolate, chopped

a heart-shaped pan, about 8 inches long from tip and just under 8 inches across the center, greased and lined on the bottom

I have yet to find a cake to better this one. It is rich and very chocolatey but not sweet or cloying; it is moist but not heavy. But however carefully it is prepared it will only be as good as the chocolate used. Top-quality semisweet chocolate, containing a lot of cocoa butter, has less sugar than lesser quality chocolate, which usually has flavorings and other additives as well.

The recipe originally came from Jean-Pierre St Martin, the chef-patron of the *Viscos* restaurant in the tiny village of St Savin, perched high up in the Pyrenees in southwestern France. For his cake, he used 8 eggs and 250 grams of everything else — butter, sugar, chocolate, and ground almonds — but gradually, through experimentation, I have reduced the sugar. There is no flour in the recipe, nor any leavening agent — the lightness comes from the beaten egg whites. The cake is covered with a ganache made from equal quantities of chocolate and cream. For a softer, more fudgy frosting use a little more cream than chocolate; for a harder, darker, and more intense coating use a little more chocolate than cream.

Although I suggest a heart-shaped pan, you can also use an 8-inch round cake pan. Double quantity cake batter will fill a 9-inch round deep cake pan — ideal for a birthday cake.

Preheat the oven to 400°F.

Very gently melt the chocolate in a heatproof bowl set over a pan of hot but not boiling water. Stir until smooth, then remove from the heat and let cool while preparing the rest of the mixture. Using an electric mixer or wooden spoon, cream the butter until light in a mixing bowl. Add the

Jean-Pierre St Martin outside his restaurant, Les Viscos, in southwestern France.

sugar and beat until fluffy, then beat in the egg yolks one at a time, beating well after each addition. Beat in the cooled chocolate, then stir in the almonds using a large metal spoon.

In a spotlessly clean, grease-free bowl, beat the egg whites with the pinch of salt until they form soft peaks. Gently fold them into the chocolate mixture in three batches using a large metal spoon.

Spoon into the prepared pan and level the surface. Bake in the preheated oven for 15 minutes, then reduce the oven temperature to 350°F and bake for about 10 minutes longer or until just cooked in the center (test with a skewer). It is important not to overcook this cake or it will not be moist. Run a round-bladed knife around the side of the pan to loosen the cake, but do not turn it out. Set the pan on a wet dish towel and let cool. When cold, unmold the cake, wrap in wax paper, and store in an airtight tin to mature for a day before icing.

To make the ganache icing, heat the cream until scalding hot but not boiling. Remove from the heat and add the chopped chocolate. Leave until completely melted and smooth, stirring occasionally. When cool and thick enough to spread, use to cover the sides and top of the cake. Let set in a cool spot – not the fridge (chilling will make the cake hard and the icing will have beads of condensation when it is served). Eat within 4 days.

1 BE SURE THE MELTED CHOCOLATE IS COMPLETELY COOLED BEFORE BEATING IT INTO THE CAKE MIXTURE.

2 ONCE THE CHOCOLATE HAS BEEN INCORPORATED, USE A LARGE SPOON TO FOLD IN THE GROUND ALMONDS.

3 IN A SPOTLESSLY CLEAN BOWL, USING CLEAN BEATERS, BEAT THE EGG WHITES JUST UNTIL SOFT PEAKS FORM.

4 TO KEEP ALL THE AIR THAT HAS BEEN BEATEN IN, FOLD THE WHITES INTO THE BATTER IN THREE BATCHES.

HAZELNUT MERINGUE CAKE

INGREDIENTS

Makes an 8-inch cake, to serve 8–10
CAKE:
1 1/3 cups (185g) skinned hazelnuts
1 cup (200g) superfine sugar
6 extra large egg whites
a pinch of salt

FILLING AND FROSTING:
2 cups (500ml) heavy cream
12oz (350g) good semisweet chocolate, chopped
unsweetened cocoa powder for sprinkling

2 baking sheets, lined with parchment paper (see recipe)
a pastry bag fitted with a 3/4-inch plain tip

This is a slightly simplifed version of one of Maison Bernachon's most famous gâteaux. It is not very difficult to make, yet tastes wonderful and looks very French and glamorous. The cake part is made from a meringue flavored with toasted and ground hazelnuts, and the filling and frosting are a thick ganache of heavy cream and dark, rich chocolate. (Be sure to use a top-quality chocolate.) The assembled cake should be chilled overnight before cutting.

Preheat the oven to 325°F.

Draw an 8-inch circle on two sheets of non-stick parchment paper. Use to line the baking sheets, turning the paper over so the drawn circle is on the underside.

Put the hazelnuts into a roasting pan or baking dish and toast in the preheated oven until a good, even brown. Cool, then work in a food processor to make a coarse powder. Mix the hazelnuts with all but 2 tablespoons of the sugar and set aside.

Put the egg whites and pinch of salt into a spotlessly clean, grease-free, non-plastic bowl – a stainless steel mixer bowl is fine. Beat the whites, starting slowly and then gradually increasing the speed, until soft peaks form. Beat in the reserved 2 tablespoons of sugar at high speed, then continue beating until the whites form stiff peaks. Using a large metal spoon, gently fold in the hazelnut and sugar mixture.

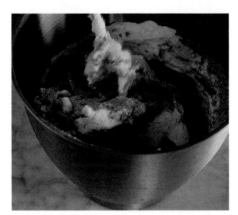

1 GENTLY COMBINE THE POWDERED HAZELNUT MIXTURE AND THE MERINGUE.

2 PIPE THE HAZELNUT MERINGUE MIXTURE IN A SPIRAL TO MAKE A NEAT DISK.

Spoon half the meringue mixture into the pastry bag fitted with the plain tip. Pipe onto one of the baking sheets in a disk inside the drawn circle: start at the center and pipe around and around in circles outward. Use the remaining mixture to pipe a second disk in the same way. Bake the disks in the preheated oven for 1–1½ hours or until golden, firm, and crisp, turning and rotating the sheets so the disks cook evenly. Let cool completely, then peel off the paper.

Meanwhile, prepare the chocolate filling. Heat the cream in a heavy saucepan until scalding hot but not boiling. Remove from the heat and gradually stir in the chocolate. Stir gently until completely melted and smooth, then let cool, stirring occasionally, until the mixture is thick enough to spread. You can hasten the process by chilling the cooled mixture. If it becomes too cold and hard to spread, warm it gently.

To assemble the cake, put one disk of hazelnut meringue on a serving platter and spread with about a third of the chocolate cream mixture, using a metal spatula. Spread gently and try not to press down on the meringue as this could crush it. Put the second meringue disk on top. Quickly spread the rest of the chocolate mixture over the top and down the sides to cover completely. It does not matter if the frosting is not completely smooth. If the chocolate becomes hard to spread it may help to dip the spatula in hot water. Wipe the excess frosting off the plate, then chill the cake overnight.

Remove from the fridge about 30 minutes before serving, unless the weather is very hot, and dust liberally with cocoa powder. Keep in the fridge in a covered container, and eat within 2 days.

A SIMPLE WEDDING CAKE

Makes a 10-inch round cake

2 cups (450g) unsalted butter, at room
  temperature

the finely grated rind and juice of 3 large unwaxed
  lemons

2¹/₄ cups (450g) sugar

8 eggs, beaten

2 cups (170g) ground almonds

1²/₃ cups (230g) self-rising flour

5 tablespoons (40g) cornstarch

³/₄ teaspoon baking powder

2—3 tablespoons milk, if necessary

TO COVER WITH MARZIPAN:

about ¹/₃ cup lemon curd (see recipe opposite)

confectioners' sugar for dusting

2lb (900g) marzipan

TO COVER WITH ICING:

a little sherry or brandy for brushing

2¹/₂lb (1.1 kg) icing fondant, prepared according to
  package directions

a 10-inch round deep cake pan, greased and
  lined with greased parchment paper (see
  pages 112–3)

a large round cake board, about 13 inches in
  diameter

flowers for decoration

1 MAKE A SOFT, DROPPING CONSISTENCY.

2 TEST THE CAKE WITH A FINE SKEWER.

I like this cake so much I made it for my own wedding two years ago. It is a lovely rich sponge, flavored with ground almonds and lemon, and is fairly quick and simple to make. Even though I covered the cake with marzipan and white icing like a traditional British wedding cake, I was anticipating a few raised eyebrows. However, most guests asked for a second piece — and the recipe. I made the cake on the Wednesday before my Saturday wedding, and it took only about two hours from start to finish. The next day I covered it in marzipan, commercially made, and left it to dry for 24 hours before covering in icing fondant. Just before the wedding party, I decorated the top and the base of the cake with roses and flowering herbs to match my bouquet.

A half quantity of the cake batter can be baked in an 8-inch round deep pan, then covered with 1³/₄lb (800g) marzipan and 2lb (900g) icing fondant. Because of the long baking time it is important to prepare the pan well — use three layers of parchment paper for lining, and cover the cake during baking if necessary.

Preheat the oven to 350°F.

Beat the butter with the lemon rind until soft and creamy, using an electric mixer. Gradually beat in the sugar, then beat until the mixture becomes very pale and fluffy. Beat in the eggs a tablespoon at a time, beating well after each addition. Add the ground almonds with the last few additions of egg, to prevent the mixture from separating. Sift the flour with the cornstarch and baking powder. Using a large metal spoon, fold into the creamed mixture in batches alternately with the lemon juice. If necessary, add a little milk to make a soft consistency that will drop from the spoon. Spoon into the prepared pan and smooth the surface.

Bake in the preheated oven for 30 minutes, then reduce the oven temperature to 325°F and bake for a further 1–1¹/₄ hours or until well risen and springy to the touch. A skewer inserted into the center should come out clean. (If baking a smaller cake, reduce the oven temperature to 300°F and bake for a further 1–1¹/₄ hours.) If the cake seems to be browning too much, cover with a double sheet of parchment paper. Leave in the pan until completely cold before turning out. The cooled cake can now be covered in marzipan, or wrapped in wax paper and foil and kept up to 5 days before covering.

To cover the cake in marzipan, first remove all your rings and bangles to prevent making marks and dents. Turn the cake upside-down and place it in the center of the cake board. Check that the top surface is level. Brush the cake all over with lemon curd. Lightly dust the work surface with sifted confectioners' sugar, then knead the marzipan until smooth. Roll it out into a round large enough to cover the top and sides of the cake (use a piece of string to measure the distance up one side of the cake, across the top and then down the other side). As you roll, move the marzipan around to prevent it from sticking, but do not turn it over. Carefully wrap the marzipan around the rolling pin, then lift it over the cake. Gently unroll the marzipan so the edge just touches the board on the far side. Then continue unrolling the marzipan over the cake so it covers the cake evenly and touches the board all around. Using the palm of your hand, smooth the marzipan on the top surface, and down against the sides of the cake to make sure it is well fixed. Trim excess marzipan. Let dry for 1–2 days.

To cover the cake with icing, first remove all your rings and bangles.

Brush the marzipanned cake with a little sherry or brandy so the icing will stick. Knead the icing fondant until smooth, then roll it out and cover the cake as for the marzipan. If air bubbles form, prick them at one side with a pin, then gently rub the bubble to expel the air. With your palm, spotlessy clean and dry, smooth and polish the surface of the icing. Do not press too hard with your fingers or there will be dents in the icing. Set the iced cake aside in a cool, dry place to dry for up to 3 days.

To finish the cake, decorate with fresh, silk, or sugar flowers. If using fresh flowers, arrange on top or use a special holder or ring available from specialist cake decorating suppliers and some kitchenware stores; the flowers will wilt rapidly if pushed into the icing. Decorate the base of the cake where it meets the cake board with foliage, ribbons, or piped icing. The cake will cut into 45 pieces, and is best eaten within a week of baking.

LEMON CURD

INGREDIENTS

Makes about 1lb (450g)

$1/2$ cup (110g) unsalted butter, diced

1 cup + 2 tablespoons (230g) sugar

the grated rind and juice of 2 large or 3 small
    unwaxed lemons

3 extra large eggs, beaten

spotlessly clean, sterilized jars

Lemon curd is used here to stick the marzipan to the lemon-flavored cake, but it can also be used to fill layer cakes, to spread on scones (see page 34), or mixed with whipped cream as a filling for cakes and pastries such as mille-feuilles (page 146) or profiteroles (page 149).

Put the butter, sugar, and lemon rind and juice into the top of a non-aluminum double boiler or into a saucepan set in a bain-marie – a roasting pan of boiling water. Cook, stirring constantly with a wooden spoon, until smooth and melted. Add the eggs and stir until very thick and opaque. If the mixture boils it will scramble, so avoid short cuts.

Spoon into prepared jars and leave until cold, then cover and store in the fridge until ready to use – up to 2 weeks

CHAPTER FIVE

PASTRIES

Pastry is not just the container for a wonderful
filling, its taste and texture should enhance the whole dish.
With the help of a food processor, superb pastry
is easy to achieve.

MAKING PASTRY SUCCESSFULLY

Rich, short pastry is easy to roll and cut if it is chilled first.

Making pastry is the exact opposite of bread making – you don't want to develop the gluten in the flour, as this makes the dough elastic, so heavy-duty kneading and man-handling are to be avoided. Also, to prevent the finished pastry from being greasy or heavy, it is important that the fats do not begin to turn oily or melt as you work the mixture; so use them cold and firm straight from the fridge where possible, and work rapidly, handling the mixture as little as possible.

For years I thought of my perpetually cold hands as a nuisance until other cooks told me I was lucky – their hot hands, the bane of their lives, hindered pastry-making. Many now make pastry in the food processor as it cuts down on handling, though it is important to run the machine only until the dough just comes together: if over-processed, the dough will become oily and sticky.

To make basic short pastry by hand, first lightly toss the flour and any other dry ingredients with the fat so the pieces of fat are coated in flour. Then cut the fat into smaller pieces about the size of your little fingernail, using one or two round-bladed knives or a wire pastry cutter. Finally, gently rub the fat and flour between the fingertips (not the palm of your hand), a small quantity at a time, until there are no visible lumps of fat and the mixture resembles fine crumbs. As you work, lift your hands up to the rim of the bowl so the mixture will become aerated as it falls back down into the bowl. (If using shortening, omit the rubbing-in stage.)

Bind the mixture together with icy cold water, or another liquid, using only just enough to make a soft dough. If the dough is dry and hard it will be difficult to roll out and use, but if it is too wet and sticky it will be tough and heavy when baked. Once the dough comes together, turn it onto a lightly floured work surface and very gently and briefly knead the dough to make it smooth and even.

To make pastry in a food processor, combine the flour and any other dry ingredients in the food processor bowl. Add the pieces of fat and process for about a minute or just until the mixture forms fine crumbs. Then, with the motor running, pour in the water or other liquid through the feed tube. The mixture should clump together within a minute. As soon as the mixture clumps together, stop the machine to prevent over-working. If the mixture doesn't come together, add more water a teaspoon at a time. Turn the dough onto a lightly floured work surface and gently knead for a few seconds to form a smooth ball.

Richer pastry doughs, such as rich short pastry and almond pastry, need to be chilled before rolling out. Basic piecrust doesn't normally need chilling, unless the kitchen is hot or the pastry dough shows signs of becoming oily. Wrap in wax paper and chill for 15–20 minutes or until firm enough to roll out. Chilling helps the dough to relax, but it is not the antidote to over-working.

Puff pastry, the richest of all the pastries, remains the biggest challenge. The only short cut is to use a food processor to make the initial dough – the *détrempe*. The tricky part, incorporating as much butter as flour, has to be achieved by rolling and folding the dough by hand in a very precise fashion. But be reassured – success comes with practice.

PREVIOUS PAGE A selection of mincemeat pies.

SHORT or PIE PASTRY

INGREDIENTS

Makes about 12oz (340g)

1²/₃ cups (230g) all-purpose flour

¹/₈–¹/₄ teaspoon salt

4 tablespoons (60g) unsalted butter, chilled and diced

¹/₄ cup (60g) lard, chilled and diced, or shortening

about 3 tablespoons icy water to bind

This pastry, with its short and light, crumbly texture, is the simplest to make and the most versatile to use. In its most basic form, pie pastry is a dough made from all-purpose flour, fat, a little salt, and some cold water. The shortness of the pastry depends on the type of fat used and the way it is incorporated into the flour. Firm unsalted butter gives the best flavor, but a mixture of lard or shortening, and butter gives the best texture — that important melt-in-the-mouth quality. Many recipes give one part fat to two of flour, by weight, that is 1oz (30g) fat to 2oz (60g) flour, the fat being made up of equal amounts of butter and lard or shortening.

To make the pastry dough by hand, sift the flour and salt into a mixing bowl. Add the diced fats and toss lightly until well coated in flour. Using a round-bladed knife, two knives, or a wire pastry cutter, cut the fats into small pieces, then rub the fats into the flour with the very tips of your fingers. (Omit the rubbing-in if using shortening.)

When the whole mixture looks like fine crumbs, with no clumps of fat, gradually pour in the water while stirring with a round-bladed knife. Keep stirring until the dough comes together – this can take a couple of minutes. If any dry crumbs still remain at the bottom of the bowl, add

1 *ADD THE FATS TO THE FLOUR AND USE A ROUND-BLADED KNIFE TO CUT THE FATS INTO QUITE SMALL PIECES.*

2 *RUB THE FLOUR AND PIECES OF FAT TOGETHER USING YOUR FINGERTIPS, LIFTING THE MIXTURE AS YOU RUB.*

3 *WHEN THE MIXTURE RESEMBLES FINE CRUMBS, SLOWLY ADD JUST ENOUGH COLD WATER TO BIND TO A DOUGH.*

4 *GATHER THE DOUGH TOGETHER IN YOUR HANDS AND FINISH BY MIXING BRIEFLY ON A FLOURED WORK SURFACE.*

more water a few drops at a time. The dough should hold together and be on the firm side of soft. If the dough is sticky or wet, stir in extra flour a little at a time. Turn onto a floured work surface and use your hand to bring the dough together to form a ball – try not to handle or work the dough too much because you don't want the fats to begin to melt and make the pastry oily. If you find that this does happen, and the dough begins to feel soft, wrap it in wax paper and chill it in the refrigerator for 15–20 minutes or until it is firm but not hard.

Alternatively, make the dough in a food processor (see page 132).

Roll out the dough on a lightly floured work surface, using a lightly floured rolling pin. Carefully lift and move the dough from time to time during rolling to check it is not sticking to the work surface; dust with extra flour as necessary.

1 PROCESS THE FATS AND FLOUR TOGETHER TO A CRUMB-LIKE TEXTURE.

2 ONCE WATER IS ADDED, THE DOUGH WILL COME TOGETHER IN A CLUMP.

RICH SHORT PASTRY

INGREDIENTS

Makes about 1lb (450g)

$1^2/_3$ cups (230g) all-purpose flour

$^1/_8$–$^1/_4$ teaspoon salt

5-6 tablespoons (60g) granulated or confectioners' sugar

$^3/_4$ cup (170g) unsalted butter, chilled and diced

1 extra large egg yolk

a little ice water to bind as necessary

Increasing the proportion of fat to flour — from half fat to flour to three-quarters fat to flour, by weight — makes the pastry taste richer. It also makes it slightly more difficult to work, so here the food processor is a blessing. Sugar, added before or after the fat is rubbed in, makes the pastry crisper as well as sweeter, but it also increases the risk of scorching during baking. Instead of water an egg yolk binds the dough and adds additional richness and color — just the yolk is used as egg white tends to make pastry tough. Rich short pastry is made in the same way as short pastry but needs to be chilled before rolling out.

To make the pastry dough by hand, sift the flour, salt, and sugar into a mixing bowl. Add the diced butter and rub in with your fingertips until the mixture resembles fine crumbs. Stir in the egg yolk using a round-bladed knife; if necessary add a little ice water to bind the mixture and make a dough that is not too soft and neither sticky nor hard and dry. Wrap the dough in wax paper and chill for 15–20 minutes or until firm but not hard.

Alternatively, make the dough in a food processor (see page 132).

To use, roll out as for short pastry.

1 TAKE THE BUTTER STRAIGHT FROM THE FRIDGE AND DICE IT QUICKLY BEFORE ADDING TO THE FLOUR AND SUGAR.

2 AFTER MIXING IN THE EGG YOLK AND WATER, STOP THE MACHINE AS SOON AS THE DOUGH COMES TOGETHER.

ALMOND PASTRY

Makes about 1lb 3oz (530g)
1²/₃ cups (230g) all-purpose flour
¹/₈–¹/₄ teaspoon salt
¹/₂ cup (40g) ground almonds
7–8 tablespoons (85g) granulated or confectioners'
   sugar
³/₄ cup (170g) unsalted butter, chilled and diced
1 extra large egg yolk

The addition of ground almonds gives rich short pastry an even richer flavor, and a good crumbly, light texture. I like to use this pastry for fruit tarts as well as for mincemeat pies. The sugar can be either confectioners' sugar – which gives the pastry a fine, crisp texture – or granulated, which makes it slightly more crumbly. Again, I prefer to make the dough in the food processor.

To make the pastry by hand, sift the flour, salt, ground almonds, and sugar into a mixing bowl. Add the diced butter and cut into the flour mixture using a round-bladed knife. When the butter has been reduced to small flakes, use your fingertips to rub it into the flour. When the mixture looks like fine crumbs, stir in the egg yolk using a round-bladed knife to make a soft but not sticky dough. If there are dry crumbs left at the bottom of the bowl, add ice water a few drops at a time. Wrap the dough in wax paper and chill for 15–20 minutes or until firm but not hard.

Alternatively, make the dough in a food processor (see page 132).

To use, roll out as for short pastry.

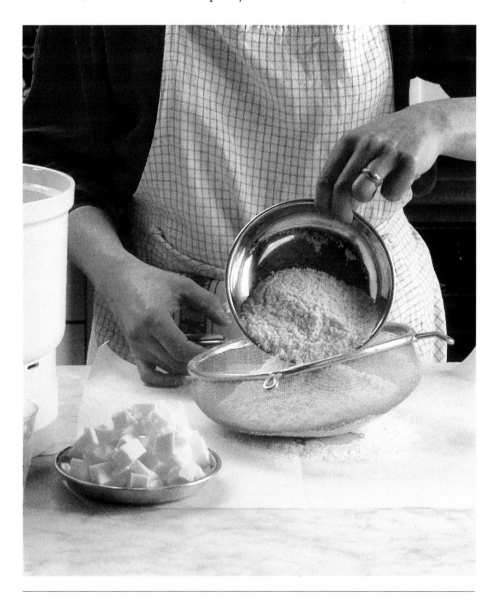

FOR THE BEST TEXTURE, SIFT THE GROUND ALMONDS WITH THE FLOUR, SUGAR, AND SALT TO REMOVE ANY LUMPS.

MINCEMEAT PIES

INGREDIENTS

Makes 12
1 batch short, rich short, or almond pastry
   dough (pages 133-135)
³/₄–1lb (340–450g) mincemeat (see recipe
   opposite)
granulated or confectioners' sugar for sprinkling

two plain or fluted round pastry or cookie cutters,
   one 4-inch and one 3-inch
a small star, leaf, or tree-shaped cutter (optional)
3-inch tartlet molds

Just as locally grown asparagus is even more of a treat because it is only in season for a few weeks in May, so the first mincemeat pies taste best because I know it is Christmas Eve. To fill me with seasonal cheer, just shut me in the kitchen with a batch of pastry, jars of homemade mincemeat, and the Festival of Nine Carols and Lessons from King's College, Cambridge, on BBC radio.

Mincemeat pies can be made with short, rich short, or, my absolute favorite, almond pastry — I find puff pastry a bit too rich. Or you can use commercially made sheets of phyllo.

Preheat the oven to 350°F.

Roll out the pastry dough on a floured work surface to about ¹/₁₆ inch thick. Cut out 12 rounds using the larger cutter and 12 rounds using the smaller cutter, re-rolling the trimmings as necessary. Line the tartlet molds with the larger rounds, gently pressing the dough against the sides of the molds with your thumb to remove any air bubbles. Put 1¹/₂–2 teaspoons of mincemeat in the center of each pastry shell.

Dampen the edges of the pastry shells using a pastry brush dipped in cold water. Cover with the smaller rounds and seal the edges by gently pressing down with an upside-down round cutter or small glass that just fits inside the rim of the mold. Make a small steam hole in the center of each top crust using a skewer.

If you like, cut a star, leaf, or Christmas tree shape out of the center of the smaller rounds before using to cover the pies. Alternatively, the pies can be decorated with shapes cut from the pastry trimmings — stick these onto the crust by dampening the undersides.

Bake the pies for 25–30 minutes or until firm and just golden — the richer pastries tend to brown very quickly so keep an eye on them. Let cool in the molds for several minutes. When the pastry firms up enough to allow the pies to be unmolded, transfer them to a wire rack. Serve warm or at room temperature, dusted with granulated or confectioners' sugar, with brandy butter (hard sauce), cream, or ice-cream. When completely cold, store in an airtight tin and eat within 5 days, or freeze.

NOTE Tartlet molds with the same diameter can vary in depth, so the size of cutter needed for the dough rounds to line the molds will depend on the depth of those you use.

1 LIGHTLY MOISTEN THE RIMS OF THE PASTRY SHELLS WITH COLD WATER BEFORE COVERING WITH THE TOP CRUST.

2 TO SEAL THE PIES, GENTLY PRESS DOWN WITH AN UPTURNED CUTTER THAT IS SLIGHTLY SMALLER THAN THE MOLD.

LUXURIOUS MINCEMEAT

INGREDIENTS

Makes about 3lb (1.35kg)

1⅓ cups (230g) currants

1½ cups (230g) large raisins

½ cup (85g) finely chopped mixed candied peel

⅓ cup (60g) chopped candied ginger

1 cup (110g) grated tart apple

½ cup (110g) shredded beef suet or vegetarian suet

¼ cup (30g) chopped blanched almonds

¼ cup (30g) chopped walnuts

the grated rind and juice of ½ unwaxed orange

the grated rind and juice of ½ unwaxed lemon

¾ cup packed (170g) dark brown sugar

½ teaspoon each ground cinnamon, grated nutmeg, and apple-pie spice

⅔ cup (140ml) brandy or ginger wine

sterilized jars and lids

I like mincemeat to be fruity and moist but not too sweet, and nicely steeped in brandy. The nuts add a crunchy texture as well as improving the balance of flavors. Mincemeat can also be used to make an easy fruit cake (see page 110) or to fill a large double-crust pie or Jalousie (page 142).

Put all the ingredients into a large mixing bowl and mix thoroughly. Cover tightly and let stand in a cool spot for a day to allow the flavors to infuse and blend. Stir from time to time.

Give the mincemeat a good mix, then spoon into the prepared jars. Cover and leave in the fridge or a cold place for several weeks to allow the mincemeat to mature. Before using, stir well. Always store opened jars of mincemeat in the refrigerator.

Christmas Eve – mincemeat pies, mulled wine, and an aromatic log fire.

RIGHT *A snow-covered church in Bavaria.*

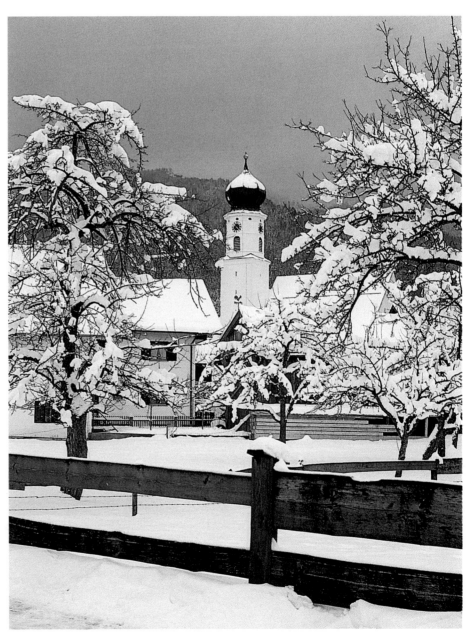

SHORTBREAD-TOPPED MINCE PIES

Makes 20
1 batch short, rich short, or almond pastry
   dough (pages 133-135)
about 1lb (450g) mincemeat (page 137)

TOPPING:
$^3/_4$ cup (170g) unsalted butter, at room
   temperature
5 tablespoons (60g) sugar
$1^1/_4$ cups (170g) all-purpose flour
$1^1/_3$ cups (110g) ground almonds

a 4-inch plain or fluted round pastry or cookie
   cutter
3-inch tartlet molds
a pastry bag fitted with a large star tip

These mincemeat pies are lighter than they appear, and disappear even faster than ordinary mincemeat pies. Although the bases can be made from short or rich short pastry, almond pastry is the most delicious when combined with good mincemeat and this rich, but not sweet, almond shortbread mixture piped on top.

Preheat the oven to 350°F.

Roll out the pastry dough fairly thinly and cut out 20 rounds using the pastry cutter (use a large cutter, according to the depth of your molds), re-rolling the trimmings as necessary. Use to line the molds. Put $1^1/_2$–2 teaspoons of mincemeat into each pastry shell.

To make the topping, beat the butter with the sugar until light and fluffy, then mix in the flour and the almonds. Use your hands to bring the mixture together, kneading gently until smooth; it should be just soft enough to pipe. Spoon the mixture into the pastry bag fitted with the star tip and pipe a swirl on the top of each mincemeat-filled pastry shell. Chill for 5 minutes.

Bake for 25–30 minutes or until a light golden brown. Let cool slightly in the molds. When the pastry is firm enough to unmold, transfer the pies carefully to a wire rack. Eat warm or at room temperature, plain or with cream or ice-cream. When completely cold, store in an airtight tin and eat within 5 days, or freeze.

PHYLLO MINCEMEAT PIES

I first discovered these on a visit to The Walnut Tree Inn, near Abergavenny in South Wales. Watching the chef and proprietor, Franco Taruschio, make petit-four mincemeat pies to serve with coffee at Christmas was a revelation — the quickest, lightest, crunchiest mincemeat pies can be made from phyllo pastry. The pastry is simply cut into squares, brushed with melted butter, and then used to line the molds and to cover the mincemeat filling.

Preheat the oven to 350°F.

If the pastry is frozen, thaw according to the package directions. Once unwrapped, keep the pastry covered with plastic wrap or a damp dish towel to prevent it from drying out. Lay one sheet of pastry on the work surface. Cut the sheet into 3¹/₂- to 4-inch squares using a large sharp knife or kitchen scissors (if your molds are deep, cut slightly larger squares) and brush them with melted butter. Use three squares, arranged at different angles, to line each mold, and lightly press into the bottom. The pastry should hang over the rim of the mold.

Put 1¹/₂–2 teaspoons of mincemeat in the center of each pastry shell. Cover with another two squares of pastry, crumpled lightly like a scarf.

Bake for 8–10 minutes or until a good golden brown and crisp. Remove from the molds and cool on a wire rack. Serve warm or at room temperature, dusted with sifted confectioners' sugar. Store the mincemeat pies in an airtight tin, and eat them within 2 days.

1 USING A PASTRY BRUSH, COAT THE CUT SQUARES OF PHYLLO WITH A THIN LAYER OF MELTED BUTTER.

2 LINE EACH MOLD WITH THREE SQUARES OF BUTTERED PHYLLO, ARRANGING THEM AT SLIGHTLY DIFFERENT ANGLES.

3 SPOON A LITTLE MINCEMEAT INTO THE CENTER OF EACH PHYLLO-LINED MOLD, WITHOUT OVERFILLING.

4 COVER EACH PIE WITH TWO MORE SQUARES OF BUTTERED PASTRY, CRUMPLED UP LIKE A CHIFFON SCARF.

LEFT Franco Taruschio making phyllo mincemeat pies in his kitchen at The Walnut Tree Inn.

QUEEN MARY TARTLETS

Makes 12

PASTRY:

¾ cup (110g) all-purpose flour

a pinch of salt

5 tablespoons (70g) margarine, butter, or a mix of fats, chilled and diced

½ teaspoon sugar

1 egg yolk

2 teaspoons ice water

FILLING:

4 tablespoons (60g) margarine or butter, at room temperature

5 tablespoons (60g) sugar

1 extra large egg

⅔ cup (110g) golden raisins

3 tablespoons (30g) finely chopped mixed candied peel

a 4-inch plain or fluted round pastry cutter

3-inch tartlet molds

Another Scottish recipe from Katie Stewart (see page 112) — simple, sweet, fruit-filled tartlets dating back to the court of Mary Queen of Scots. The pastry can be made with margarine, butter, or a mixture of either with lard or shortening.

Preheat the oven to 375°F.

Make the pastry: sift the flour and salt into a mixing bowl, add the fat, and cut and rub in with your fingertips until the mixture looks like fine crumbs (do not rub in shortening). Stir in the sugar. Mix together the egg yolk and water, then stir into the mixture to make a firm dough.

Roll out the dough fairly thinly on a lightly floured work surface. Cut out 12 rounds using the pastry cutter, re-rolling the trimmings as necessary. Use the rounds to line the tartlet molds, pressing the dough gently against the bottom and sides of the molds to eliminate any air bubbles. Try not to stretch the dough as you do this.

For the filling, beat the margarine or butter with the sugar until light and fluffy, then beat in the egg. When thoroughly blended, stir in the raisins and the chopped candied peel. Divide the filling equally among the tartlet shells and smooth the surface.

Bake for 15–20 minutes or until the pastry under the filling is cooked — to test, carefully loosen and lift out the filling from one tartlet using a small round-bladed knife.

Remove the tartlets from the molds and let cool on a baking sheet. Eat warm or at room temperature, within 24 hours of baking.

ROUGH or QUICK PUFF PASTRY

INGREDIENTS

Makes about 12oz (340g)

1²/₃ cups (230g) all-purpose flour

¹/₄ teaspoon salt

4 tablespoons (60g) butter, chilled and finely diced

4 tablespoons (60g) lard, chilled and finely diced,
  or shortening

about 4 tablespoons ice water to bind

Rough puff is quicker, simpler, and less rich than puff pastry, but it still has plenty of layers of crisp, light pastry, and it is ideal for deep-dish fruit pies as well as tarts. Although you can use all butter for a richer taste, I find a combination of butter and lard or shortening helps the dough to rise more during baking and makes a lighter pastry. To make rough puff, flakes of fat are combined with flour and water to make a soft, lumpy dough, which is then rolled out and folded six times, just as with puff pastry. This incorporates the fat into the dough in hundreds of layers.

Sift the flour and salt into a mixing bowl. Add the fats and stir gently with a round-bladed knife until the pieces are thoroughly coated in flour. Stir in enough ice water to bind the dough, adding it a tablespoon at a time. The dough should be lumpy, soft, and moist, but not sticky or wet.

Turn the dough onto a lightly floured work surface and form it into a brick shape by gently patting with floured fingers. Using a floured rolling pin, roll out the dough away from you into a rectangle 18 x 6 inches. Fold the dough in three like a business letter: fold the bottom third of the dough up to cover the center third, then fold the top third down to cover the other two layers. Gently but firmly seal the edges by pressing down with the rolling pin. This is the first "turn."

Lift up the piece of dough and give it a quarter turn counterclockwise, so that the folded edges are now at the sides. Roll out and fold in three again, then give the dough a quarter turn counterclockwise; repeat. After this third "turn," wrap the dough and chill for 20 minutes, then do three more "turns," to make a total of six. Chill for 20 minutes before using.

1 THE DOUGH SHOULD LOOK LUMPY, SOFT, AND MOIST BUT NOT WET OR STICKY.

2 SHAPE THE DOUGH INTO A BRICK, THEN ROLL IT OUT TO MAKE A RECTANGLE.

3 FOLD THE RECTANGLE OF DOUGH IN THREE LIKE A BUSINESS LETTER.

4 PRESS THE EDGES OF THE FOLDED DOUGH WITH THE ROLLING PIN TO SEAL THEM.

CARAMELIZED MANGO JALOUSIE

Serves 4

1 batch rough puff pastry dough (page 141)

2 medium to large, ripe mangoes

2 tablespoons sugar

2 pieces of candied ginger, minced (optional)

GLAZE:

a little egg white, lightly beaten, for brushing

1 tablespoon sugar for sprinkling

a baking sheet, lightly greased

Instead of mangoes, you can use lightly poached, forced spring rhubarb for this delicious pastry. Other possible fillings include ripe cherries, pitted and tossed with sugar; quartered apricots; apple slices mixed with mincemeat; or some very good preserves.

Heat the broiler.

Wrap the prepared pastry dough and let rest in the fridge while making the filling (this will help the gluten in the flour to relax).

Peel the mangoes and cut the fruit away from the central pit, taking two pieces from each mango. Slice each piece lengthwise like a fan so the slices remain attached at one end. Arrange the four mango "fans" on the prepared baking sheet and sprinkle with the sugar. Broil for a few minutes or until the tops of the fruit become golden and caramelized. Remove and let cool completely.

Preheat the oven to 425°F.

On a lightly floured work surface, roll out the pastry dough to a rectangle 12 x 10 inches. Using a large sharp knife, trim the edges to make them straight, then cut the rectangle in half lengthwise to make two long

1 FOLD THE PASTRY STRIP IN HALF AND CUT SLITS ACROSS THE FOLD.

2 MOISTEN THE PASTRY EDGES USING A PASTRY BRUSH DIPPED IN COLD WATER.

3 SCORE THE SIDE SO THE PASTRY WILL RISE EVENLY DURING BAKING.

narrow strips. Cut cleanly without dragging the dough. Put one strip on the clean, greased baking sheet. Lightly dust the other strip of dough with flour and fold it in half lengthwise. Cut slits across the fold, about 3/8 inch apart, leaving an uncut border about 3/4 inch wide along the top, bottom, and sides. When opened the strip should look like a Venetian blind.

Arrange the cold caramelized mango fans in a line down the center of the strip of dough on the baking sheet. Scatter the ginger over, if using. Dampen the edges of the strip with a brush dipped in cold water. Lay the cut strip of dough on top and carefully unfold to cover the base and filling. Gently press the edges to seal, then trim to neaten. Using a small knife, score the sides: hold the knife parallel to the assembled pastry and gently knock the blade against the pastry sides to make a series of horizontal marks — the pastry sides will look like the closed pages of a book. Using two fingers and the small knife, flute the edges all around by gently pressing the fingertips down and drawing the knife up between them to form small scallops.

Chill the pastry for 5 minutes, then bake for 20 minutes or until golden and crisp. Remove the baking sheet from the oven. Brush the jalousie lightly with egg white, then sprinkle with sugar. Return to the oven and bake for a further 5 minutes.

Serve warm, with cream, ice-cream, or crème fraîche.

PUFF PASTRY

Makes about 1lb 5oz (600g)
1³/₄ cups (250g) all-purpose flour
¹/₂ teaspoon salt
1 cup (250g) unsalted butter, cold
1 teaspoon lemon juice
about ¹/₂ cup (125ml) ice water

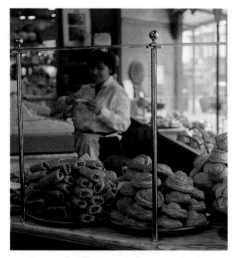

A selection of puff pastry confections and other tea-time treats at Betty's of Harrogate, in northern England.

This, the lightest, richest, flakiest, and most delicious of all pastries, is time-consuming to make and tricky to master. Oh, but the taste is worth it! Nothing can compare to its butteriness, for this pastry contains as much butter as flour, incorporated into the dough by rolling and folding six times, to form seemingly hundreds of airy layers. It makes a fine mille-feuilles layered with cream and fruit, or it can be used for chaussons (fruit turnovers) or a Pithiviers — a pastry filled with a rich almond frangipane.

As with all pastry it is important to avoid developing the gluten in the flour (this is only desirable when making bread dough, where the resulting elasticity is essential). With puff pastry, over-working and stretching the dough would result in it shrinking alarmingly and becoming tough. Although lemon juice helps to prevent this, I prefer to make the détrempe — the initial dough — in the food processor, to cut down on handling, and I stick religiously to the chilling times.

The butter is most easily incorporated if it is cold — the same temperature as the détrempe — but pliable rather than hard. So I use it straight from the fridge and beat it with a rolling pin to get the right consistency. It is vital not to let the butter get warm and start to ooze out of the dough or the pastry will not rise during baking and will be end up greasy and heavy.

For convenience, the dough can be stored in the fridge for 4 days, or frozen, after you have given it four "turns." Then the last two "turns" can be completed when you want to use the dough.

Sift the flour and salt and tip into the bowl of a food processor. Add 2 tablespoons (30g) of the butter, cut into dice, and process until the mixture resembles fine crumbs. Mix the lemon juice and water. With the machine running, pour the liquid in via the feed tube in a steady stream, to make a ball of soft dough that is fairly moist but not sticky or wet. If the dough seems dry or there are crumbs left in the bottom of the bowl, add a little extra water a teaspoon at a time. Turn the dough onto a lightly floured work surface and shape into a ball, then cut a deep cross in the top (this helps reduce the elasticity). Wrap and chill for 15 minutes.

Dust the remaining slab of butter with a little flour, then place it between two pieces of plastic wrap. Pound with a rolling pin until the butter is half as thick as it was. Remove the plastic. Fold the butter in two, then place between the plastic and pound again. Keep pounding and folding in this way until the butter is pliable but not soft, then fold and beat the butter to make a square with 5-inch-long sides.

Set the ball of dough on a lightly floured work surface. Using a floured rolling pin, roll out the dough to make four flaps with a thick square of dough — the size of the square of butter — in the center. Lift the dough and give it a quarter turn after rolling each flap. Put the square of butter, dusted with flour, on the central square of dough and fold the four flaps over the butter so it is completely enclosed. Gently press the seams to seal. Turn the piece of dough upside down, then lightly press with the rolling pin several times to flatten the dough — do this gently because the fat must not be forced out of its dough wrapping.

Lightly roll out the dough into a rectangle 18 x 6 inches, rolling away from your body in short, brisk movements. Fold the dough in three like a business letter: fold the bottom third up to cover the center third, then fold the top third down to cover the other two layers, making a neat square of dough. Lightly press the edges with the rolling pin to seal. This completes the first "turn."

Lift up the piece of dough and give it a quarter turn counterclockwise, so that the folded edges are now at the sides. Roll out the dough into a rectangle and fold it in three again, just as before. Use two fingers to mark the dough with a couple of dents, to indicate that it has had two "turns," then wrap the dough and chill for 15 minutes.

Give the dough two more "turns," and mark with four little indentations. Wrap and chill the dough as before. At this point the pastry can be stored in the fridge for 4 days or frozen. Before using, give the dough two more "turns," to make a total of six.

1 DUST THE SLAB OF CHILLED BUTTER WITH FLOUR, THEN POUND WITH THE ROLLING PIN UNTIL PLIABLE BUT FIRM.

2 ROLL OUT THE BALL OF DOUGH IN FOUR DIRECTIONS TO MAKE FOUR FLAPS WITH A THICK SQUARE IN THE CENTER.

3 SET THE FLOURED BUTTER SQUARE IN THE CENTER AND FOLD THE FLAPS OF DOUGH OVER TO ENCLOSE IT.

4 LIGHTLY PRESS THE SQUARE OF DOUGH WITH THE ROLLING PIN TO FLATTEN IT, THEN ROLL OUT INTO A RECTANGLE.

5 FOLD THE RECTANGLE IN THREE – THE BOTTOM THIRD UP, THEN THE TOP THIRD DOWN – TO MAKE A SQUARE SHAPE.

6 MAKE DENTS IN THE PASTRY WITH YOUR FINGERS AS A REMINDER OF HOW MANY "TURNS" YOU'VE COMPLETED.

MILLE FEUILLES

INGREDIENTS

Serves 6–8

¹/₂ batch puff pastry dough (page 144), about
   10¹/₂oz (300g)

3–4 tablespoons good raspberry preserves

²/₃ cup (140ml) heavy cream, chilled and whipped

1¹/₄ cups (150g) raspberries

confectioners' sugar for dusting

a large baking sheet, lightly greased

This recipe shows off puff pastry to its best advantage – it is simply baked in a sheet, then sliced into three, and layered with cream and fruit. You can use a variety of fillings to suit the season: pastry cream (see recipe page 166) instead of whipped fresh cream, strawberries, fresh sliced peaches or apricots, pitted cherries, fresh currants, or lightly poached and well-drained fruit like rhubarb or pears. Once assembled, eat as soon as possible because the pastry quickly becomes soggy.

Preheat the oven to 425°F.

Roll out the pastry dough to a square with 12-inch sides, then trim the edges to straighten them using a large sharp knife. Avoid dragging the knife or pulling the dough as this will distort the shape. Put the square of dough upside down on the prepared baking sheet and prick the dough all over with a fork.

Bake for 10 minutes or until well risen, golden, and crisp. Remove from the oven and cool on a wire rack.

Cut the cold pastry into three equal rectangles, each measuring 4 x 12 inches. If necessary, trim the sides to neaten them. Put one pastry rectangle on a serving plate and spread with the jam, then cover with half of the whipped cream. Spread the rest of the whipped cream on a second pastry rectangle and place this on top. Arrange the fruit on the cream very gently, then cover with the third rectangle of pastry. Dust with sifted confectioners' sugar, and serve.

CHOUX PASTRY

Makes a 3-egg quantity

³/₄ cup (110g) all-purpose flour

³/₄ cup + 1 tablespoon (185ml) water from the
    cold tap

¹/₈ teaspoon salt

5 tablespoons (75g) unsalted butter, diced

3 eggs, beaten

Unlike short pastry and other rubbed-in pastries, choux is cooked in a saucepan before it is baked in the oven. The soft dough – made from butter, water, flour, salt, and egg – is piped or dropped in spoonfuls onto a baking sheet. In the oven it rises and puffs up to make a crisp, hollow container. Choux pastry is used for éclairs and profiteroles (cream puffs) to be filled with pastry cream (crème pâtissière), whipped cream, or ice-cream, or beignets, which are deep-fried fritters served with a fruit sauce.

To make successful choux pastry it is important to measure the ingredients very carefully and accurately. In addition, the water must not boil and begin to evaporate before the butter in it has melted. The eggs should be added gradually because if too little is beaten into the dough it will be hard and flat; if too much is added the dough will be too soft to pipe and will not hold a shape.

Sift the flour onto a piece of paper. Put the water, salt, and butter into a medium-sized saucepan and heat gently until the butter has completely melted. Rapidly bring the mixture to a boil, then immediately remove from the heat and tip in all the flour. Beat vigorously with a wooden spoon – the mixture will look a complete mess and a failure at the start but will come together to make a smooth, heavy clump of dough. Return the pan to a low heat and beat the dough for half a minute to dry it slightly. It should come away from the sides of the pan to form a smooth ball.

Turn the dough into a large mixing bowl and let cool until tepid. Then, using an electric mixer – you can use a wooden spoon if you prefer, but it is hard work – gradually beat in the eggs, beating well after each addition. Beat in just enough egg to make a smooth and shiny, paste-like dough that falls from the spoon when lightly shaken. Keep covered until ready to use.

1 DO NOT LET THE WATER BOIL BEFORE THE BUTTER HAS COMPLETELY MELTED.

2 OFF THE HEAT, BEAT IN THE FLOUR VIGOROUSLY USING A WOODEN SPOON.

3 RETURN TO A LOW HEAT AND BEAT THE DOUGH TO DRY IT SLIGHTLY.

4 BEAT IN JUST ENOUGH EGG TO MAKE A FAIRLY STIFF, PASTE-LIKE DOUGH.

TINY ÉCLAIRS

INGREDIENTS

Makes about 24
1 batch choux pastry (page 147), with a
  pinch of sugar added with the salt

COFFEE PASTRY CREAM:
3 egg yolks
5 tablespoons (60g) sugar
2 heaped tablespoons (20g) all-purpose flour
2 tablespoons (15g) cornstarch
1¼ cups (280ml) whole milk
2 teaspoons instant coffee or to taste
a small piece of butter

GLACÉ ICING:
1½ cups (170g) confectioners' sugar, sifted
2 teaspoons instant coffee dissolved in 2 tablespoons
  boiling water

a pastry bag fitted with a ⅝-inch plain tip
2 baking sheets, greased and dampened

Clare Cave, a friend who caters parties for the Duke of Westminster and up, cooked the most heavenly food for my wedding party, but I can only remember eating the miniature, lighter than air, utterly delicious éclairs. The finger-size choux pastry cases must be well-cooked and crisp before they are filled, otherwise they quickly become soggy. Whipped cream, chocolate mousse (see the Chocolate Macaroons on page 24), or pastry cream can be used to fill them — here I've used coffee pastry cream, and coated the tops with a coffee glacé icing. Eat as soon as possible after assembling.

Preheat the oven to 375°F.

For éclairs, choux paste should hold its own shape and be stiff enough to pipe, so add the last spoonfuls of egg very slowly. Spoon the choux paste into the pastry bag fitted with the plain tip and pipe éclairs the size of your little finger on the prepared baking sheets. Space the éclairs well apart to allow for rising and spreading.

Bake for 20 minutes or until crisp and golden. Remove from the oven, and make a small hole in one end of each éclair, using a skewer or toothpick, to let out the steam. Return the éclairs to the oven and bake for a further 3–4 minutes. Cool on a wire rack.

To make the pastry cream, beat the egg yolks with the sugar in a heatproof mixing bowl until light and creamy. (To avoid spills set the bowl on a damp cloth.) Sift in the flour and cornstarch and mix until smooth. Heat the milk in a heavy saucepan until scalding hot, then add the coffee and stir until dissolved. Pour onto the egg mixture, stirring briskly to make a smooth, creamy liquid. Tip into the rinsed-out saucepan and cook, stirring constantly, until the mixture boils, then beat vigorously until smooth. Turn into a bowl and rub the surface with a little butter to prevent a skin from forming, then let cool.

Spoon the cold pastry cream into the clean, dry pastry bag fitted with the plain tip. Pipe into the éclairs through the steam hole (if necessary, enlarge the steam hole slightly so you can insert the tip).

For the coffee glacé icing, put the sifted sugar into a small mixing bowl and stir in the hot coffee to make a smooth icing. Dip the top of each filled éclair in the icing and let set. Eat within 4 hours.

1 PIPE THE ÉCLAIRS, CUTTING THE DOUGH
OFF NEATLY WITH A SMALL KNIFE.

2 TO ENSURE CRISP PASTRY, MAKE A SMALL
STEAM-HOLE IN EACH BAKED ÉCLAIR.

VARIATIONS: CHOCOLATE ÉCLAIRS Omit the coffee in the pastry cream. Melt 4oz (110g) good semisweet chocolate and add to the cooked pastry cream, off the heat, before transferring it to the bowl. Replace the coffee powder in the icing with 1 tablespoon unsweetened cocoa powder.

PROFITEROLES Put the choux pastry into the pastry bag fitted with the plain tip and pipe rounded mounds about 1 inch wide and ¹/₂ inch high onto the prepared baking sheets. Lightly brush with beaten egg, making sure that it does not drip down and glue the pastry to the sheet. Bake as above. When cold, fill with coffee, vanilla, or chocolate pastry cream, whipped cream, or, my favorite, vanilla ice-cream. Serve with a sauce – chocolate, caramel, or fruit, depending on the filling.

LEFT Rena Salaman works rapidly to assemble her baklava.

ABOVE The finished baklava (see recipe on next page).

PHYLLO PASTRY

These wafer-thin sheets of pastry, spelled phyllo or filo, are now used for all kinds of sweet and savory dishes. Traditional Greek baklava (see page 152) and mincemeat pies (page 139) are just two delicious examples. Strudel, pastis, and brik doughs are similar to phyllo, though slightly thicker; all become crisp, light, and flaky when baked.

While you can make strudel and pastis doughs at home – kneading, stretching, rolling, and pulling a soft and very pliable dough of flour, egg, and water to make a sheet so thin you can read the newspaper through it – phyllo is always bought commercially made. Supermarkets and specialty gourmet stores sell frozen brands. The quality of frozen phyllo varies from the abysmal to the wonderful, and I have been disappointed many times, but it is only through trial and error that you will find a good brand.

When using frozen phyllo, it is important to follow the directions on the package. Thawing should be at room temperature, and once thawed and unwrapped the pastry sheets must be kept covered with a damp dish towel or plastic wrap while you are working on the recipe. This is vital, because if the pastry dries out, it hardens, cracks, and crumbles and becomes almost impossible to fold.

RENA'S BAKLAVA

Cuts into about 24 pieces

1lb 2oz (500g) phyllo pastry

3$\frac{1}{4}$ cups (380g) coarsely chopped walnuts
    (see recipe)

2 tablespoons sugar

1 teaspoon ground cinnamon

$\frac{3}{4}$ cup + 1 tablespoon (185g) unsalted butter,
    melted

2 tablespoons water from the cold tap

SYRUP:

1$\frac{2}{3}$ cups (330g) sugar

1$\frac{1}{4}$ cups (300ml) water

1–2 cinnamon sticks, depending on their size and
    your taste

2 teaspoons lemon juice

3 tablespoons clear honey, preferably Greek and
    thyme-scented

a roasting pan, about 12 inches in diameter if
    round or 14$\frac{1}{2}$ x 9$\frac{3}{4}$ inches if rectangular
    (see recipe)

This is a real mouth-opener, and nothing like commercial baklava. The recipe comes from the distinguished Greek cook and food writer, Rena Salaman. It is made with commercial phyllo pastry, plenty of walnuts, and some cinnamon. Other cooks use pistachios or almonds, but Rena prefers walnuts because they have a greater depth of flavor and a little sharpness to counterbalance the sugar syrup. No special equipment is needed as Rena bakes the baklava in a roasting pan.

If the pastry is frozen, thaw according to package directions. Once unwrapped, keep it covered with plastic wrap or a damp dish towel to prevent it from drying out.

Preheat the oven to 350°F.

The walnuts should be chopped to the consistency of coarse bread crumbs. Mix them with the sugar and cinnamon in a bowl. Set aside.

Unfold the phyllo sheets and choose a roasting pan that best fits their shape: round or rectangular. The sizes of pans suggested usually fit almost perfectly, but you can use other size pans and then just fold in the edges of the phyllo sheets a little. Using a pastry brush, grease the pan liberally with melted butter to prevent sticking.

Cover the bottom of the pan neatly with a sheet of phyllo and brush it with butter. Continue adding sheets, buttering each one. When you have layered about six sheets of phyllo, spread with about a third of the walnut

1 BRUSH THE PHYLLO SHEETS WITH BUTTER BEFORE OR AFTER ARRANGING THEM IN THE PAN, AS YOU WISH.

2 WHEN THERE ARE SIX SHEETS IN THE PAN, SPRINKLE IN A THIRD OF THE WALNUT FILLING AND SPREAD EVENLY.

3 COVER WITH TWO MORE BUTTERED PHYLLO SHEETS BEFORE ADDING MORE OF THE WALNUT FILLING.

4 AFTER ADDING THE FINAL LAYER OF FILLING, FOLD IN THE EDGES OF THE PHYLLO SHEETS OVER THE SURFACE.

filling. Cover with two more sheets of buttered phyllo and spread with half of the remaining filling. Place two sheets of buttered phyllo on top and spread evenly with the rest of the filling. Fold in the edges of the phyllo sheets all around to enclose the filling, rather like a parcel. Place the remaining phyllo on top, buttering each sheet before lifting it. Trim the excess pastry around the edges using a small knife or a pair of scissors – remember that phyllo pastry tends to shrink so do not trim too much.

Now comes the tricky part. Phyllo pastry is too brittle to be cut neatly after it has been baked, so the pieces have to be cut before it goes into the oven. Using a sharp knife cut the baklava carefully into oblong pieces. Ideally the pieces should be the same size, but if not, it is not the end of the world. Sprinkle the cold water all over the surface with your fingertips: the moisture will prevent the pastry edges curling up in the oven.

Bake in the preheated oven for 15 minutes, then turn up the temperature to 375°F and bake for a further 15–20 minutes or until the surface is crisp and light golden. Remove from the oven and let cool while you make the syrup.

Put the sugar and water in a saucepan and heat, stirring, until the sugar dissolves, then bring to a boil. Add the remaining ingredients, cover, and simmer for about 10 minutes to make a light, syrupy consistency. Remove from the heat and let the syrup stand for 10 minutes.

Pour the syrup slowly through a fine strainer over all of the warm baklava. Leave it to absorb all the syrup. The baklava is delicious freshly made, but it will also keep well for 3–4 days, covered with plastic wrap.

5 *AFTER COVERING WITH THE REST OF THE PASTRY, TRIM OFF THE EXCESS AT THE EDGE WITH A SHARP KNIFE.*

6 *CUT THROUGH THE BAKLAVA TO MARK OUT SMALL SQUARES OR OBLONGS, THEN SPRINKLE WITH WATER AND BAKE.*

7 *ONCE THE SUGAR HAS DISSOLVED, BRING THE SYRUP TO A BOIL AND ADD THE CINNAMON, JUICE, AND HONEY.*

8 *LET THE SYRUP COOL SLIGHTLY BEFORE POURING IT, THROUGH A STRAINER, EVENLY OVER THE WARM BAKLAVA.*

CHAPTER SIX

PIES & TARTS

Making a clear distinction between a pie and a
tart isn't easy: both have a pastry base and a
filling, but both may also have a pastry crust
or other topping. Whatever you call them,
the case and its contents should not
merely share a plate — they ought
to make a good marriage.

LEMON MERINGUE PIE

Makes an 8-inch pie, to serve 6
PASTRY:
1¼ cups (170g) all-purpose flour
a pinch of salt
1½ tablespoons (20g) sugar
½ cup (110g) unsalted butter, chilled and diced
1 egg yolk, mixed with 2 teaspoons ice water

FILLING:
the grated rind and juice of 3 large unwaxed lemons
5 tablespoons (40g) cornstarch
1¼ cups (280ml) water
2 egg yolks
7 tablespoons (85g) sugar
3 tablespoons (45g) unsalted butter, diced

MERINGUE TOPPING:
3 egg whites
⅔ cup (140g) superfine sugar

an 8-inch loose-based tart pan

It may be corny, but this is my favorite dessert. The lemon filling is nicely sharp and well-flavored, and unlike most recipes it is made rich and creamy with butter. To keep the pastry base from going soggy, bake it thoroughly before adding the filling. If you cannot find unwaxed lemons, give the fruit a good scrub with hot, soapy water before grating the rind.

Note that the recipe uses three eggs: one yolk for the pastry, the other two yolks for the filling, and the three whites for the meringue topping.

Make the pastry: sift the flour and salt into a mixing bowl and stir in the sugar. Add the diced butter and rub into the dry ingredients, using the tips of your fingers, until the mixture resembles fine crumbs. Using a round-bladed knife, stir in the egg yolk mixture to make a slightly firm dough – it should not be dry and crumbly nor soft and sticky. The dough can also be made in a food processor (see page 132). Chill the dough until firm – about 15 minutes.

Turn the dough onto a lightly floured work surface and knead for a couple of seconds or until smooth. Roll out to a round about 10½ inches in diameter. Roll the dough up around the rolling pin and lift it over the tart pan. Gently unroll the dough so it drapes over the pan. Carefully press the dough onto the bottom of the pan and up the sides so there are no pockets of air. Roll the rolling pin over the top of the tart pan to cut off the excess dough.

The sides of the pastry shell should stand slightly above the rim of the tart pan, just in case the pastry shrinks during baking. So use your thumbs to press and ease the pastry sides upward to make a neat rim that is about ¼ inch higher than the pan. Curve your forefinger inside this rim and gently press the pastry over your finger so the rim curves inward rather

1 ROLL THE DOUGH AROUND THE ROLLING PIN AND LIFT IT OVER THE TART PAN.

2 CUT OFF THE EXCESS DOUGH BY ROLLING THE PIN OVER THE TOP OF THE PAN.

3 POUR THE HOT FILLING INTO THE BAKED PASTRY SHELL AND SPREAD EVENLY.

4 SPOON THE MERINGUE ON TOP AND SPREAD GENTLY WITH A KNIFE.

PREVIOUS PAGE *Summer Fruit Tart.*

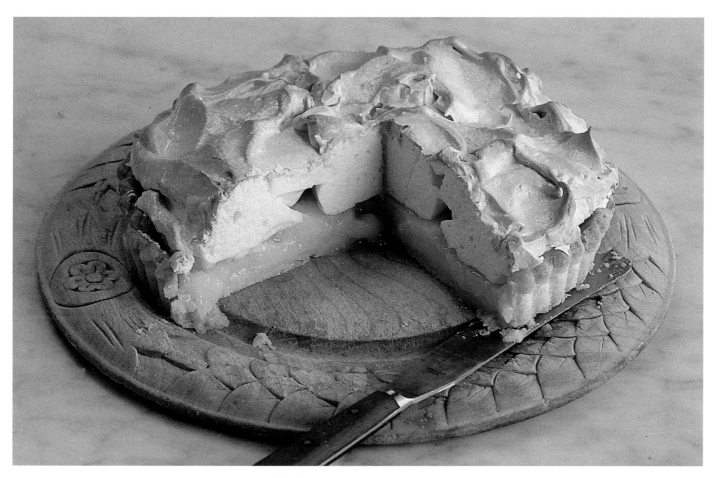

than over-hanging the rim of the pan. (This makes unmolding easier.) The pastry rim can be fluted with your fingers to match the fluting of the pan sides. Prick the bottom of the pastry shell all over with a fork to prevent the pastry from bubbling up during baking. Chill for 10–15 minutes or until the pastry is firm.

Preheat the oven to 400°F.

Bake the pastry shell (see page 158). Remove from the oven and let cool slightly while you make the filling. Leave the oven on at 350°F.

Put the grated lemon rind and juice into a small heatproof bowl with the cornstarch. Add 2 tablespoons of the water and stir well. Bring the rest of the water to a boil in a medium-sized saucepan. Pour the boiling water onto the cornstarch mixture, stirring constantly, then tip the contents of the bowl into the saucepan. Cook, stirring constantly, until the mixture boils. Reduce the heat and simmer for 2 minutes, stirring frequently, to make smooth, thick paste.

Remove from the heat and beat in the egg yolks and sugar, and then the butter. When thoroughly combined and there are no streaks in the mixture, spoon it into the baked pastry shell and spread evenly.

To make the meringue topping, put the egg whites into a non-plastic, spotlessly clean, grease-free bowl and beat until soft peaks form. Gradually beat in the sugar, then beat well to make a stiff, shiny meringue. Spoon the meringue over the lemon filling to cover completely, spreading it out gently with a knife or metal spatula.

Bake for 15–20 minutes or until the meringue is just firm and a good golden brown. Serve at room temperature, within 24 hours of baking.

HOW TO BAKE PASTRY SHELLS

FILL THE PAPER-LINED PASTRY SHELL WITH A LAYER OF PIE WEIGHTS OR DRIED BEANS.

Cut a round of non-stick parchment paper about the same size as the round of pastry dough used to line the pan. Crumple up the paper, then open it out and gently press it into the pastry shell to cover the bottom and sides – this is easy if the pastry is chilled and firm. It is important to press the paper into the angle where the sides meet the bottom. Fill the paper-lined shell with enough pie weights, dried beans, uncooked rice, or dry bread crusts to weigh it down. Bake the pastry shell in a preheated 400°F oven for 15 minutes or until lightly golden and just firm. Carefully remove the paper and beans, lower the oven temperature to 350°F, and bake the pastry shell empty for a further 5–7 minutes or until the bottom is crisp and lightly golden.

TREACLE TART

INGREDIENTS

Makes an 8-inch tart, to serve 6
ROUGH PUFF PASTRY:
1 cup (140g) all-purpose flour
1/8 teaspoon salt
2 1/2 tablespoons (35g) butter, chilled and diced
2 1/2 tablespoons (35g) lard, chilled and diced, or shortening
2–3 tablespoons ice water to bind

FILLING:
about 6 rounded tablespoons golden syrup (see recipe)
about 2 1/2 cups (110g) fresh white bread crumbs
the grated rind and juice of 1 large unwaxed lemon, or to taste

an 8-inch loose-based tart pan

ARRANGE THE PASTRY STRIPS ON THE FILLING TO MAKE A NEAT WOVEN LATTICE.

This is an old-fashioned English dessert. The recipe here has plenty of lemon to flavor the filling of golden syrup (which has replaced the original treacle) and bread crumbs. I like to use rough puff pastry for the tart shell, but you can also use a simple short pastry (see page 133) or a slightly sweet rich short pastry (see the recipe for Lemon Meringue Pie on page 156).

To make the rough puff pastry, sift the flour and salt into a mixing bowl. Add the fats and stir gently with a round-bladed knife until the pieces are coated with flour. Stir in just enough icy water to bind the dough – it should be very lumpy and soft but not sticky or wet.

Turn the dough onto a lightly floured work surface and form it quickly into a rough brick shape. Using a floured rolling pin, roll out the dough away from you into a rectangle about 3/8 inch thick. Fold the dough in three like a business letter: fold the bottom third of the dough up to cover the center third, then fold the top third down to cover the other two layers. Gently but firmly seal the edges by pressing down with the rolling pin. This completes the first "turn."

Lift up the piece of dough and give it a quarter turn counterclockwise, so that the folded edges are now at the sides. Roll out and fold in three again, just as before, then give the dough a quarter turn counterclockwise; repeat. After this third "turn," wrap the dough and chill for 20 minutes, then complete three more "turns" – to make a total of six. Chill the dough for 20 minutes.

Roll out the dough to a round about 10 inches in diameter and use to line the pan. Roll the pin over the top of the pan to cut off the excess dough. Reserve the trimmings to make the lattice. Chill the pastry shell and trimmings while you make the filling.

Preheat the oven to 400°F.

Gently heat the syrup until it becomes runny, then remove from the heat and stir in the bread crumbs and lemon rind and juice. Let stand for 10 minutes. If the mixture seems very sloppy, add another spoonful of crumbs; if the mixture seems stiff and dry, add another spoonful of syrup.

Treacle Tart (left), Croustade aux Pommes (see recipe on page 176).

Treacle Tart (left), Croustade aux Pommes (see recipe on page 176).

NOTE Golden syrup, in jars or cans, is found in most gourmet shops or better supermarkets.

Taste the mixture and add more lemon juice if necessary.

Spoon the filling into the pastry shell; don't press down to level the surface. Roll out the dough trimmings ¼ inch thick and cut into thin strips. Lay the strips across the filling to make a lattice pattern, sticking the ends to the rim of the pastry shell with a little cold water. The pastry strips can be twisted before sticking the ends down if you want to make the tart look fancier.

Bake for 15 minutes, then reduce the oven temperature to 375°F and bake for a further 10 minutes or until golden. Serve warm.

LEMON TART

Makes a 9-inch tart, to serve 6
PASTRY:
1 cup (140g) all-purpose flour
a pinch of salt
6 tablespoons (85g) unsalted butter, chilled and
    diced
2½ tablespoons (30g) sugar
1 egg yolk
1–2 tablespoons ice water
a little egg white, lightly beaten, for brushing

FILLING:
3 eggs
1 egg yolk
⅔ cup (140ml) heavy cream
½ cup + 1 tablespoon (110g) sugar
the grated rind of 2 unwaxed lemons
the juice of 3 lemons

a 9-inch loose-based tart pan
a baking sheet

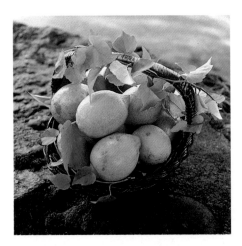

In a weekend newspaper, I once read a review of fashionable restaurants rated according to the quality of the lemon tarts they served! It is hard to get the balance right when making this dessert — the pastry must be crisp, and the filling should be lemony, creamy, fresh-tasting, and fairly light. In the simple recipe here, the filling is like a light lemon curd made with cream rather than butter. Serve the tart with fresh strawberries or raspberries, and crème fraîche. Use unwaxed lemons if possible; otherwise scrub the fruit well with hot, soapy water before grating the rind.

To make the pastry dough, sift the flour and salt into a bowl, add the diced butter, and rub into the flour, using the tips of your fingers, until the mixture resembles fine crumbs. Stir in the sugar. Add the egg yolk and 1 tablespoon of water and stir into the flour mixture to bind, using a round-bladed knife; add more water if necessary. Quickly bring the mixture together with your hands, without kneading, to make a firm but not sticky ball of dough. Alternatively, you can make the dough in a food processor (see page 132). Wrap the dough and chill for about 30 minutes.

Roll out the dough on a lightly floured work surface to a round about 11 inches in diameter and use to line the tart pan. Trim off the excess dough by rolling the rolling pin across the top of the pan, then neaten the rim with your fingers. Prick the bottom of the pastry shell all over with a fork, then chill for 15 minutes.

Preheat the oven to 375°F.

Bake the pastry shell (see page 158). It is important to cook the pastry thoroughly or the base of the finished tart will be soggy. Remove from the oven but do not unmold. Immediately brush the bottom of the pastry shell with a little egg white, and let cool. (The egg white helps to keep the pastry from turning soggy once the filling is added.) Reduce the oven temperature to 325°F and put a baking sheet in the oven to heat up.

To make the filling, put all the ingredients into a large measure and whisk, by hand, just until thoroughly combined.

Set the pastry shell, still in the pan, on the hot baking sheet and pour in three-fourths of the filling. Put into the oven, then carefully pour in the rest of the filling — this way you avoid spilling the filling as you put the tart into the oven. Bake for 25–30 minutes or until the filling is firm when the tart is gently shaken. Let cool before unmolding. Serve the tart at room temperature or chilled.

RIGHT The display of luscious tarts at La Boîte à Dessert in Lyons, France.

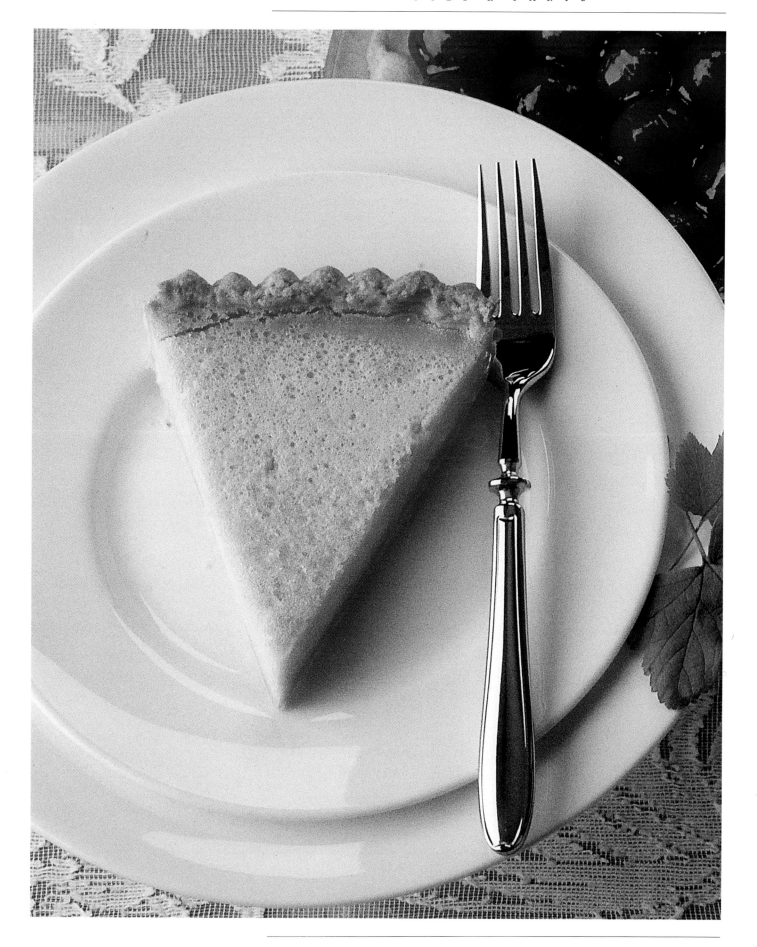

STRAWBERRY CHEESE TART

INGREDIENTS

Makes a 25.5cm (10in) tart, to serve 8
PASTRY:
210g (7¹/₂oz) plain flour
1 tablespoon caster sugar
a pinch of salt
110g (4oz) unsalted butter, chilled and diced
2–3 tablespoons orange juice to bind

FILLING:
340g (12oz) cream cheese – Philadelphia brand
   seems to work best
100g (3¹/₂oz) caster sugar
2 eggs, size 2, beaten
1 tablespoon grated orange rind
150g (about 5oz) strawberries, thinly sliced

GLAZE:
3 tablespoons apricot or strawberry conserve
1 tablespoon lemon juice

a 25.5cm (10in) loose-based flan tin

This light summery dessert, a cross between a cheesecake and a creamy fruit flan, comes from Rosemary Underdahl of Yarmouth, Maine (see pages 18-19 for her wonderful cookie recipes). She says that out of season the strawberries can be replaced with pears lightly poached in — leftover — sparkling wine or champagne, rosé for choice, or with sliced nectarines. The pastry for the tart is very rich so it is best rolled out between sheets of cling film or baking parchment.

To make the pastry, mix the flour with the sugar and salt, then rub in the butter, using your fingertips, until the mixture resembles fine crumbs. Add 2 tablespoons orange juice and stir into the flour mixture to bind, using a round-bladed knife; add more orange juice if necessary. Quickly bring the mixture together with your hands, without kneading, to make a fairly firm dough that is not dry or crumbly. Alternatively, you can make the dough in a food processor (see page 132). Shape the dough into a flat disc, then wrap and chill for 10 minutes.

Roll out the dough between two sheets of cling film or non-stick baking parchment to a round about 30.5cm (12in) in diameter. Peel off the top sheet of film or paper, turn the round of dough over and lay it over the tin. Gently press the dough into the tin to line the bottom and sides evenly, then peel off the remaining cling film or paper. Do not cut off the excess pastry dough, but instead fold it back into the tin and press gently, to make the sides twice as thick. Prick the bottom of the pastry case all over with a fork, then cover and chill in the freezer for 30 minutes.

Preheat the oven to 400°F.

Line the chilled pastry shell with non-stick parchment paper and fill with pie weights (see the instructions for baking pastry shells on page 158). Bake for about 10 minutes or until just firm, then remove the paper and weights and bake for a further 8–10 minutes or until lightly browned. Let the pastry shell cool completely.

Lower the oven temperature to 350°F.

To make the filling, beat the cream cheese with the sugar until smooth and creamy, then gradually beat in the eggs followed by the orange rind.

Pour the filling into the cold pastry shell. Bake for 30 minutes or until set. Let cool on a wire rack before unmolding.

Arrange the sliced strawberries on top. To make the glaze, heat the preserves with the lemon juice until runny, then strain into a clean pan. Warm gently and then brush over the fruit to glaze it lightly. Chill for about 1 hour before serving.

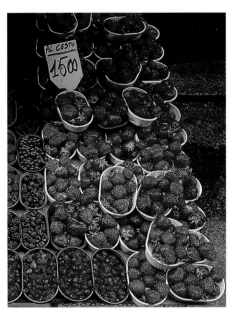

Strawberries in the market in Lyons, France.

STRAWBERRY MARZIPAN TART

INGREDIENTS

Makes a 9-inch tart, to serve 6–8
PASTRY:
1¼ cups (170g) all-purpose flour
7 tablespoons (100g) unsalted butter, chilled and diced
2½ tablespoons (30g) sugar
1 egg yolk
about 1 tablespoon ice water

FILLING:
1 cup (230g) unsalted butter, at room temperature
7 tablespoons (85g) sugar
2 eggs, beaten
the grated rind and juice of 1 unwaxed orange
2⅔ cups (230g) ground almonds

TOPPING:
½lb (230g) ripe strawberries, hulled and sliced

a 9-inch loose-based tart pan

I am very fond of the combination of strawberries and almonds, which makes this a favorite dessert. It is quite a substantial tart – the pastry case is filled with an almond sponge flavored with orange and then topped with sliced fruit. For a glossy finish the arranged strawberries can be brushed with a glaze of hot red-currant jelly, but if the fruit is loaded with flavor I prefer to leave it plain. As with most almond desserts, this tart improves on keeping a day or so before the fruit is added.

To make the pastry dough, sift the flour into a bowl, add the diced butter, and rub into the flour, using the tips of your fingers, until the mixture resembles fine crumbs. Stir in the sugar. Add the egg yolk and water and stir into the flour mixture to bind, using a round-bladed knife; add more water if necessary. Quickly bring the mixture together with your hands, without kneading, to make a soft but not sticky ball of dough. Alternatively, you can make the dough in a food processor (see page 132). Wrap the dough and chill for 20 minutes.

Preheat the oven to 350°F.

Roll out the pastry dough on a lightly floured work surface to a round about 11 inches in diameter and use to line the tart pan. Chill while preparing the filling.

Beat the butter until creamy, then beat in the sugar and continue beating until light and fluffy. Gradually beat in the eggs, beating well after each addition. Beat in the orange rind and juice, then fold in the ground almonds using a large metal spoon. Spoon the filling into the pastry shell and level the surface.

Bake in the preheated oven for 45 minutes to 1 hour or until golden and firm to the touch. Let cool before unmolding. If possible, wrap the tart and store in an airtight tin overnight before finishing.

Arrange the sliced strawberries in overlapping circles on top of the tart just before serving. Serve at room temperature.

TARTE TATIN

INGREDIENTS

Makes a 12-inch tart, to serve 8–10
PASTRY:
1 1/2 cups (200g) all-purpose flour
a pinch of salt
2 1/2 tablespoons (30g) sugar
7 tablespoons (100g) unsalted butter, chilled and
    diced
1 egg yolk
2 tablespoons ice water

FILLING:
1/2 cup (110g) unsalted butter
1 cup (200g) sugar
about 4 1/2lb (2kg) apples, such as Granny
    Smith, Golden Delicious, McIntosh, Pippins

a 12-inch heavy frying pan or skillet with
    an ovenproof handle, or a tarte tatin mold

This upside-down apple tart, traditionally cooked in a heavy cast-iron frying pan, can be made with puff pastry or a sweet short pastry. I find the classic French recipe slightly too rich, heavy, and sweet to enjoy at the end of a meal, so mine uses less butter and sugar. Here you can really taste the fruit as well as the caramel. It is best to use tart, crisp apples for the filling and to pack them together tightly. Do not put the pastry on top of the apples until they are sitting in a good brown caramel or the tart will be soggy and insipid-tasting.

Make the pastry dough by hand (see page 132) or in a food processor: put the flour, salt, and sugar in the bowl of the processor and process until mixed. Add the diced butter and process until the mixture resembles fine crumbs. With the machine running, add the egg yolk and ice water through the feed tube, and process until the mixture binds together to form a firm but not dry dough. If there are dry crumbs, gradually add a little more water. Wrap and chill while preparing the apples.

1 COOK THE APPLE HALVES IN THE FRYING PAN WITH THE BUTTER AND SUGAR UNTIL A RICH CARAMEL IS FORMED AND MOISTURE FROM THE APPLES HAS EVAPORATED.

2 COVER THE CARAMELIZED APPLES WITH THE PASTRY CRUST, GENTLY UNROLLING IT FROM THE ROLLING PIN, THEN TUCK THE EDGES DOWN INSIDE THE PAN.

Cut the butter into thin slices and arrange on the bottom of the frying pan to cover completely. Sprinkle over the sugar to make an even layer. Peel, halve, and core the apples. Arrange in the pan, on top of the butter and sugar, so the apple halves stand up vertically. Pack the apples tightly together so the tart will not collapse in the oven.

Put the pan over a medium heat on top of the stove and cook for 20–30 minutes or until the butter and sugar have formed a richly colored caramel, and all the moisture from the apples has evaporated. Remove from the heat.

While the apples are cooking, preheat the oven to 425°F.

Roll out the dough on a lightly floured surface to a round to fit the top of the pan. Roll up the dough around the rolling pin and lift over the pan. Gently unroll the dough so it covers the apples completely. Quickly tuck the edges of the crust down inside the pan, then prick the crust all over with a fork. Bake for 20–30 minutes or until golden brown and crisp.

Cool slightly, then loosen the edges of the crust and turn out the tart upside down so the pastry is under the caramelized apples. Eat warm or at room temperature, with ice-cream or crème fraîche.

SUMMER FRUIT TART

Makes a 9- to 10-inch tart, to serve 8

½ batch puff pastry dough (page 144), about 10½oz (300g)

2 tablespoons liqueur de noisette, eau de vie, or kirsch

2–3 large, ripe peaches

about 12 ripe apricots

2 cups (230g) ripe, sweet cherries

3 tablespoons red-currant jelly

1 tablespoon toasted sliced almonds

black-currant leaves for decoration (optional)

PASTRY CREAM:

1¼ cups (280ml) rich creamy milk

1 vanilla bean, split, or 1 teaspoon pure vanilla extract

4 extra large egg yolks

5 tablespoons (60g) sugar, plain or vanilla-flavored

2 tablespoons all-purpose flour

a 9- to 10-inch loose-based tart pan

ABOVE Katie Barber proudly shows off her Summer Fruit Tart.

OPPOSITE Juicy, aromatic summer fruits being prepared for sale in the market in Lyons, France.

This pretty, fresh fruit tart comes from Katie Barber, who moved from England, where she ran a successful restaurant, to central France. There she has opened her house to bed-and-breakfast guests, and has gained a reputation among the local population for cooking very good dinners.

Preheat the oven to 400°F.

On a floured work surface, roll out the pastry dough to a round about 2½ inches larger than your tart pan. Use the dough to line the pan, letting the excess dough drape over the rim. Chill for 15 minutes, then cut off the excess dough with a very sharp knife, taking care not to stretch it. Prick the bottom of the pastry shell all over with a fork, then bake (see page 158). Leave until completely cold. (It is important to cook the pastry shell well or the tart will become soggy soon after assembling.)

To make the pastry cream, put the milk and the split vanilla bean (but not the extract) into a heavy saucepan and heat slowly until scalding hot. Remove from the heat, cover the pan, and let infuse for 20 minutes. Whisk the egg yolks with the sugar until very light and thick, then whisk in the flour until there are no lumps. Remove the vanilla bean, then whisk the milk into the egg mixture. Tip the mixture into the saucepan and cook over medium heat, whisking constantly, until the mixture boils and thickens to a smooth, creamy consistency. Cook gently, whisking, for a couple of minutes or until there is no raw flour taste. Remove from the heat and stir in the vanilla extract, if using. Sprinkle the top of the pastry cream with a little sugar or melted butter to prevent a skin from forming, then let cool.

Add half the liqueur to the cold pastry cream and beat until completely smooth. Spread over the bottom of the cold pastry shell.

Prepare the fruit: slice the peaches; halve or quarter the apricots; pit the cherries, leaving a few whole and joined by the stems in pairs for decoration. Arrange the fruit attractively over the pastry cream.

Heat the red-currant jelly with the rest of the liqueur and stir vigorously until smooth, then brush over the fruit to glaze it. Scatter the almonds over and serve as soon as possible, decorated with black-currant leaves and the reserved cherries.

NOTE To make a lighter pastry cream, you can stir in ⅔ cup (140ml) heavy cream which has been lightly whipped just before it is to be used.

VARIATIONS: MIXED FRUIT TART Make the pastry shell and pastry cream as above, but omitting the liqueur. Decorate with small whole fruits, such as tiny apricots and figs, grapes, cherries, strawberries, red currants, raspberries, and blackberries, plus tiny vine leaves and wild roses. Let your imagination run riot.

APRICOT TART Make the pastry shell and pastry cream as above, but omitting the liqueur. Add 1 tablespoon each of ground almonds, almond or apricot liqueur, and whipped cream to the pastry cream. Decorate with poached apricot halves and sliced almonds, and glaze with the apricot poaching liquid, well reduced, or apricot jelly.

TARTE À LA CRÈME

INGREDIENTS

Makes a 10½- to 11-inch tart, to serve
   8–10

½ batch puff pastry dough (page 144), about
   10½oz (300g)

1 quart (1 liter) UHT French cream (see note)

7 tablespoons (80g) sugar

a 10½-11-inch loose-based tart pan

NOTE: The only cream that works
is UHT (Ultra Heat-Treated) long-
life French cream. It is available
from some gourmet food shops.

This recipe comes from restaurateurs Max Renzland and his twin brother, the late Marc Renzland, whose friendliness and skills as a chef are sadly missed. Their first restaurant, in Kew in Surrey, England, quickly gained a reputation for some of the best, and most scrupulously French, food in London. Their hospitality overwhelmed their customers...and eventually their restaurant because portions were more than generous, extra courses were added at no extra charge, and wine was used in sauces by the magnum rather than by the ladle. The restaurant closed, but a while later they turned up farther down the Thames, cooking at a café restaurant, Le Petit Max, in Hampton Wick. There is now also a larger place in London, called Chez Max. This tart has been on every one of their menus since they first opened. A combination of light, buttery pastry and pure cream, it is wonderful.

Roll out the pastry dough to a large, thin round about 13¾ inches in diameter and use to line the tart pan. Let the excess dough hang over the edge of the pan – do not cut it off. Chill for 25 minutes.

Preheat the oven to 400°F.

Prick the bottom of the pastry shell all over with a fork, then bake until crisp and golden, about 15 minutes. Let cool in the pan.

Put the cream and sugar in a heavy-based saucepan and slowly bring to a boil. Simmer until reduced by 60% – about 1 hour – stirring frequently. Pour into the baked tart shell and carefully slide into the oven (at the same temperature). Bake for about 15 minutes or until golden.

Let cool, then use a sharp knife to trim off the excess pastry around the edge. Serve the tart at room temperature.

CAREFULLY POUR THE HOT, THICKENED
CREAM INTO THE BAKED PASTRY CASE.

RIGHT Marc Renzland with a Tarte à la Crème –
the pastry edges are trimmed after baking and
cooling.

DANISH STRAWBERRY SHORTBREAD

INGREDIENTS

Serves 6–8
SHORTBREAD BASE:
1 2/3 cups (230g) all-purpose flour
a pinch of salt
1/2 cup + 1 tablespoon (70g) confectioners' sugar
3/4 cup (170g) unsalted butter, chilled and diced
2 extra large egg yolks
a few drops of pure vanilla extract

TOPPING:
1lb (450g) ripe strawberries, hulled
about 2/3 cup (230g) raspberry or red-currant jelly
1–2 tablespoons water

a large baking sheet, greased

Above SHAPE, FLUTE, AND PRICK THE PASTRY BASE, THEN CHILL IT WELL BEFORE BAKING.

Top right BRUSH THE JELLY GLAZE OVER THE STRAWBERRIES. FOR AN EVEN, THIN COVERING THE JELLY GLAZE MUST BE BOILING HOT.

This gorgeous summer dessert, of rich, crisp shortbread topped with whole strawberries under a shiny glaze, is adapted from a Cordon Bleu recipe. With a food processor the base is so simple to make, and you can use any soft fruit in season – raspberries, large sweet blackberries, peaches, apricots – with a suitable jelly or strained jam to glaze.

To make the shortbread, sift the flour, salt, and confectioners' sugar into the bowl of the food processor. Add the diced butter and process until the mixture resembles fine crumbs. With the machine running, add the yolks and vanilla extract through the feed tube. When the mixture has come together, remove it, shape into a ball, and wrap. Chill until the dough is firm enough to roll out – about 30 minutes.

Roll out the dough on the prepared baking sheet to a round about 10 inches in diameter and about 1/4 inch thick. Flute the edge by pinching the dough between your fingers, then prick the base all over with a fork. Chill for about 10 minutes.

Preheat the oven to 350°F.

Bake the shortbread base for 20–25 minutes or until just firm and lightly golden. Leave on the baking sheet until cool and quite firm before attempting to transfer to a wire rack. When the shortbread base is cold, place it on a serving platter or bread board.

To prepare the topping, check the strawberries for blemishes, then wipe gently to clean them – wash only if the berries look gritty or muddy or you are dubious about them. Put the jelly into a small saucepan with 1 tablespoon of water. Heat gently, stirring frequently as the jelly melts, then beat vigorously with a wooden spoon to make a smooth, thick syrup.

Brush a little hot jelly over the shortbread base. Arrange the strawberries upright on the base with the pointed ends upward – I find it easiest to start at the edge. The berries should cover the shortbread base completely. Brush the berries with the boiling hot jelly glaze to coat them thoroughly. If the glaze becomes thick and difficult to use, reheat it and add a little extra water. Let set – about 20 minutes – then serve with cream or ice-cream. Eat within about 4 hours of assembling.

PLUM TART

Makes an 8-inch tart, to serve 6
PASTRY:
5 tablespoons (70g) unsalted butter, at room
     temperature
$^1/_3$ cup (40g) confectioners' sugar, sifted
the grated rind of $^1/_2$ unwaxed lemon
1 egg yolk
1 cup (140g) all-purpose flour

FILLING:
10 ripe plums, about 1lb 2oz (500g)
2 tablespoons ground almonds
2 tablespoons (30g) unsalted butter, cut into small
     pieces
2 tablespoons granulated or raw brown sugar, or to
     taste, for sprinkling
$^1/_4$ cup (30g) slivered almonds

an 8-inch cast-iron frying pan or skillet or a loose-
     based tart pan

This recipe is based on a tart I enjoyed in Düsseldorf. It arrived at the table in a small cast-iron pan, and tasted as wonderful as it looked. Fully ripe purple plums that are juicy and sweet are the best to use; you can also use yellow or green plums, although you may have to add extra sugar. The tart can also be made in a loose-based tart pan.

To make the pastry, beat the butter until creamy, then beat in the sugar and lemon rind. When the mixture is light and fluffy, beat in the egg yolk. Work in the flour, first stirring and then gently kneading to bring the dough together. It should be soft but not sticky. Wrap and chill until firm – about 1 hour.

Roll out the dough on a lightly floured surface to a round about 10 inches in diameter and use to line the pan or tart pan. (If using a pan, it is easiest to cut out a neat round of dough for lining.) Prick the bottom of the pastry shell all over with a fork, then chill for 20 minutes.

Meanwhile, rinse and quarter the plums, discarding the pits. Preheat the oven to 375°F.

Sprinkle the ground almonds over the bottom of the pastry shell. Arrange the plum quarters on top so the fleshy side is uppermost. Dot with the butter and sprinkle with the sugar. Bake for 30 minutes or until the fruit is almost tender. Scatter the almonds over the plums and bake for a few more minutes or until the almonds are golden. Serve the tart warm or at room temperature.

1 PUT THE ROUND OF DOUGH IN THE PAN AND PRESS ONTO THE BOTTOM AND SIDES TO REMOVE ANY AIR BUBBLES.

2 SPRINKLE IN THE GROUND ALMONDS. THEY WILL ABSORB THE PLUM JUICE AND PREVENT THE PASTRY BECOMING SOGGY.

3 ARRANGE THE PLUM QUARTERS ON THE LAYER OF GROUND ALMONDS, WITH THE SKIN-SIDE UNDERNEATH.

4 DOT THE PLUMS WITH SMALL PIECES OF BUTTER AND SPRINKLE WITH SUGAR TO GIVE A MOIST TOPPING.

ENGLISH DEEP-DISH FRUIT PIE

Makes a medium pie, to serve 6
PASTRY:
1¼ cups (170g) all-purpose flour
½ cup (110g) unsalted butter, chilled and diced
about 4 tablespoons ice water

FILLING:
about 2½lb (1.1kg) apples (see right)
about 3 tablespoons light brown sugar, to taste
2 tablespoons water or orange or lemon juice
sugar for sprinkling

an oval deep pie dish, about 8¾ x 6¼ inches, or a
    casserole

The traditional English fruit pie is made in a special oval china or ovenproof glass dish, deep enough for plenty of filling. Apples, preferably those that are crisp and tart, make the most popular filling (often tossed with grated orange or lemon rind and juice). For variety, they can be flavored with cinnamon and dark brown sugar, or mixed with raisins or toasted nuts. Other fruits can be mixed with the apples: blackberries, of course, but also cranberries — fresh, frozen, or dried — or fresh or frozen blueberries. Another excellent combination is pear and raspberry. I also like rhubarb (or gooseberries) with sliced oranges, or rhubarb and red currants. The pastry, a top crust only, is usually short pastry, though rough puff makes an excellent covering for cherry or rhubarb pies.

Preheat the oven to 400°F.

Make the pastry dough by hand (see page 132) or in a food processor: put the flour and butter into the bowl of the processor and process until the mixture looks like fine crumbs. With the machine running, gradually add the water through the feed tube, to make a soft but not sticky dough. Wrap and chill while preparing the fruit.

Peel, core, and thickly slice the apples. Toss them with the sugar and water or juice. Add spices, grated orange or lemon rind, or dried fruit to taste and mix well.

Pile the fruit into the pie dish, mounding it slightly in the center. Some cooks like to use a china pie bird, putting it in the center of the dish so the top sticks up above the fruit filling. A pie bird is good if you are short of filling because it prevents the crust sagging in the middle. Also, if the filling is likely to become very juicy during cooking, the pie bird will prevent the crust becoming soggy.

Roll out the dough on a floured work surface to an oval about 3 inches larger all around than the dish. Cut off a strip of dough about ⅜ inch wide and long enough to fit around the rim of the dish. Dampen the rim of the dish and press the strip of dough onto the rim, joining the ends neatly. Dampen this pastry rim.

Lay the remaining piece of dough over the dish, centering it so it completely covers the pie. Press the dough onto the strip on the rim to seal the top crust to the pie dish. Trim off the excess dough with a sharp knife — the trimmings can be kept for decorations.

The sides of the crust can be scored to give a good-looking edge as well as sealing them: use the back of a small knife held horizontally to make small knocks, or cuts, into the side of the crust all around. The edge can

1 PRESS A STRIP OF PASTRY ONTO THE DAMPENED RIM OF THE DISH TO HELP THE CRUST STAY IN PLACE.

2 TO AVOID STRETCHING THE DOUGH, USE THE ROLLING PIN TO SUPPORT IT AS YOU LIFT IT OVER THE PIE.

3 AFTER SCORING THE SIDE OF THE CRUST, GIVE THE EDGE AN ATTRACTIVE SCALLOPED FINISH WITH A SMALL KNIFE.

Apple and Raspberry Pie.

then be fluted by placing two fingertips on the pastry rim and gently drawing a small knife between them to give a scalloped look. If decorating the crust with dough trimmings, cut out the shapes and stick them on with a little water.

Make a steam hole in the center of the pie with the tip of a knife or a skewer (directly over the pie bird, if using), then bake for about 30 minutes or until the pastry is golden and crisp. Sprinkle with sugar, and serve hot, warm, or at room temperature.

VARIATIONS If you would rather use rough puff pastry, follow the recipe given on page 141, using 1¹/₄ cups (170g) all-purpose flour and 3 tablespoons (40g) each butter and lard or shortening.

If using another fruit with the apples (or pears), use about 2lb (900g) apples plus about ¹/₂lb (230g) blackberries, blueberries, cranberries, or raspberries, and toss with the water and sugar to taste.

MRS. BUSH'S PRIZE-WINNING PIE

Makes a 9-inch pie, to serve 6
FILLING:
2 large Bramley apples, about 1lb (450g)
1 tablespoon water
sugar to taste

PASTRY:
1²/₃ cups (230g) all-purpose flour
4 tablespoons (60g) hard lard, chilled and diced
4 tablespoons (60g) salted butter, chilled and diced
8 teaspoons ice water
1 egg, beaten with a pinch of salt, for glazing
1 tablespoon sugar for sprinkling

a shallow 9-inch pie pan, about ³/₄ inch deep

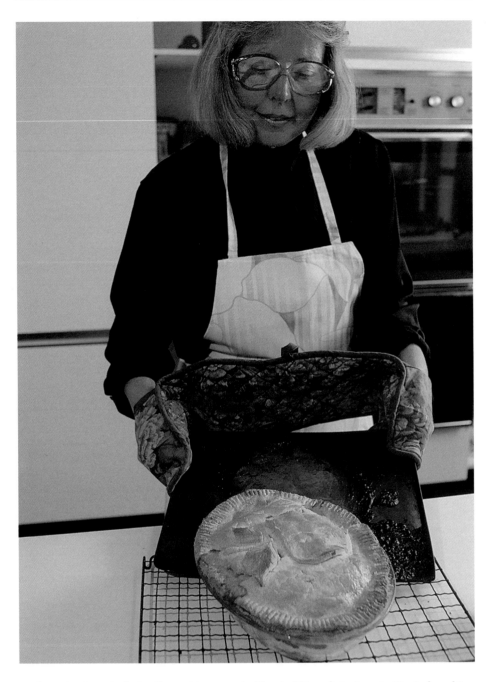

RIGHT Mrs. Jean Bush with her prize-winning
apple pie. As she says, this pie served with fresh
cream is the true taste of Nottinghamshire,
England.

In the 1994 Open Apple Pie Competition, organized by the Women's Institute in Nottinghamshire, England, Jean Bush won first prize with this recipe. The competition was held near where the first Bramley apple tree was grown. Hundreds of pies, all made with Bramley apples, were entered.

Mrs. Bush gave me some sound advice about baking apple pie. She cooks the apples first and then leaves them to cool before putting them into the pie. Bramleys make a good pie filling because they have three times more malic acid than Golden Delicious. It is this, and a lower sugar content, that gives them their tangy flavor, which isn't lost during cooking. The unique texture of the Bramley is caused by air trapped in the cells of the apples; this helps the flesh turn wonderfully fluffy as the cells expand with heat. American varieties such as Gravenstein and Greening can be substituted for Bramleys.

JEAN BUSH USES A CARDBOARD PATTERN
TO CUT PERFECT PASTRY DECORATIONS
FOR HER PIE.

AFTER PUTTING THEM IN PLACE, SHE
BRUSHES THE PIE VERY EVENLY AND
LIGHTLY WITH EGG BEFORE BAKING

Peel, core, and slice the apples. Put into a microwave-proof dish with the tablespoon of water and cook in the microwave on high setting for 2 minutes. Let cool, then add sugar to taste.

While the apples are cooling, make the pastry dough. Sift the flour into a large mixing bowl, add the fats, and cut into very small pieces, then rub into the flour, using your fingertips, until the mixture resembles fine crumbs. Add the water and toss with a round-bladed knife to bind the ingredients. Knead lightly to make a soft but not sticky dough, then wrap and chill for 20 minutes, if necessary.

Preheat the oven to 425°F.

Roll out half of the pastry dough on a cold, floured work surface to a round about 12 inches in diameter. Use to line the pie pan, leaving the excess dough hanging over the edge. Spoon in the apple filling. Roll out the rest of the pastry dough to a round as before. Brush the rim of the bottom crust with water, then cover the pie with the top crust. Press the edges together to seal, then trim off the excess dough and flute the edges with a fork. This makes the pie look attractive as well as helping to seal together the top and bottom crusts.

Gather up the dough trimmings, knead them together lightly, and then roll out thinly. Cut out decorations such as leaves, apples, or an apple tree. Stick the decorations to the pie with a little water, then brush the top crust all over with the beaten egg. Cut a slit in the middle of the crust.

Bake in the preheated oven for 30 minutes or until golden and crisp. Sprinkle with sugar, and serve hot, warm, or at room temperature.

BELOW Judges Wendy Whittaker and Olympic swimmer Duncan Goodhew examine the entries in the 1994 Open Apple Pie Competition. The judging took several hours.

BELOW RIGHT Judge Margaret Foss takes a closer look at one of the entries.

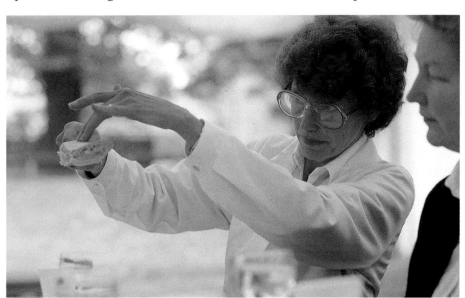

CROUSTADE AUX POMMES

The beauty of this apple pie, from the southwest of France, is its simplicity: there is no pastry to make, just sheets of phyllo to butter and arrange in the pan. The filling is simply apples cooked in butter and sugar until golden and slightly caramelized. The best pan to use is a springform, although you could also use a deep tart pan, taking care not to let the pastry stick to the rim.

If the pastry is frozen, thaw according to the package directions. Once unwrapped, keep the pastry covered with plastic wrap or a damp dish towel to prevent it from drying out.

Melt 4 tablespoons (60g) of the butter in a large heavy pan. Peel, core, and thickly slice the apples, then put into the hot butter and cook until almost tender. The slices should keep their shape as much as possible, so don't stir, but shake the pan from time to time to prevent them from sticking. Sprinkle over about half of the sugar and cook, tossing and shaking the pan, until the sugar starts to caramelize the apples. Remove from the heat, sprinkle with the Calvados, and let cool.

Preheat the oven to 425°F.

1 LINE THE PAN WITH OVERLAPPING SHEETS OF PHYLLO, BRUSHING THEM WITH BUTTER AND SPRINKLING WITH SUGAR.

2 SPOON THE COOLED CARAMELIZED APPLE AND CALVADOS FILLING INTO THE PHYLLO-LINED PAN.

3 FOLD IN THE EDGES OF THE PASTRY TO COVER THE FILLING, THEN BRUSH WITH BUTTER AND SPRINKLE WITH SUGAR.

4 GENTLY ARRANGE THE CRUMPLED SHEETS OF PHYLLO PASTRY ON THE TOP, PILING THEM UP.

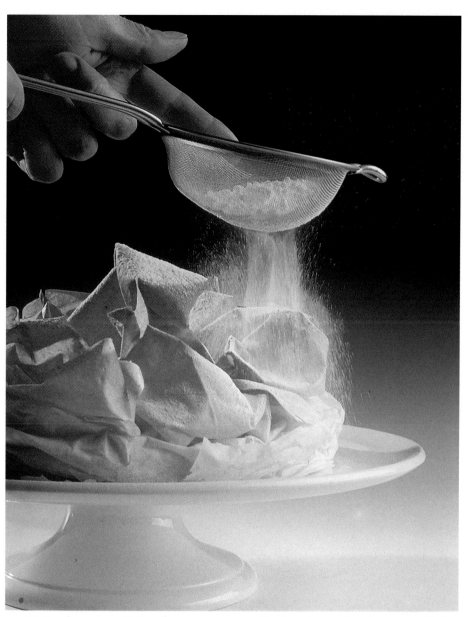

DUST THE WARM CROUSTADE WITH CONFECTIONERS' SUGAR BEFORE SERVING.

Melt the rest of the butter in a small pan. Line the bottom of the prepared pan with two or three sheets of phyllo pastry, overlapping them where necessary and letting the edges flop over the rim of the pan. Brush the layered pastry with a little melted butter and sprinkle with some of the remaining sugar. Add another two or three sheets of phyllo; brush with butter and sprinkle with sugar. Repeat once more so that about half the phyllo has been used. Spoon in the apple filling, then fold the edges of the phyllo in over the filling as if wrapping a parcel. Brush the folded-in pieces of phyllo with butter and sprinkle with sugar. Lightly brush the remaining sheets of phyllo with butter, then cut or tear them in half, across or diagonally. Crumple up each piece, rather like a chiffon scarf, and gently arrange in a pile on top of the apples – the whole thing should resemble a big, silly, frilly hat.

Sprinkle with any remaining butter, then bake for about 20 minutes or until golden and crisp. Carefully unmold and dust liberally with sifted confectioners' sugar. Serve warm, with ice-cream or crème fraîche, or an apple and Calvados sorbet.

177

DOUBLE-CRUST FRUIT PIES

YOU CAN SEAL THE PASTRY RIM BY
CRIMPING WITH THE BACK OF A FORK.

As in the English Deep-Dish Fruit Pie on page 172, the fruit and pastry in the double-crust fruit pies here can be varied to suit the season and your fancy. A metal pie pan will give the crispest pastry base because it conducts heat the best, although ovenproof glass and china pie pans can also be used. It is best to bake these pies on a baking sheet to catch any juices that bubble out. Some cooks like to toss very juicy fruit – peaches and cherries, for example – with a little cornstarch so the filling will hold together instead of running out when the pie is cut. You can make a plain closed top crust or a lattice top (see below). For a plain top crust, roll out the larger portion of dough into a round 1 inch larger than the diameter of the pie pan and use to cover the pie. Firmly press the top crust onto the dampened border of the bottom crust to seal, then cut off the excess dough with a sharp knife. Score the sides (see page 172), then finish the edge by crimping – pressing down with the back of a fork – or fluting with your fingers. Make a steam hole in the center of the top crust and decorate, if desired, with leaves cut from the dough trimmings.

RHUBARB AND ORANGE PIE

Both short and rough puff pastry are suitable for this irresistible pie. When red currants are in season, use them instead of orange, as an unusual companion for the rhubarb.

Preheat the oven to 400°F.

To make the pastry dough, sift the flour and salt into a bowl, add the fat, and cut and rub into the flour, using the tips of your fingers, until the mixture resembles fine crumbs. Stir in the sugar. Add 3 tablespoons of water and stir into the flour mixture to bind, using a round-bladed knife; add more water if necessary. Quickly bring the mixture together with your hands, without kneading, to make a soft but not sticky ball of dough. Alternatively, you can make the dough in a food processor (see page 132). Wrap the dough and chill while you make the filling.

Wash the rhubarb, then cut into pieces about ³/₄ inch long. Grate the rind from the orange and reserve. Cut off all the peel and white pith, then either slice the orange thinly or cut out sections, depending on the quality of the flesh. Mix the rhubarb with the grated orange rind, orange slices or sections, and the sugar.

Divide the dough into two portions, one slightly smaller than the other. Roll out the smaller portion on a lightly floured work surface to a round about 11 inches in diameter and use to line the pie pan, letting the excess dough drape over the rim of the pan. Spoon in the filling, leaving the border around the rim of the pan clear and mounding the fruit neatly in the center. Brush the pastry border with cold water. Roll out the rest of the dough to a round about 10 inches in diameter and stamp out a lattice with a special cutter. Put the lattice crust in place and press the edges to seal. (Alternatively, cut strips and arrange them in a lattice pattern as in the

INGREDIENTS

Makes a 9-inch pie, to serve 6
PASTRY:
2 cups (280g) all-purpose flour
a pinch of salt
5 tablespoons (70g) unsalted butter, chilled and
   diced
5 tablespoons (70g) lard, chilled and diced, or
   shortening
1 tablespoon sugar plus more for sprinkling
about 4 tablespoons ice water to bind

FILLING:
1¹/₂lb (680g) trimmed young rhubarb
1 unwaxed orange
about 4 tablespoons sugar, to taste

a shallow 9-inch pie pan, about ³/₄ inch deep
a baking sheet

OPPOSITE Rhubarb and Orange Pie. The lattice topping on this pie was made using a lattice cutter.

Blueberry Pie on page 180.) Finish by scoring and then crimping or fluting the edge (see opposite).

Set the pie pan on a baking sheet and bake for 20 minutes. Reduce the oven temperature to 350°F and bake for a further 10–15 minutes or until the pastry is golden. Sprinkle with sugar, and serve warm.

BLUEBERRY PIE

INGREDIENTS

Makes a 9-inch pie, to serve 6
PASTRY:
2 cups (280g) all-purpose flour
¼ teaspoon salt
1¾ tablespoons sugar
¾ cup + 1 tablespoon (185g) unsalted butter,
  chilled and diced
3 tablespoons cold milk plus more for glazing

FILLING:
3 cups (450g) fresh or frozen blueberries
½ teaspoon ground cinnamon
7 tablespoons (60g) all-purpose flour
1 cup + 2 tablespoons (230g) sugar, or to taste
1 tablespoon (15g) butter

a shallow 9-inch pie pan, about ¾ inch deep
a baking sheet

Wild blueberries taste better than cultivated ones, so look out for them for this luscious pie, even frozen wild berries. The rich pastry, bound with milk rather than the more usual water, is best rolled out between sheets of plastic wrap or parchment paper.

Make the pastry in a food processor: sift the flour, salt, and sugar into the processor bowl, add the butter, and process until the mixture resembles fine crumbs. With the machine running, add enough milk through the feed tube to make a soft but not sticky dough. Wrap the dough in plastic wrap and chill for 30 minutes.

Divide the dough into two portions, one slightly larger than the other. Roll out each portion between two sheets of plastic wrap or non-stick parchment paper to a thin round; the round from the larger portion should be about 11 inches in diameter and that from the smaller portion should be about 9½ inches. Chill the smaller round, and use the other to line the pie pan: peel off the top sheet of plastic or paper, turn the round of dough over, and lay it over the pie pan. Gently press the dough into the pan to line the bottom and sides evenly, then peel off the remaining plastic wrap or paper. Do not cut off the excess pastry dough.

To make the filling, mix together all the ingredients except for the butter. Spoon into the bottom crust and dot with the butter, cut into small pieces. Brush the pastry rim with a little water. Peel the plastic or paper from the remaining dough round. Cut into strips about ⅜ inch wide and arrange over the filling to make a lattice, sticking the ends of the strips to the bottom crust with a little water. (Alternatively, you can leave the top crust plain – see page 178 – but don't make a steam hole in the center. Trim and seal the edges together firmly, then score the sides (see page 172) and flute or crimp the edges neatly.) Chill the pie for 30 minutes.

Preheat the oven to 425°F.

Brush the pastry lattice or top crust with milk to glaze. If the crust is plain, use a small sharp knife to make eight or nine slits, evenly spaced. Set the pie pan on a baking sheet and bake for 25–30 minutes or until the pastry is golden and the filling is bubbling through the lattice or slits. Serve warm, with ice-cream.

SHEILA'S PEACH PIE

This recipe comes from an American friend, Dr. Sheila Rossan, whom I met every day for years at the local swimming pool. We used to swap recipes, and bring in samples to aid recovery from our exertions. This is her masterpiece – the best peach pie you are ever likely to eat. It has a very rich and delicate pastry that is quite hard to handle and which is best made in a food processor. The filling needs good ripe peaches, and the cornstarch helps to thicken the juices released during baking. You can make this in a pie pan or a loose-based tart pan.

Make the pastry dough in a food processor: put the flour and the diced butter into the bowl and process just until the mixture resembles coarse crumbs. Add the ground almonds and sugar and process or pulse briefly just to mix. With the machine running, add the egg yolk and milk through the feed tube and process until the mixture comes together to make a soft but not sticky dough. Wrap and chill for 30 minutes.

Roll out the dough between two pieces of plastic wrap or non-stick parchment paper to a thin round about 12 inches in diameter. Peel off the top sheet of plastic or paper, turn the round of dough over, and lay it over the pie pan. Gently press the dough into the pan to line the bottom and sides evenly, then peel off the remaining plastic wrap or paper. If any cracks or tears appear, push the dough together to seal the hole. Trim off the excess dough and keep to make the lattice, then chill the pie shell and trimmings while you make the filling.

Preheat the oven to 375°F.

Peel the peaches, then slice thickly into a bowl to catch all the juices. Sprinkle over the sugar, cinnamon, and cornstarch and toss gently to combine. Sprinkle the ground almonds over the bottom of the pie shell and spoon the peach mixture on top. Gently knead together the dough trimmings, then roll out thinly and cut into strips about 3/8 inch wide. Arrange over the top of the pie to make a lattice, sticking the ends of the strips to the rim of the bottom crust with a little cold water.

Bake the pie for 25 minutes, then brush the pastry lattice with egg white and sprinkle with the sugar. Return to the oven and bake for a further 20–25 minutes or until the pastry is golden and the filling is bubbling. Serve warm, with vanilla ice-cream.

INGREDIENTS

Makes a 9-inch pie, to serve 8
PASTRY:
1 1/2 cups (200g) all-purpose flour
1/2 cup + 2 tablespoons (140g) unsalted butter, chilled and diced
1/2 cup (40g) ground almonds
1/3 cup (40g) confectioners' sugar, sifted
1 egg yolk
2 tablespoons cold milk

FILLING:
2lb (900g) peaches
5 tablespoons (60g) sugar
1/2 teaspoon ground cinnamon
3 tablespoons cornstarch
3 tablespoons (15g) ground almonds

TO FINISH:
1 egg white, beaten, for brushing
sugar for sprinkling

a 9-inch pie pan, about 1 1/2 inches deep, or loose-based tart pan
a baking sheet

BETTY'S SHOO FLY PIE

INGREDIENTS

Makes a 9-inch pie, to serve 8–10
PASTRY:
1⅓ cups (185g) all-purpose flour
¼ teaspoon salt
¼ cup (60g) lard, chilled and diced, or shortening
2 tablespoons (30g) butter, chilled and diced
2–3 tablespoons icy water

CRUMB TOPPING:
1 cup (140g) all-purpose flour
¼ cup (60g) lard or butter, chilled and diced, or
 shortening
½ cup packed (100g) light brown sugar

FILLING:
¼ teaspoon salt
1 teaspoon baking soda
1 cup (230ml) boiling water
1 cup (340g) light or unsulfured molasses

a 9-inch pie pan, about 1½ inches deep

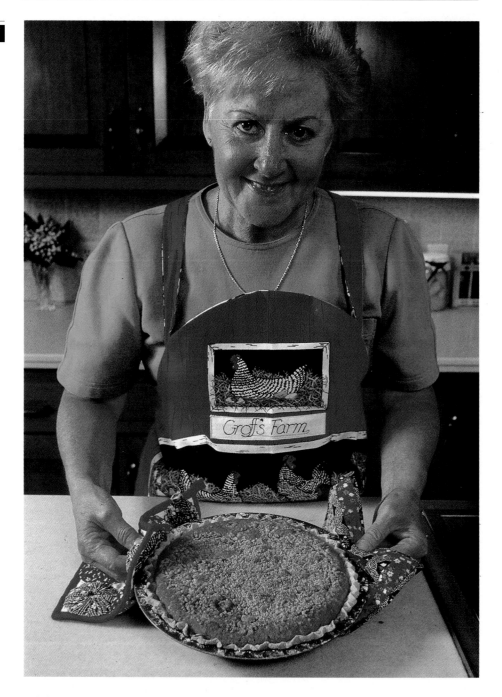

Betty Groff and her favorite Shoo Fly Pie.

While we were in the United States, we were told several times that we had to meet Betty Groff, "the Julia Child of the Pennsylvania Dutch." Encouraged by James Beard, she has done more than any other food writer to modernize and publicize the food of her community: "I cook old family dishes with a lighter touch: less cream, butter, and stodge. What with central heating, cars, and office work, few people want to eat as our grandparents did." Cooking is in her blood — her grandmother had a butcher's shop; her father cured hams and air-dried beef; her mother made the pies. It was a strict Mennonite upbringing — Betty had to keep to the dress code — "but every meal was a party." The family farmhouse is now a restaurant — called Groff's Farm — and Betty still serves meals family-style. This and the pie on page 184 are her favorite desserts.

Preheat the oven to 375°F.

To make the pastry dough, put the flour into a mixing bowl and add the salt and fats. Rub the fat into the flour with the tips of your fingers, or cut it in with a wire pastry cutter, until the mixture resembles crumbs. Gradually add enough water just to bind the crumbs together (it will need less on a damp day), tossing the mixture gently with your hand. Press lumps of the dough gently against the sides of the bowl so it comes together. The less the dough is handled, the lighter it will be. Alternatively, you can make the dough in a food processor (see page 132).

Turn the dough onto a generously floured work surface. Gently pat it into a ball, then flatten it lightly and pat the edges to smooth out the rough sides. Roll out the dough into a round about 12 inches in diameter and use to line the pie pan. Crimp the edges with your fingers. Put the pastry shell into the oven, just as it is, to part-bake for 6–10 minutes; it will just be starting to puff up. (This part-baking helps prevent the pastry from becoming soggy when the filling is added.) Let cool while preparing the crumbs and filling.

To make the crumb topping, put all the ingredients into a mixing bowl and rub the fat into the flour and sugar, using your fingertips, until the mixture looks like fine crumbs.

To make the filling, dissolve the salt and baking soda in the boiling water in a small saucepan. Then add the light molasses and mix thoroughly. Bring back to a boil, then remove from the heat and set aside to cool slightly.

Pour the filling into the pie shell – it should not be more than two-thirds full or the filling will boil over. Sprinkle evenly with the crumb topping. Bake for 10 minutes, then reduce the oven temperature to 350°F and bake for a further 30 minutes or until the center of the filling doesn't wobble when the pie is shaken.

Let cool completely, and serve at room temperature.

1 BETTY CRIMPS THE PIE EDGE USING THE THUMB AND FOREFINGER OF ONE HAND AND THE FOREFINGER OF THE OTHER.

2 SHE SPRINKLES THE CRUMB TOPPING EVENLY OVER THE SYRUP FILLING AND BAKES THE PIE IMMEDIATELY.

THE · BAKING · BOOK

BETTY'S AMISH VANILLA PIE

Makes a 9-inch pie, to serve 8–10
PASTRY:
1¹/₃ cups (185g) all-purpose flour
¹/₄ teaspoon salt
¹/₄ cup (60g) lard, chilled and diced, or shortening
2 tablespoons (30g) butter, chilled and diced
2–3 tablespoons ice water

FILLING:
2 cups (455ml) water
¹/₂ cup (100g) sugar
2 tablespoons all-purpose flour
1 cup (340g) light unsulfured molasses
1 egg, beaten
1 teaspoon pure vanilla extract

CRUMB TOPPING:
1 cup (140g) all-purpose flour
¹/₂ cup (100g) sugar
4 tablespoons (60g) butter, chilled and diced
¹/₄ teaspoon baking soda
¹/₄ teaspoon cream of tartar

a 9-inch pie pan, about 1¹/₂ inches deep

Preheat the oven to 375°F.

Make the pastry dough, line the pie pan, and part-bake the shell as for Shoo Fly Pie (see page 183). Let cool.

To make the filling, heat the water in a saucepan over medium heat until it is fairly hot but nowhere near boiling. Mix the sugar with the flour and whisk into the hot water. Whisk in the molasses. As soon as it has melted and the mixture is smooth, whisk in the egg. Continue whisking until the mixture thickens – it should barely come to a simmer and must not boil. Remove from the heat and let cool before stirring in the vanilla.

To make the crumb topping, put all the ingredients into a mixing bowl and rub between your fingertips until the mixture resembles fine crumbs.

Pour the filling into the cooled pie shell, and sprinkle the surface evenly with the crumb topping. Bake for 10 minutes, then reduce the oven temperature to 350°F and bake for a further 30 minutes or until the center of the filling is firm when the pie pan is gently shaken. Serve at room temperature.

An Amish horse and buggy in Lancaster County, Pennsylvania.

RIGHT Shoo Fly Pie and an uncut Amish Vanilla Pie.

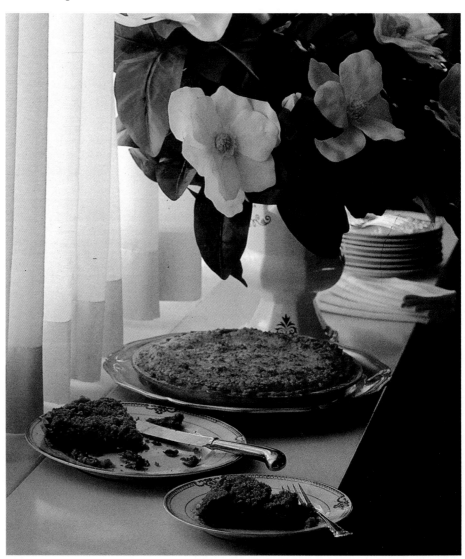

STEPHEN BULL'S PECAN BUTTER TART

Makes a 10-inch tart, to serve up to 16
PASTRY:
1²/₃ cups (230g) all-purpose flour
a pinch of salt
2¹/₂ tablespoons (30g) sugar
¹/₂ cup + 3 tablespoons (155g) unsalted butter,
  chilled and diced
1 extra large egg yolk, mixed with 1 tablespoon ice
  water

FILLING:
1¹/₄ cups packed (280g) dark brown sugar
1 cup (230g) unsalted butter
¹/₂ cup (170g) maple syrup
¹/₂ cup (170g) golden syrup
5 extra large eggs
1 teaspoon pure vanilla extract
1 cup (170g) raisins
4¹/₂ cups (500g) roughly chopped pecans

a 10-inch springform cake pan

ABOVE A piece of wonderful Pecan Butter Tart.
TOP RIGHT Stephen Bull and his Pecan Butter
Tart in the Fulham Road restaurant.

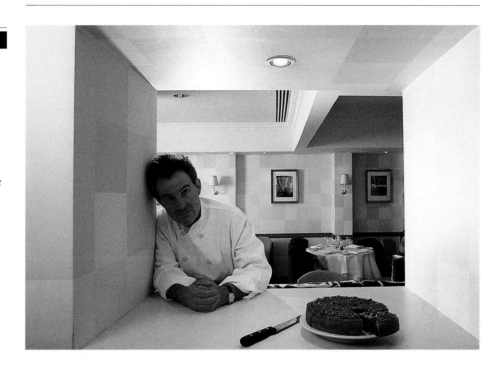

I first tasted this most wonderful of traditional butter-rich pecan pies at Vivian's, our local gourmet shop. Vivian is an old friend of the chef and restaurateur, Stephen Bull, who once had a restaurant nearby and now has three in London – Fulham Road, the restaurant in Blandford Street, and The Bistro in St. John Street. I decided to take the bull by the horns, as it were, and ask for the recipe. It requires a lot of nuts, but the pie is very large and cuts into 16 slices.

Make the pastry dough by hand (see page 132) or in a food processor: sift the flour, salt, and sugar into the processor bowl, add the diced butter, and process until the mixture resembles fine crumbs. With the machine running, add the egg and water mixture through the feed tube. Run the machine until the dough comes together in a ball. It should be soft but not sticky. If this has not happened after a minute and there are dry crumbs, add more water, a teaspoon at a time. Wrap and chill for 15 minutes.

Preheat the oven to 400°F.

On a floured work surface, roll out the dough to a round about 13 inches in diameter and use to line the pan. Prick the bottom of the pastry shell all over with a fork, then chill for 10 minutes. Bake the pastry shell (see page 158), then let cool while making the filling. Reduce the oven temperature to 300°F.

Put the sugar, butter, and both syrups into a large saucepan and bring to a boil. Cook over medium heat for 5 minutes, stirring frequently to prevent sticking, then remove from the heat and set aside. Put the eggs into a large bowl and beat well, then stir in the vanilla extract, the raisins, and, finally, the nuts. When thoroughly blended, add the syrup mixture and mix well.

Pour the filling into the baked pastry shell and bake for 1 hour or until the filling is fairly firm to the touch.

Let cool completely, and serve with cream or vanilla ice-cream.

DIANE'S CHOCOLATE PECAN PIE

INGREDIENTS

Makes a 9-inch pie, to serve 8
PASTRY:

1 cup (140g) all-purpose flour

¹/₂ teaspoon salt

6 tablespoons (85g) fat (*see recipe*), chilled and
    diced if using butter or lard

2-3 tablespoons icy water

FILLING:

¹/₂ cup (110g) margarine or butter, melted

¹/₄ cup (35g) all-purpose flour

¹/₄ cup (30g) unsweetened cocoa powder

1 cup (200g) sugar

¹/₄ teaspoon pure vanilla extract

2 eggs, beaten

1 cup (100g) pecan halves

TO FINISH:

¹/₂ heaped cup (60g) pecan halves

a 9-inch pie pan, about 1¹/₂ inches deep

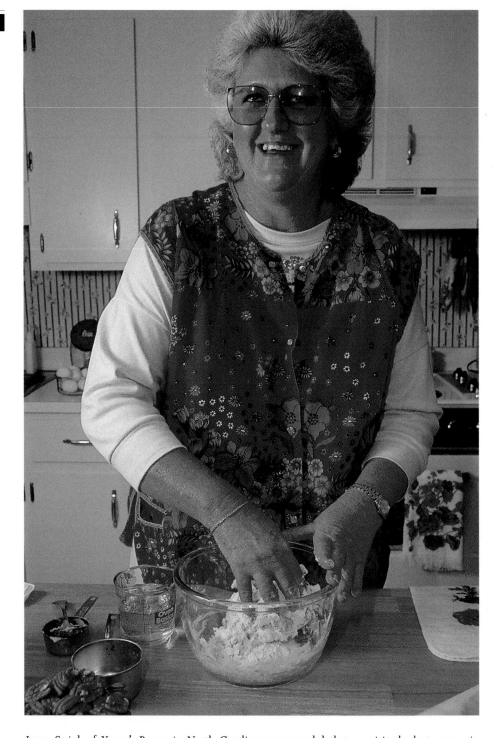

*Diane Dorsey makes light, melt-in-the-mouth
pastry for her pecan pie.*

James Swink of Young's Pecans in North Carolina recommended that we visit the best pecan pie baker he knew — Diane Dorsey. Diane was very matter of fact about her unusual pecan pie, the recipe for which is much sought after locally. Diane said she made it up by combining her favorite fudge and traditional pecan pie recipes. The result is like a very nutty brownie in a pastry shell. Diane makes her pastry with shortening, but you can use butter, lard, or margarine, or a combinations of fats instead.

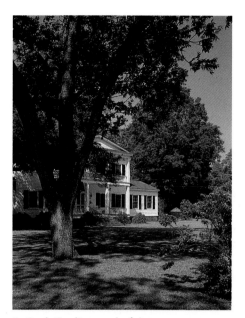

In South Carolina, much of the pecan crop comes from yard trees rather than commercial orchards.

ABOVE At Young's Pecans, the nuts are graded for size and then checked for damage before shelling.

RIGHT Chocolate Pecan Pie, combining the best of traditional pecan pies with chocolate fudge.

Preheat the oven to 350°F.

To make the pastry dough, put the flour and salt into a mixing bowl and add the fat. If using shortening, mix it into the flour with a spoon or round-bladed knife; hard fats should be rubbed in with your fingertips until the mixture resembles fine crumbs. Then add the water and mix, using your hands or a round-bladed knife, to make a soft but not sticky dough. Knead very gently until the dough just comes together.

Turn the dough onto a lightly floured work surface. Roll out fairly thinly into a round about 12 inches in diameter. Rather than roll up the dough around the rolling pin, Diane uses this method: fold the dough in half and in half again, into quarters, and lift it into the pie pan. Unfold the dough and press it gently onto the bottom and sides to line the pan completely. Decorate the rim of the pie shell by pressing down all around with the back of a fork, then cut off any excess dough. Leave in a cool place – not the fridge – while preparing the filling.

Mix the melted fat with the flour using a metal or wooden spoon; don't worry if the mixture looks slightly lumpy. Add the cocoa and mix well. Stir in the sugar, then the vanilla, and, finally, the eggs. When thoroughly blended, stir in the pecans.

Pour the filling into the pastry case. Decorate with the extra nuts. Bake for 25 minutes or until the filling feels just firm to the touch. Let cool completely, and serve at room temperature.

APPLE ALMOND CREAM PIE

INGREDIENTS

Makes a 9-inch pie, to serve 8
PASTRY:
1²/₃ cups (230g) all-purpose flour
a pinch of salt
4 tablespoons (60g) unsalted butter, chilled and
    diced
¹/₄ cup (60g) lard, chilled and diced, or shortening
2–3 tablespoons ice water to bind

ALMOND CREAM:
8oz (230g) almond paste (marzipan), crumbled
¹/₂ cup (110g) unsalted butter, at room
    temperature, diced
2 tablespoons all-purpose flour
2 eggs, beaten

TOPPING:
4 large, tart apples
1 tablespoon lemon juice
2 tablespoons sugar

a 9-inch metal pie pan, about 1¹/₂ inches deep

ABOVE The Isaac Randall House in Freeport,
Maine, home of the Friedlanders.

TOP RIGHT (from left to right): Apple Almond
Cream Pie, Bayberry Bread, Granny Glyn's Lemon
Loaf (recipes for the breads are on pages
100–101).

OPPOSITE Jim Friedlander takes a freshly baked
Apple Almond Cream Pie from the oven.

This is one of the best apple pies I have ever tasted. The recipe comes from Jim Friedlander of Freeport, Maine (also see the two quickbread recipes on pages 100-101). The pie is much easier to make than it first appears, though a food processor is essential. You also need good, tart apples, such as Granny Smiths or Pippins.

Preheat the oven to 450°F.

Make the pastry dough by hand (see page 132) or in the food processor: put the flour, salt, and fats into the processor bowl and process until the mixture looks like fine crumbs. With the motor running, slowly pour in 2 tablespoons of the water through the feed tube. If the dough has not come together to form a ball within a minute, gradually add more water, to make a soft but not sticky dough.

Turn the dough onto a lightly floured work surface. Cut off a third of the dough; wrap and chill the larger portion. Roll out the smaller piece to a round about 12 inches in diameter and use to line the pie pan. Let the excess dough hang over the rim. Put on one side.

Now prepare the almond cream. Put the almond paste and butter into the bowl of the food processor and process until smooth. Add the flour and the eggs and process once more, until the mixture is smooth, creamy, and thoroughly blended.

Peel, halve, and core the apples, then cut into slices ³/₈ inch thick. Cut each slice crosswise into three. Put the apples in a bowl and toss with the lemon juice and sugar.

Spoon the almond cream mixture into the bottom of the pastry shell, then cover with the apples, mounding them slightly in the center. Roll out the remaining dough to a round about 11 inches in diameter to make the lid. Dampen the rim of the pie shell, then cover the pie with the top crust. Press the edges together to seal firmly. Using a sharp knife, cut off the excess dough, then cut 6 slits in the top crust.

Put the pie in the preheated oven, then immediately reduce the oven temperature to 375°F. Bake for 45–50 minutes or until golden brown. Sprinkle with a little sugar and let cool.

Serve the pie warm or at room temperature.

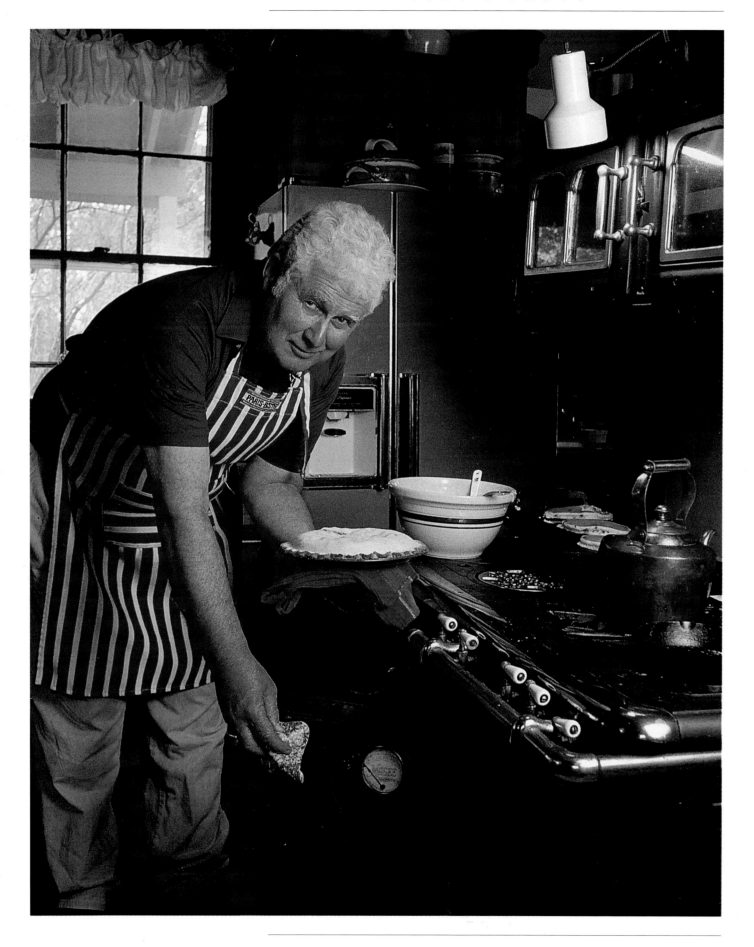

A LIST OF SUPPLIERS

Bridge Kitchenware
214 E. 52nd Street
New York, NY 10022
800-274-3435
(catalogue available)

Broadway Panhandler
520 Broadway
New York, NY 10012
212-966-3434

Dean & Deluca, Inc.
Mail Order Department
560 Broadway
New York, NY 10012
800-221-7714
(catalogue available)

King Arthur ® Flour Baker's Catalogue
P.O. Box 876
Norwich, VT 05055
800-827-6836
(catalogue available)

Kitchen Krafts
P.O. Box 805
Mount Laurel, NJ 08054
800-776-0575
(catalogue available)

La Cuisine
323 Cameron Street
Alexandria, VA 22314
800-521-1176
(catalogue available)

Maid of Scandinavia
3244 Raleigh Avenue
Minneapolis, MN 55416
800-328-6722
(catalogue available)

Williams-Sonoma
P.O. Box 7456
San Francisco, CA 94120-7456
800-541-2233
(catalogue available)

Zabar's
2245 Broadway
New York, NY 10024
212-496-1234
(catalogue available)

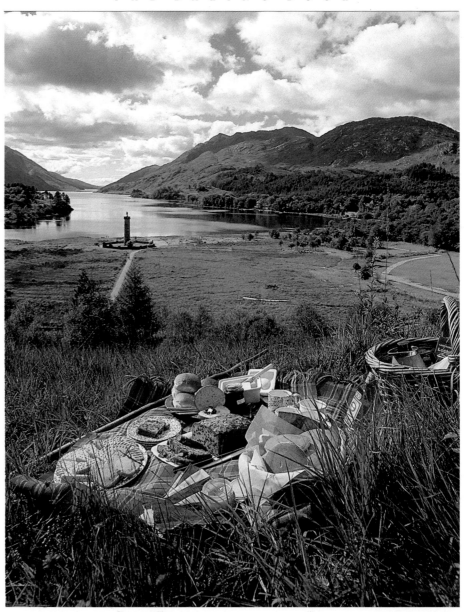

ACKNOWLEDGMENTS

Linda Collister and Anthony Blake would like to thank the following people and companies:

IN THE UNITED STATES:
Lucinda Hampton (Pennsylvania Dutch Visitors Bureau), Dottie and Andy Hess, Betty and Abe Groff, Dee Dee and Jack Meyer, Will and Annette Hertz, Rosemary Underdahl, Jim Friedlander, Lois and Ezia Lamdin, Caroll Boltin, and at Young's Pecans, Florence, South Carolina, James Swink, Helen Watts, Diane Dorsey, Shawn Price, and Mac Davenport.

IN FRANCE:
Kate and John Barber, Jean-Jacques Bernachon, and Jean-Pierre St Martin.

IN GREAT BRITAIN:
Joy Skipper, Barbara Levy, Norma MacMillan, Paul Welti, Sharon Turner and Yvonne Jenkins, Stephen Bull, Max Renzland and the late Marc Renzland, Brigitte Friis, Zeynep Stromfelt, Katie Stewart, Sallie Morris, Alan Hertz, Michael Sealey, Rena Salaman, Betty Charlton, Jean Bush, Alice Portnoy at Neff, and Sheila Rossen.

IN GERMANY:
Nürnberg Tourist Office.

FOR PHOTOGRAPHY:
Uli Hintner at Leica Cameras;
for dishes and flatware: Villeroy and Boch; for equipment: The Kitchenware Company; for kitchen appliances: Neff, Braun, Kenwood, Magimix.